The Political Economy of Global Sporting Organisations

At the global level, sport is ruled by a set of organisations including giants such as the IOC (Olympics), FIFA (soccer) and the IAAF (athletics) as well as sporting minnows such as the World Armsport Federation (arm wrestling). Many of these organisations have been surrounded by controversy during their histories, after having to adjust to the realities of commercial sport.

This important book analyses the evolution of modern sport examining the ways in which sporting organisations have adapted over the years to accommodate changing environments. Themes covered in this impressive volume included:

- sources of sports revenue;
- organising global sporting events such as the Rugby World Cup;
- differences and similarities between global sporting organisations.

Forster and Pope have created an important book that seriously analyses sports organisations from a political economy vantage point for the first time. Of interest to students and academics studying the economics of sport, the book is also written in a style that makes it accessible for those with a general interest, as well as for global sporting organisations themselves.

John Forster is Senior Lecturer in the School of Economics at the Griffith Business School, Australia.

Nigel K.Ll. Pope is Associate Professor of Marketing at the Griffith Business School, Australia.

Routledge frontiers of political economy

The Political Economy of Global Sporting Organisations

John Forster and Nigel K.Ll. Pope

Routledge
Taylor & Francis Group

LONDON AND NEW YORK

First published 2004
by Routledge
2 Park Square, Milton Park, Abingdon, Oxon, OX14 4RN

Simultaneously published in the USA and Canada
by Routledge
270 Madison Ave, New York NY 10016

Routledge is an imprint of the Taylor & Francis Group

Transferred to Digital Printing 2007

© 2004 John Forster and Nigel K.Ll. Pope

Typeset in Sabon by
Newgen Imaging Systems (P) Ltd, Chennai, India

British Library Cataloguing in Publication Data
A catalogue record for this book is available from the British Library

Library of Congress Cataloging in Publication Data
A catalog record for this book has been requested

ISBN10: 0–415–26773–0 (hbk)
ISBN10: 0–415–45931–1 (pbk)

ISBN13: 978–0–415–26773–1 (hbk)
ISBN13: 978–0–415–45931–0 (pbk)

Contents

Figures

1 Global sports organisations
Ringmasters or alphabet boys?

Sport: a commodity without weight

Sport is simultaneously a cultural and an economic activity. It is also a set of highly organised and structured global phenomena. Our interest lies in the role and nature of the global sports organisation (hereafter GSO). The GSOs exist to control sports at the world level and take many shapes and forms. In essence they are the supreme governing body of a sport or some other aspect of sport such as doping. Some are massive in their impacts and influence while others are much less so, even though their claim to global control may be legitimate. Whatever their size within their own circuit they all have some claim to be the ringmasters of sport. To date, there has been little investigation of them as a group but there are some interesting studies of them as individuals. It is our intention to begin to rectify this omission.

Sport as an economic sector is massive. In 1995, sport was the eleventh largest industry in the USA (Harverson, 1997). Also in the USA the sport industry was estimated in 1996 to be worth US$100 bn a year, and projected to reach US$139 bn by 2000 (Pitts and Stotlar, 1996). To suggest a figure for the present of US$200 bn a year is reasonable. In Europe soccer was estimated to be a US$10 bn business in 1997 (Giulianotti, 1999, p. 86). This seems likely to be a gross underestimate when a small number of clubs individually generate close to US$100 mn annually. The British Sports Council (1995) estimated that it accounts for 2.5 per cent of world trade. This figure includes both physical goods such as equipment and intangibles such as earnings and royalties.

There are further figures, all disparate in their nature. Sport-related activities generate $1–1\frac{1}{2}$ per cent of regional 'value added' and $1\frac{1}{2}$ per cent of employment in Britain (Lewney and Barker, 2002). More than $798 mn entered Indiana's economy through fishing and more than $280 mn was expended on hunting in 1996, according to the US Fish and Wildlife Service and the US Census Bureau (Polston, 1997). The 2000 US Tennis Open contributed $699 mn to the New York economy. But the problem is that these figures only give us glimpses of various parts of sport, not of a whole, global phenomenon. As Statistics Canada has observed:

> ...the amount of sport data currently available is insufficient to pro-vide a comprehensive profile of the nature, benefits and value of sport ...the data that are available are difficult to compare due to conceptual and definitional differences.
>
> (Ogrodnik, 1997, pp. 4–5)

Sport and sport-related production are a part of what Alan Greenspan has referred to as the 'weightless' economy (1996). For a variety of reasons that are in dispute material production has fallen dramatically as a proportion of GDP around the world – hence the term 'weightless economy'. Greenspan paid special attention to the IT industry but a general move from manufac-turing to service industries is also recognised. Sport, principally a service industry, is part of that movement. This factor, in addition to the magnitude of the revenues generated, the capital invested and circulating, and the indi-rect economic impacts, allows us to talk of a global sport economy.

More than any other part of the world economy, with the exception of global financial markets, sport is intermediated by its own set of institutions and organisations. These were designed to formalise and further the inter-ests of individual sports, events and culture rather than to be commercial enterprises. They have remained non-profit organisations in a stridently commercial activity. So when examined from the perspective of the mass of non-profit global organisations with cultural or humanitarian objectives, a major difference becomes apparent: the GSOs are organisations with the capacity to control, contest or commercially generate hundreds of billions of dollars. Nevertheless, despite the fact that the revenues, either under the immediate control or indirectly under the influence of the GSOs are enor-mous, these organisations are largely ignored as a group. Perhaps this is precisely because of a fundamental element in their political economy, their non-profit status. Many of the GSOs have tremendous power to generate revenues, but their ambiguous 'ownership' of a sport combined with their non-profit status makes distribution of any surplus difficult. This is part of what makes them singularly interesting.

The GSOs are the outcome of processes that precede the formation of the global sport economy. They are one of that economy's main actors but their importance stems from the size of that economy. Both the sport economy and the GSOs rely on the prior formalisation of sport. Without that for-malisation sport could not be treated as a commodity. While some previous civilisations, China, Greece and Rome had highly organised, commer-cialised sports, before the eighteenth-century sport can be regarded as lim-ited in extent, and almost entirely localised, non-professional and informal. So while the global sport economy is now a useful category, it is meaning-less in an examination of eighteenth-century sport. After all, it was not until the mid-to-late eighteenth century that many sports began to be formalised and standardised in ways that would eventually allow sport commodities to be identified.

To become a commodity, sport not only had to be producible, but also to be re-producible within a standard format, yet maintain uniqueness for each game, match or event. We argue that what is less recognised is that a pool of players, and teams in some cases, had to be created that could play each other on a more than casual basis. This is standardised and trained labour as an input to a commodity production. This requires that games be played under identical rules and is equally true for both amateur and professional sport. Equally important for standards of play, but less recognised, is that the required training for players (often from childhood) be performed under identical and stable rules.

The existence of a readily identifiable, well-defined and discrete commodity is central to the economist's standard theoretical and applied analyses of markets. Of course, if such commodities are not identified, this does not mean that a market does not exist. Rather it points to the inadequacy of our concepts of commodity. In addition it is likely that market behaviour will vary from the theoretically expected norms. Allowing that sport does not supply commodities that are well defined, readily identifiable or even discrete, there is a prima facie case that sports market behaviour will depart from the theoretical norms. This is entirely consistent with the previous argument concerning formalisation and reproducibility – formalised sport will give rise to reproducible but not always simple, discrete and readily identifiable commodities. This is also consistent with the work of Rosa *et al.* (1999) who examined the development of the automobile market. Much of what they say can be applied to the sports market and sport commodity. Rosa *et al.*, write:

> Starting as unstable, incomplete, and disjointed conceptual systems held by market actors – which is revealed by the cacophony of uses, claims, and product standards that characterise emerging product markets – product markets become coherent as a result of consumers and producers making sense of each others' behaviors.
>
> (Rosa *et al.*, 1999, p. 64)

In the political economy sense, we go somewhat further than this arguing that this is not an equal set of transactions. Instead, a variety of power and control frameworks come into play that can manipulate the decisions of the players in both groups.

Placing sport within this context, it is not necessarily the individual game or match that need be regarded as the commodity. This is recognised within the early classic economic analyses of league sports such as Rottenberg (1956) and Quirk and El Hodiri (1974). For most team sports it is the league that is the production unit. For individual sports such as tennis or squash it may be a series of tournaments as well as the individual matches. This is because consumers do not see a game or match in isolation. Rather, they see it in relation to the season or tournament as a whole. Spectators consume the sport commodity over a period of time, with different degrees of intensity of consumption. Thus the standardisation of the time length of games and events, and the calendarisation of sport goes hand in hand with its commodification. Consequently some games are enormously more important than others, with different meanings to different viewers or fans. The on-field competition is almost entirely symbolic from a league's point of view. The commodity instead is a season of games that can be consumed in a variety of ways (attendance, broadcast, print, word-of-mouth, etc.). The league or tournament is both the corporate entity and the production unit.

Consequently, codification, the creation of explicit codes of rules, is only one step in the overall formalisation of sport. Yet neither codification nor overall formalisation relies on sport being a commodity. Continuing and finalising the codification process was one of the first functions of early sports organisations, and was important for amateurs. This process was necessarily one that had begun before the organisations were formed. It was the prior creation of codes, and the competitions and events using those codes that became the catalyst for the creation of sports organisations. In global terms the operation of the calendar and the maintenance of the code and rules becomes one of the most important operational functions of a GSO.

The formalisation process first began in Britain, particularly England. It was, of course, no accident that this happened to be the most economically and industrially developed nation in the world. At first the movement towards formalisation was driven by individuals or by special interest groups. In some cases this was for purely sporting reasons while in others, including horse racing, bare-knuckles and cockfighting, there were also economic imperatives driving formalisation. The economic imperative intervened far earlier than is often realised. And while there were sporting clubs, it was only later into the eighteenth century that embryonic sports governance bodies begin to develop. International events began to occur sporadically after the Napoleonic wars and towards the middle of the nineteenth century. It was in this period that the embryonic development of national, international and ultimately global sports governance began.

The GSOs

But the global sport economy is much more than an economic system. So while sport is anything but insignificant in economic terms, it is misunderstood when considered solely in those terms. It embodies sets of cultural values that intermingle with economics, and with which individuals, whole communities and groups of nations identify.

The Olympic Games, soccer's World Cup and Formula 1 (hereafter F1) motor sport dominate all other sports competitions. Attracting audiences of many billions, they are closer to encompassing the entire human race than any other entertainments. The organisations that own and govern these events, The International Olympic Committee (IOC), Le Federation Internationale de Football Associations (FIFA) and Le Federation Internationale de L'Automobile (FIA) have extraordinarily high global levels of recognition. Even their acronyms are well known.

Their world is not a gentle one. The GSOs, non-profit organisations in a commercial environment, are caught in a web of contradictions that they struggle to resolve. As sport has become immensely financially rewarding so the GSOs have found themselves increasingly involved in off-field competition: drug-related activities, commercial disputes and legal controversies that have led to the formation of specialist global sports bodies to combat these problems. The World Anti-Doping Agency (WADA) is just one of these. Increasingly, nation states have become involved. The International Intergovernmental Consultative Group on Anti-Doping in Sport (IICGADS) in many ways represents several governments' desire not to leave anti-doping entirely in the hands of an International Non-Government Organization (INGO). This reality belies the image of harmony, such as that nurtured by the Olympic movement and its construct of the 'Olympic family'. Rumours and accusations of corruption, malfeasance and an apparent lack of ethical standards have damaged the IOC, FIFA, FIA and other GSOs. The behaviour of the GSOs in this ungentle world often appears at odds with the behaviour that they impose upon individual athletes.

But what exactly makes a GSO? Virtually without exception, the GSOs claim a legitimate control over their respective sports or some global sporting event. And often it is both. Yet these organisations are self-appointed, as is the case for the IOC. GSOs often point to current and founding member national associations for their legitimacy, for example, FIFA and the International Amateur Athletics Federation (IAAF). This might be considered a circular claim since the national associations, in their own search for legitimacy, point to their membership of the GSO!

Not surprisingly new entrants have challenged these organisations in a variety of forms. CART (Championship Auto Racing Teams) is centred on the USA but has competed for much the same world market as Formula One (hereafter F1), while rejecting the authority of FIA. At present the organisation of motor sport is intensely fluid. Control of major elements of this sport is fought out in the financial markets and the law courts. This is neither a unique nor a new story.

In the 1970s World Series Cricket (WSC) rejected the authority of the International Cricket Council (ICC) and its associated national bodies such as the Australian Cricket Board (ACB). While the WSC no longer operates, it had major impacts on cricket. The intended but minor effect was that it gave its owners an entrée into broadcasting cricket in Australia. The major effect was that it dramatically changed the economics and commercial practices of cricket as a global sport. Many argue that it changed the nature of the game itself. In North America where the GSOs are much less powerful, sports such as football, baseball and ice hockey have seen rebel leagues and competitions come and go. Some have failed but others have ultimately amalgamated with the incumbent leagues. While the ICC was powerless to intervene despite its supposed monopoly of control in cricket it is not clear that this powerlessness would extend to all sports. FIFA's ability to exclude nations and individual players from international competition is much stronger although potentially contested (e.g. under labour laws in the European Community (EC)).

In other sports there is no single controlling body. Professional boxing is the prime example. Boxing organisations claiming to be world governing bodies are legion. Bernath in assessing the World Athletic Association (WAA), World Boxing Association (WBA), World Boxing Board (WBB), World Boxing Council (WBC), World Boxing Federation (WBF), World Boxing Organization (WBO), World Boxing Union (WBU), International Boxing Board (IBB), International Boxing Council (IBC), International Boxing Federation (IBF), International Boxing Organization (IBO) and so on, most of them meaningless shells, refers to them as 'the alphabet boys' (Bernath, 2002). He attributes this splintering to the commercial opportunities offered by the electronic media, especially the TV. Unfortunately for Bernath's argument, if it were correct the splintering would have appeared throughout the sports world and this has not been the case generally.

However, there are some examples. Chess, a very different form of combat to boxing, has over the last few years been split by rebellion against FIDE (Federation Internationale des Echecs). Viner puts it succinctly:

> The task of reunifying the official and unofficial world chess championship titles is akin to putting Humpty Dumpty together again after his great fall.
>
> (Viner, 2003)

Some of the factors affecting chess are those that affect boxing. The implication is that GSOs need to be examined as a group.

Difficulties arise in describing and interpreting the GSOs. In most instances GSOs are readily describable as the supreme governing bodies of their respective sports, but not all are of this type. While GSOs have a defining role as sport governance bodies, they also play major roles as management and administration bodies. In addition many are critically involved in global sporting events, running their respective world championships or the equivalent in their sport. Some are also involved in global events through an association, usually a subordinate one, with the IOC and Olympic Games. Another element in describing them is that they are global rather than national or even international. The reason for this is that the sport economy is now a global one; it is global events that are significant both economically and culturally, as well as fitting within the larger framework of globalisation. Thus national sport bodies and even international or supra-national bodies such as Union of European Football Associations (UEFA) do not qualify within our terms as GSOs.

In some cases, such as decisions about rules of the game, part of the governance function, can be carried out relatively easily. In other areas such as drugs, arbitration, corruption and disputes between member nations, the governance function is not only critical but also difficult. There are enormous ethical and moral dimensions to punishing some players for transgressions against a sport code (as opposed to some governmentally instituted law) that can destroy their livelihood. So it is here that the nature of the GSOs as independent, unbiased and non-partisan governance bodies is most tested. And yet more and more of these organisations are not just governance and administrative structures but profit-making organisations, through global events. This is despite their non-profit status. This makes conflicts of interests in their actions and decisions all the more likely.

There are several possible reasons why the GSOs have become involved in the profit making side of sport, thereby changing their nature. These are listed here:

(i) The organisations have been forced into revenue raising through global events they construct because they have relatively few alternative sources of funds to support their functions. There is a limit to their ability to raise funds from member nations, especially when the basis upon which the level of fees raised is inevitably contentious given different levels and types of participation across nations and huge differences in per capita GDP.

(ii) The growth of commercial opportunities at all levels may require organisations to be independently profitable just to be effective in bargaining and negotiation (this may increasingly be the situation if clubs become more and more powerful vis a vis their national associations).

(iii) Commercial opportunities have increasingly become global, and national and local organisations are not best placed to accomplish in this area.

This is problematic when the GSOs were originally designed to play their role with respect to the symbolic rather than commercial action in a sport. Quite apart from this most GSOs do not fit as private enterprise in that they

(i) have different formal primary objectives, such as the furtherance of a specific sport;

(ii) operate within different legal frameworks, governance and managerial structures to profit corporations; and perhaps most fundamentally;

(iii) are not 'owned' in the same way as private enterprise.

The contradiction between their desire, need and ability to engage in profitable activities and their non-profit status is crucial to understanding them and their political economy. Their lack of ownership occurs in several ways compared to private corporations. GSOs do not generally have direct owners or even shareholders. In some sports there is a legally recognised private ownership and in others there is a variety of forms of beneficial ownership at the international organisational level. Equally importantly, they often do not have a specified means by which owners receive dividends such as exists for multinational corporations (MNCs). Lack of ownership of the profits generated offers enormous areas of discretion to these governance bodies as a whole, and their executives in particular, in the ways they disburse them and the locations to which they are disbursed. These include developmental funds to different points on the globe, the perks of office and inflated remuneration packages, patronage and influence.

Some of the reasons for the problems of the GSOs relate to the embryonic nature of the global sports economy. In most cases, they predate the early 1950s and many were founded before the Second World War. But the sports world is now very different from the 1930s and even the early postwar world. Before then the economic rewards provided little to fight and cheat about for the GSOs. The major North American sports – baseball, basketball, football and ice hockey were intensely commercial but did not have an international following. The major exception was golf. Tennis and athletics were largely amateur at even the highest international levels: all of the Grand Slam events were amateur as were the Olympics. But now, in an irony of ironies what was until recently the IAAF (see Appendix) is now the supporter and promoter of elite professional athletics, while the Grand Slams are 'open' tournaments. Many international cricketers were amateurs and the pay for its professionals was low until the advent of the WSC (Forster and Pope, 2002). But the commercial power of sport was becoming recognised, especially TV. This has dramatically changed the world of the GSOs.

Global civil society

We now turn our attention to the nature of the GSOs with respect to a collective role in global society rather than purely within the sport economy. In doing so, we now interpret sport as popular culture rather than as a commodity. The two interpretations, of course, are entirely compatible in that popular culture is often commodified. As a group, the GSOs play a role in the development of a global culture within global civil society. In this we adhere to Giddens' suggestion that:

> The emergence of a global civil society is perhaps one of the most momentous developments taking place in the world today, and its exploration one of the major challenges for the social sciences in the years to come.
>
> (Anheier *et al.*, 2001)

International non-government organisations (INGOs) play an enormous role in the development of global civil society and the GSOs were among the first of the INGOs to be founded. Nevertheless we do not wish to overstate the case as some of the GSOs appear to have done. The Olympic Movement in particular appears to make statements that portray itself as a force for world peace. There is absolutely no evidence to support any success on its part in this role but it is one that needs to be taken seriously. The IOC, for example, has recently begun an attempt to reinstate 'Ekecheira', the concept and use of the Olympic truce. In part this allowed all attending the Olympic Games to travel to and from them in safety. To this relatively limited end 'and to promote peace in areas of conflict around the world' the IOC has instituted the IOTC, the International Olympic Truce Centre (www.olympic.org, press release, 19 June 2002). In general the GSOs can be viewed as a more limited part of global civil society. Global sport is now one of the most important of all cultural outlets. In addition, because of the longevity of the GSOs compared to most INGOs, they may be regarded as part of the establishment.

In that regard, they manifest what Bowles and White (1994) call the 'complex interactions between political and economic forces' (p. 236). In the case of the GSOs the 'political' refers not only to the global polity, but to the polity that exists and acts within the GSOs as well as at all other scales right up to the global. It is the interactions between the political and economic that many political economists treat as both intrinsic and central to any understanding of the real world. Given this stance, according to Gilpin, 'Proponents of this broad approach to the subject are eclectic in their choice of subject matter and methods (economic, historical, sociological, political etc.)' (2001, p. 31). The very nature of the GSOs implies that the political and the economic are not readily separated, even for analytical purposes. One consequence is that there is little conventional economics has to say about organisations such as the GSOs and the institutions that surround them.

They move in an economic sphere where organisational structures flow freely across the globe, much as capital does. The GSOs are generally free to choose physical locations in order to ensure their independence in terms of political and economic non-intervention by their host nation. In practice they have mostly chosen political, financial and social regimes that provide them non-accountability and secrecy as well as congenial living environment for the officers of the GSO. It is not surprising that Switzerland is a heavily favoured headquarters location and it is even less surprise that this host allows the non-publication of accounts that has become the hallmark of the major GSOs.

This lack of accountability applies not only to the external world, but also often to member federations. The arguments for this are that they are cultural, global and not-for-profit and hence there is little need for such arrangements, as they do not have profits to distribute. Rather, each GSO appears to regard itself as the 'apolitical guardian' (Bowles and White, 1994, p. 238) of the sport and that sport's interests. It is extraordinarily difficult to get financial information about these bodies, often sheltering behind their non-profit status and lack of shareholders, as well as the secrecy laws of their host nations. The problems this engenders are exacerbated by the increasing revenue potential of these organisations – and by their associated ability to influence the revenues of their member organisations.

A lack of clear mandates and non-accountability as well as self-perpetuation of bodies are seemingly generic to these sports bodies. These problems would not matter outside the arena of individual sports and their multiplicity of organisations if the stakes were not so high. The organisations and forms of sports governance, both in terms of their structures and processes, have the potential to be major points of change in the political economy of sports. The global sporting economy can have dramatic effects on individual nations. There is a concern with the governance and accountability in global sports governing bodies. Despite the presence of formal governance mechanisms, such as general assemblies of delegates from national affiliated bodies, there is frequently a lack of accountability of both the bodies and their individual offi-cers and, to a lesser extent, the member organisations' delegates to them.

Individual GSOs have frequently been analysed, but never as a group. Most approaches concentrate on the history of a GSO or the individual politics within international and global sports organisations. Their gover-nance role is taken as given and treated as background in many ways. Each organisation, individually analysed, is treated as an artefact of sport. Their impacts upon sport and their role in sport are largely ignored espe-cially in economic terms. Such analyses quite legitimately take governance structures as given and as external to their analysis, but they cannot help but stray into examining the creation and the impacts of governance struc-tures. In the sociological literature, Giulianotti (1999) and Sugden and Tomlinson (1998), both texts dealing with soccer and FIFA, are exemplars of this approach.

Even less attention has been paid to GSOs as a group. This is particularly difficult to reconcile with the considerable attention paid to specific GSOs, most notably the IOC and FIFA. Examples range from Jennings (1996) in his critique of the actions and ethics of the IOC, Sugden and Tomlinson (1998) and Giulianotti (1999), both of whom deal specifically with FIFA. Maguire (1999) uses both the IOC and FIFA.

Much of the literature dealing with the economics of sport is North American and here the GSOs are, almost literally, in a foreign territory. One such is Scully (1995). The global institutions and organisations litera-ture, be it concerned with global civil society as a whole or with INGOs in particular leaves the roles of the GSOs largely unexplored. Yet this is a role long claimed by the Olympic movement in particular. Their economic roles are also ignored, largely perhaps because traditional sports economics lies almost entirely in the neoclassical economics tradition. All of these litera-tures essentially ignore the existence of this network of organisations. Almost ritually in some of the literature on global and international non-government organisations, sporting organisations are mentioned, their significance is noted, and they are then ignored. Two recent examples are Boli and Thomas (1999) and Strange (1996).

Maguire (1999) is different from these in being centrally concerned with sport. But his interest is with sport per se rather than sports organisations, although he examines the IOC and FIFA in pursuing his arguments, seeming to recognise the importance of GSOs although not pursuing this issue. Boli and Thomas (1999) argue for the importance of INGOs, as opposed to what they regard as the mainstream view, INGOs being 'treated as marginal, even epiphenomenal' (p. 2). Boli and Thomas present data on the proliferation of INGOs (pp. 23–34 and 41–5). In this endeavour their empirical evidence on INGOs by sector of activity (pp. 41–5) suggests at least a prima facie case that sports organisations are extraordinarily important. Indeed, their arguments suggest that they are extraordinarily important to what they term the 'world polity' (pp. 41–2), suggesting that '…sports and leisure above all, strongly reify the world polity through ritualised global events' (p. 46). Surprisingly then, the GSOs are ignored from this point on without explanation. This is particularly odd given that they have both a commercial and cultural significance, no mention being made of their commercial roles. Strange's viewpoint is rather different, arguing for their importance and that the reason for their omission is only because of her lack of expertise in the area. But in her all too brief consideration of sport, particularly soccer, Strange (1996) refers to international sports bodies as:

> …those transnational authorities who, more than states, manage various multinational sports and thereby affect the options open to the participants, spectators, and those who provide the necessary finance. The political economy of football has been much less seriously researched than the psychology of the game and its devotees.
>
> (p. 96)

This lack of research with respect to the political economy of sport and international sports organisations is a key reason for this text, along with an appreciation of the extraordinary cultural importance of the area.

Outline of the book

In this work, we examine, as a group, the nature of the GSOs. In part, this is because these organisations have never before been analysed as a group. These include what might be called the hegemonic GSOs. These include the IOC, FIA and FIFA, but of perhaps around 200 hundred and more GSOs in existence the vast majority are very different from these. They are small and insignificant outside their individual sports. Consequently we also address the middle and lower ranks of this group. What can be described as the middle rank includes organisations such as the International Ice

Hockey Federation (IIHF), founded in Paris in 1908 but now headquartered in Zurich with sixty affiliated national federations; the International Judo Federation (IJF), also founded in Paris, in 1951, and now headquartered in Seoul with English and Korean as its official languages. It has over 180 affiliated national federations. At the lower end of the scale is arm-wrestling. Its governing body is the World Armsport Federation (WAF). Founded in the USA, in 1967, it is now headquartered in Calcutta and has seventy-two affiliated organisations. The WAF's official languages are Hindi, English, Spanish and Russian.

Some GSOs do not serve a specific sport but are specialised in other ways. They include such diverse organisations as WADA and the International Association for Blind Sports (IBSA). IBSA, concerned with sport for the blind and visually impaired, was founded in 1981 and is headquartered in Madrid, its official languages being Spanish, English and French. Others are much smaller and less central to the arguments here, including world organisations for ancillary specialists such as sport statisticians and sport medicine. The Appendix lists GSOs referred to on this text with their major details, although the proliferating alphabet boys of professional boxing organisations are omitted.

One of the things that we hope to show is that the economics of sport cannot be entirely disentangled from these organisations either on an individual basis or taking them as a group. One element of our critique of the economics of sport is that it nevertheless has had some successes in analysis of sport and these cannot be overlooked. This must be incorporated into any political economy approach rather than being rejected. One of the main issues that comes through our interpretation of the economic theory is the tension between competitive balance and superstardom. At the moment the economics of sport appears to be moving away from competitive balance and replacing it with dominant teams and individuals, the superstars.

What we have also done wherever possible is to incorporate the GSOs' vision of themselves. Some of this comes from the individual organisations' own materials, as with the IOC material discussed earlier. Others come from secondary sources such as Sugden and Tomlinson (1998) who point to the problem of Article 58 of FIFA's statutes:

> National associations, clubs or club members shall not be permitted to refer disputes with the federation or other associations, clubs or club members to a court of law and they shall agree to submit each one of such disputes to an arbitration tribunal appointed by common consent.
> (Article 58/1) (Sugden and Tomlinson, 1998, p. 49)

This approach to governance is frequent in GSOs, not only in formal expression as in the FIFA rule, but in their behaviour. We interpret much of their behaviour as autocratic.

We will also examine the structures of the GSOs. An extreme example is the IOC which has a very different, if not unique, organisational and administrative history to other sports organisations. It began as a conscious creation at the centre or top and worked its way outwards and down to the national levels. This is particularly important in relation to the possibility of the formation of self-perpetuating oligarchies. In other words the IOC is seen as being a law unto itself. It is in this area that the most visible governance problems appear in globally organised and governed sports. Those within the IOC have ignored these potential structural problems, tending instead to argue that it is individual members who have 'strayed' while suggesting relatively small changes in rules, such as those governing the acceptance of hospitality and gifts which will prevent such behaviour.

Consequently we suggest that the commonalities among the governance structures of sports codes, as well as the nature of those codes, argues for a systematic and integrated understanding of the political economy of these structures. They cannot be studied in isolation from each other. Here a systematic viewpoint across the GSOs and their similarities and differences, is adopted, arguing that rules and structures order and channel behaviour at both the organisational and individual human level. This is despite the fact that this often occurs in unintended ways.

In this first section Chapter 1 provides an overall introduction to what is essentially a new topic – GSOs as a group. As such it attempts to outline some of the main themes with respect to the GSOs. One question that is implicit in analysing them is if they will continue to have much power into the twenty-first century, or will other global arrangements, institutions and organisations in sport eclipse them either individually or as a group? Chapter 2 provides a brief historical background to GSOs, arguing that an evolutionary approach is necessary to understand them. This provides insights into the nature of the common factors affecting these organisations. In part it also begins to explain why the GSOs are potentially such contested territories, a potential most amply realised in professional boxing's fractured organisations. This potential for fracturing and for invasion of a GSO's territory is a theme that recurs through the text.

The Chapters 3, 4 and 5 analyse some of the economic imperatives that are affecting the GSOs, as well as discussing the economic theory used to analyse sport. In Chapter 3 it is argued that these tools, largely those of neo-classical economics have had some enormous successes, especially in analysing professional sports leagues. However, they have largely not been concerned with the organisation of sport. Political economists who were more likely to be interested have until recently ignored this area of sport. Sociologists and political scientists have largely taken the lead in analysing the organisational structures of sport. But, again, the GSOs as a group have not been identified as worthy of analysis. In the one area where this might be expected, global political economy, they have not been considered at all. This raises the question in Chapter 4 of the market that the GSOs face. It is a market that in many ways they have helped create but may now be running beyond their ability to control while still providing them with enormous revenues. One aspect of this that is extraordinarily important for the GSOs is the idea of global events covered in Chapter 5. This has been the area where the GSOs have found themselves able to create both a global role and sources of income independent of their membership and which has often placed their member organisations in a subordinate and supplicatory role if they wish to be part of the global events. Some of these events have clearly reached extraordinary proportions where nations vie with each other to obtain those events. Chapter 6 deals with the relationship of structures and processes in the GSOs. It argues that the structures of the GSOs are important in understanding the decision-making of the GSOs but that different types of sports tend to give rise to certain types of structure.

Chapter 7 continues the theme of the internal workings of the GSOs but is a more speculative and less empirically based analysis. Together Chapters 6 and 7 suggest that the nature of these organisations is that they are very porous but are also often autocratic at the centre. Lack of accountability, patronage and sometimes outright corruption are hallmarks of many of the GSOs. In this respect the opacity of the workings of the GSOs is both remarkable and entirely to be expected. The great difference between the GSOs and other INGOs as we suggest is that the GSOs often have commercial imperatives, operations and opportunities that place them in a very different category and give them enormous financial and other freedoms. In defending and even increasing these freedoms and economic prerogatives the GSOs have to manage their relationships with each other and with national or international governmental bodies with considerable care. Thus Chapter 8 looks at the external relationships of the GSOs. It examines mundane squabbles between GSOs within a single and economically unimportant sport, and that sport's relationship to the IOC, to the rather grander stages where individual rights, national and supra-national governments and major GSOs clash.

Chapter 9 looks at the future of sport in terms of its past and future evolutionary prospects. The role of technology is especially examined but it is also made clear that the GSOs can have a role as guardians of a sport and its participants. The inability to create such an organisation deprives a sport of considerable powers and influence. It suggests likely avenues for that evolution and indicates that the roles that the GSOs are likely to play will potentially be diminished. However, they are not entirely at the mercy of these changes but as they have done in the past they have opportunities to mitigate, mediate and even instigate some of them. The final chapter attempts to draw some conclusions from a large variety of strands. It not only tries to suggest what the role of the GSOs will be in globalisation but also examines the means by which these influential and sometimes high-income organisations will survive and prosper or become irrelevant and die.

2 A product of history
The creation and evolution of GSOs

The GSOs in context

The GSOs appeared as the result of a temporally unique set of conditions. In that sense, they are a product, if not an accident of history. As a result they have some claim to be the first coherent group of INGOs in the evolution of a global civil society. They appeared only a little later than the earliest of the INGOs. The International Committee of the Red Cross (ICORC) traces its conception to the Swiss Henri Dunant's improvised help to wounded combatants after the Battle of Solferino in 1859 (Moorehead, 1998). Other INGOs were also created during the early part of the last half of the nineteenth century. In this context, the GSOs appear as part of a broader movement. Probably the first among the GSOs was the International Gymnastics Federation (IGF) in 1881, although with other early GSOs it was European in its affinities rather than global.

Growth in the number of INGOs was rapid, both in size and importance. By 1910 the Nobel Prize had already gone to two such organisations: the International Peace Bureau (founded 1891) won it in 1910 and the Institute of International Law (founded 1873) had already won it in 1904. ICORC received it in 1917 (www.nobel.se). So de Courbetin's specific conception and creation of the Olympic movement in 1895 fitted well with this civil climate. To de Courbetin the Olympics were internationalist in purpose. It is also the case that it was in Europe rather than anywhere else in the world that these developments were taking place. Despite being global these organisations were predominantly European in creation, development and outlook. The same was true in the sporting area. Sport and the games were seen as a means to this internationalist end, rather than the event being an end in itself. Since that time many of the GSOs have adopted this internationalist position and its rhetoric, perhaps as a tool for achieving broader acceptance and legitimacy. Their original raison d'être may have been sport but it was arranged with other broader societal objectives. And as we will explain later, the GSOs may have inverted means and ends again in their evolution. Finance was a tool to achieving sporting ends, and sport has evolved within an environment that has made it the means to achieving financial ends.

Growth in the number of GSOs – as with other INGOs – is a function of two factors. The first is a changing world environment and the second their own internal dynamics. This presents a problem in discussing their evolution as almost all GSOs have histories of less than a hundred years. So the nature of global sports as a set of institutions and organisations is certainly still in its formative stages on historical time scales. A century is perhaps little time for the evolutionary mechanisms to be entirely apparent. Nevertheless a sketch can be given. In this respect the GSOs and INGOs are very different from private enterprise corporations whose structures, such as Boards of Directors and indirect ownership by shares, are mandated by bodies of corporate law that have evolved over many centuries. There are companies now in existence that have histories several times longer than any INGO or GSO. The Hudson's Bay Company, for example, was established by a group of entrepreneurs through the mechanism of royal charter in 1670. By comparison, the IAAF, one of the oldest of the GSOs was founded only in 1912 – by a group of national level athletics federations as its members and no clear ownership structure. We discuss in a later chapter how this lack of clear and evolved ownership structures helps create problems of legitimacy and of distribution of surpluses that shareholder corporate entities rarely have. This should not be seen as a normative argument in favour of privately owned GSOs – far from it. It does, however, suggest that some GSOs may have evolved in that direction if the environment at the end of the nineteenth century had been different.

Consistent with an evolutionary interpretation – as opposed to the approaches of mainstream economics and the possibility that they might have begun life as private enterprises – we do not see the creation of the GSOs solely as a response to market forces. Such a limited economic view of the GSOs would fit far better with neoclassical institutionalism and public choice theory (Gilpin, 2001). The basis of our argument is that once created, the GSOs again did not respond solely to market forces. If that were the case, the GSOs could be seen as rational choice responses rather than as evolutionary. However, the GSOs, as with the INGOs, enjoy a degree of autonomy from the constraints of national economies and even from the international economy. In examining them therefore it is necessary to look at their evolution and to treat them in political economic terms. But regardless of which approach is used to interpret the genesis and early development of the GSOs, their degree of autonomy is critical to understanding them. It is this that gives them their ability to shape not only sport culture but also the sport economy, its markets, consumers and producers.

We do not want to overstate the case and do not pretend that the evolution of modern sport was entirely due to the GSOs. In fact, in many ways it is the other way round. The formalisation of sport and its explicit governance, sometimes by individuals and sometimes by national or even highly localised organisations began well before the GSOs came into existence. Indeed their prior existence was a precondition for the appearance of the GSOs. At the same time an evolutionary approach does not mean that the GSOs have to be treated as passive in their own development either individually or as a group. And they have been and remain the most influential instruments in the creation of sport as a global cultural phenomenon.

We now proceed to a discussion of the political economy of the evolution of the GSOs, beginning the discussion with a developmental history of modern sport.

Genesis: the beginnings of modern sport

Sports are imbued with cultural meaning, both jointly and severally. This meaning is often co-opted by – but distinguishable from – its economic elements. For example, surf and beach sports have elements connected with youth life styles in South Africa, California, Hawaii and Australia. These cultural elements are readily co-opted in visual form and surf filmmaking has become a specialist genre with a commercial imperative of its own. Competitions, championships and sponsorships arise for commercial reasons and then take on cultural significance. But while co-opted these cultural elements are not entirely within the control of commerce or even the sports organisations and global governing bodies. So by combining changing cultural meanings with the formalisation, commercialisation and organisation of sport we can identify a link from early sport to the forms of the present. In the case of surfing the reasoning is especially straightforward as the cultural meaning is lost beyond certain coastal areas and so the commercial evolution is limited.

At this point we need to make a methodological point. It has been suggested that the terms 'traditional', 'modern' and 'postmodern' apply in the context of soccer and, presumably, sport in general (Giulianotti, 1999). In our analysis, we avoid this conceptual framework and the consequent 'periodization' that it implies (Giulianotti, 1999, pp. xiii–xv). We do this in order to more clearly keep to an evolutionary analysis – what Dennett calls 'Darwin's Dangerous Idea' (Dennett, 1995). Thus, while some might see a particular sport as postmodern, we consider them all as springing from the same wellsprings and subject to the same evolutionary mechanisms as other sport forms. The assumption of evolutionary mechanisms also provides the link between this analysis of the past and the treatment of the future of the GSOs and sport that is discussed in Chapter 9.

There is in addition the role of early sporting organisations to be examined. These are largely ignored in discussions of the development of sport. In the context of the GSOs however, they play an important dual role. They first and foremost established the relevance and need for permanent organisations in sport. In other words they were successful as a group and in most individual cases. This led to a situation where major sport without organising bodies became unthinkable. This acquired need for organisation was critical to the formation of the GSOs as sport becomes international and then global. Second, in a few cases the early organisations went on to become de facto GSOs, some retaining that role to the present day.

It is difficult to present a continuous time line for this organisational evolution. The early developments are too random for this to be sensible and products of the human mind such as de Courbetin's conception of the Olympic movement are not understandable rather than predictable in their time and environmental context. But it is clear that the early stages of (a) sport organisations; (b) the formalisation of some sports; (c) the professionalisation of at least some players and (d) the commercialisation of sport, were all occurring at about the same time. We locate its beginning approximately in the eighteenth century particularly in England in common with most discussions of the creation and rise of contemporary sport and its economic mechanisms. The temporal location of modern sport's evolution at the juncture of the eighteenth and nineteenth centuries was influenced by the revolutionary and Napoleonic wars. These wars, lasting a quarter of a century slowed down the development of both international and domestic sport. The physical location in England (or perhaps Britain) is for good reason. Partly this was because it was the centre of the industrial revolution with its related improvements in communication, urbanisation and increasing formalisation of employment and work. England was the most globally committed of all nations in this period. Many of the current world sports became such because of the spread of empire. The title of Guha's text on Indian cricket, *A Corner of a Foreign Field: The Indian History of a British Sport*, is telling in this respect. It is also the case that many attitudes if not practices of eighteenth-century England carried over into global sport and its organisation.

Importantly, the development of sport ran from the local, largely unorganised and informal condition at the beginning of the eighteenth century, to be international, organised and formal by the end of the nineteenth. From being open at the beginning of this period (i.e. with a mix of amateur and a very few professionals) the distinction between these groups grew and this distinction was reflected in many of the GSOs. However, by the last quarter of the twentieth century sport was once again called 'open' (as in the tennis 'opens'), but purely amateur sport now exists in a different and in many ways a culturally as well as economically subordinate sphere to commercial sport. The commercial version of sport now dominates. The English soccer 'pyramid' exists as a concrete and formalised example of this, with the lower leagues largely amateur and the higher leagues completely professional and commercial.

Sports such as soccer, boxing, athletics, martial and equestrian sports and others existed around the world for considerable periods before the eighteenth century, some apparently for millennia. Some died out through isolation or through conquest as in South and Central America. Some had already undergone an evolution of their forms of play before the eighteenth century. This is true of golf, while a recognisable form of cricket had already evolved and was being played in the south west of England by 1550 (Varney, 1999, p. 558). Yet while acknowledging the existence of these precursor and fossil sports the early evolution of modern, formal sport occurred within the time frame and locations we have noted.

Two elements are critical in the formalisation of any sport. These are codification of rules and the calendarisation of events. The first, codification, is widely recognised and for a degree of permanence and acceptance requires some formal organisation. The second element, calendarisation, presupposes the existence of interested parties who wish to meet regularly for purposes of sport and competition. A commonly understood and written formal code of game rules is possible without a formal organisation, but as a sport develops some of the rules and governance mechanisms will ultimately prove inadequate. They then require modification. Without some form of organisation that is given responsibility for those rules, or gives itself such authority or is regarded as authoritative there can be a breakdown into separate codes. Or the sport may cease to hold interest and die. This has been seen as some codes have fissioned, even after formalisation, with separate codes or even separate sports evolving. Examples include rugby union, which gave rise to American Football, initially at college level. The same sport also gave rise to the rugby league offshoot, while rugby itself had previously evolved from soccer. These evolutionary movements arose in part because of the absence of an effective governance body.

The possibility of an evolutionary split continues to the present day but has been avoided by some organisations. For example, St Andrews, founded in 1754, promulgated universal rules of golf by 1822. It avoided a later international split through recognition that the USA had become the economic heartland of golf. Consequently in the present day it shares the role of codification with the United States Professional Golf Association (USPGA). By contrast, some organisations have in some way or another ceded authority to other bodies as sports developed. Brailsford points out that: articles governing cricket matches were set out in 1727 (1988, p. 8). This was by the rural Hambledon Cricket Club, which became the recognised authority of the period. Nevertheless, as the axis of the sport shifted to London and commercial elements became more important, so the Marylebone Cricket Club based at Lord's became the central organisation for the sport, including its later, international components.

Codification does not necessarily occur simultaneously with calendarisation, although it can. It *always* precedes it, sometimes by a lengthy period. So, while The Jockey Club (Horse racing, founded 1752) was afforded the authority for '...forming and applying the Rules of Racing and licensing individuals and racecourses' (www.thejockeyclub.co.uk/jockeyclub/html/home/history.asp), the establishment of what were to become the classic races would take another quarter of a century (the St Leger in 1778, the Oaks in 1779 and the Derby in 1780). But, as with present-day creation of sport competitions such as Frisbee and Xtreme sports, codification has historically seen occurrences where it was combined with calendarisation. For example, Thomas Doggett's Boat Race for Thomas Doggett's Coat and Badge has been rowed since 1717 when it appeared with its own specific set of rules.

Calendarisation requires a level of social stability not available in either America or France in the eighteenth and nineteenth centuries. Indeed, it is to the English upper classes and, in particular, their privileged education system, that sport owes a great debt. For calendarisation suggests that not only a governing body exists but also bodies capable of organising and taking responsibility for teams. This occurred in the English university and public school system well into the nineteenth century. According to Quercetani (1964):

> The first school to promote inter-class athletics was Eton in 1837. Exeter College, Oxford, followed in 1850. The earliest inter-collegiate sports were held at Cambridge in 1857 and at Oxford in 1860.
>
> (p. xv)

In the case of cricket an annual Oxford vs Cambridge game was being held by 1855 at the latest, denoting the increasing use of sport by non-sporting organisations that helped create sport's organisational base. Some of the first modern athletics meets in a modern form were Oxford vs Cambridge with eight events in 1864. In 1866, the Amateur Athletics Club organised the English Championships with twelve events and a new body, the Amateur Athletics Association would do the same in 1880. In the USA, a similar championship would not be created until 1876 (organised and hosted by the New York Athletic Club). That country had then only recently emerged from a civil war.

Organisations serve another purpose in addition to codification, calendarisation and cohesion. They serve to protect the sport against predatory competitors. In the modern day we see the various codes of football and martial arts competing for 'market share' or some other form of dominance, with the various associations playing leading roles. And some 200 years ago in England the Elizabethan fencing masters guild fended off challenges from the Italian style of sword and sword play (Varney, 1999). This success was short lived, the guild and the art or sport eventually collapsing when the underlying need for their skills disappeared.

Our preceding paragraphs have sought to establish that three preconditions of the formalisation of sport (codification, calendarisation, cohesion and, implicitly, teams) can be directly established as an evolutionary trend beginning in England in the eighteenth century. The reasons for this lie in the political, social and economic climate of that period in that place. Each of these elements continues to the present day. While these conditions were developing, one of the vital components of commercial sport had already been fashioned. This was the development of the professional athlete.

Individuals had been able to make a living as professional athletes before sport itself became a commodity. In eighteenth-century England aristocrats had employees who might be nominally footmen but who were pugilists, road racers, jockeys, oarsmen or cricketers. In addition a few professional coaches made a living from wealthy amateurs who were prepared to pay to increase their ability and their competitiveness. Coaches existed in activities that were sport or sport-related such as fencing and dancing, where their functions were similar to those of the drawing masters, that is, the skills attained were seen as a part of a rounded genteel cultured individual. In these proto-sports the distinction between amateur and professional emerged relatively early and was not dependent on the late nineteenth-century commercialisation of sport. It was, however, in the earlier period that the concept of professional athlete began to crystallise and, whereas sport had previously been open, it began to become a distinguishable amateur vs professional activity.

In cricket, there were increasing numbers of professional players by the late eighteenth century (Brailsford, 1988). The professional–amateur distinction had already occurred. In England, this was described as a player–gentleman distinction, owing its roots to the English upper classes. This continued for some long time: a professional would not be captain of England's cricket team until 1953, and the player–gentleman distinction only died in 1963 (Varney, 1999). The concept of professionals as indicated above was also associated with the use of trainers. In the case of boxing, Broughton's rules were established, at least for his own 'amphitheatre' in August 1743 (Brailsford, 1988). At about the same time 'mufflers', that is, training gloves were brought in for teaching and training. The training and coaching element therefore began to become more important and increasingly a permanent part of some sports from this earlier period. This has more recent international echoes, such as the IAAF, which for a long period either ignored or denigrated professionals. It now promotes professional sport in the open era that emerged in the 1960s–1980s.

Formalisation and other social and economic changes made commercialisation easier, while commercialisation led back to more formalisation and organisation. In understanding the evolution of commercial sport, the distinction between professional sport and commercial sport is rarely made. That distinction is crucial in understanding the evolution of modern sport. The existence of professional sport long preceded that of commercial sport, but commercialisation requires a much larger set of preconditions than paying athletes, it required that sport be a commodity. This has required the creation of the paying spectator.

Paid viewing of sport for recreation has a short history compared to sport itself. While viewing contests free of charge has been a feature of many societies, the audience directly compensating the entrepreneur for the provision of sport is recent. In Rome's gladiatorial contests audiences entered for free, but they did bet on the outcomes. It is not surprising therefore, that some of the first episodes of paid viewing of sport included particularly brutal activities that were also conducive to gambling, as well as to buying drink and food. This is true of Elizabethan fencing contests, which also took place in theatres as well as open spaces, with the potential for admission to be charged, sometimes remuneration being by the expedient of appealing for donations to be thrown by the crowd (McElroy and Cartwright, 1986). The English Civil Wars, the influence of the Puritans and the Commonwealth made the seventeenth century a bare patch for sport, theatre and the arts. The Restoration changed the situation completely. James Figg's London amphitheatre was founded in 1719 and used for animal baiting and bare-knuckle fighting. Charging entrance is one early example of commercial sport delivery. Significantly, differences in spectator prices were substantial. It cost 2d or 3d to watch a day's cricket in 1720 as opposed to 2/6d for a bare-knuckle contest (Brailsford, 1988), indicating a price and class differentiated audience for sport. Nevertheless the implication of this is that sports were paid entertainment available to most classes within the population. Sport was already a commodity before the formalisation process had been completed and provided an impetus for that process to go forward.

All of the ingredients for GSOs have now been described with the crucial exception of international sport itself.

Becoming global: early stages of international sport

Despite its relatively late development into the contemporary open form, tennis has claims to be one of the earliest international games. Cox (England) played Charrier (France) in Paris in 1819 in what appears to have been a non-representative game. Pigeon racing between Belgium and England was established in 1830. Despite these examples, Brailsford (1988) claims boxing as '...the first world sport...', '...the peripatetic James Mace himself sailing nonchalantly between England, Australia and the United States' (p. 139) during the 1850s–1860s. Brailsford also claims that although there '...was no vestige of international organisation behind the sport...the concept of a world championship had begun to take root' (p. 139).

As the British created empire, so their sports spread with different but lasting effect in each place. Governor Macquarie allocated land for cricket in Hyde Park in Sydney in 1810 establishing perhaps the most successful of all cricket nations. Singapore Cricket Club was founded in 1852 but no non-Europeans were allowed as members until after the Second World War.

> But much as they might have tried, the British could not completely control cricket once it had been transplanted to the colonies, and in many countries – most notably those in the West Indies – it became the focus of a strong nationalism that helped resist the colonial powers.
>
> (Varney, 1999, p. 559)

And in India, the second most populous nation in the world, it became the national game to the point of obsession. Somewhat surprisingly then the first cricket international was between the USA and Canada in 1844.

There was an English cricket tour of Canada and USA in 1859 and Australia in 1861.

In athletics the first club-level international match was held between the New York Athletic Club and the London Athletic Club in 1895 (Quercetani, 1964). This was only a year before the first Olympic Games. So two related processes were at work – matches were becoming international, and some sports were becoming both international and global in their support. Despite the presence of America in these examples it was to be largely absent from international sport in a major portion of this critical period. The Civil War, and its relatively long recovery period and the development of baseball independent of other major sports led to a relative sporting isolation that meant a separate development in its major commercial team games. With the major exceptions of Olympic sports, amateur tennis and professional golf, North America was a place apart.

Almost certainly the first attempt at a genuinely global event was the Olympics in 1896 in Athens. In many ways the games were a little out of their time as other international regional groupings came later as ideas, organisational capabilities and regional identities spread. Crucially in athletics and in part prompted by the prominence given to athletics by the Olympics, seventeen national athletics associations in 1912 founded the IAAF '...who saw the need for a governing authority, for an athletic programme, for standardised technical equipment and world records' (IAAF website, 1999). This also helped the development of international events on a regional basis. In terms of athletics meets, the first Far Eastern Games were held in Manila in 1913. Then came the First World War, the influenza pandemic immediately after, as well as the Russian Revolution and civil disorder in a number of nations. This slowed the spread of international events in athletics as in other sports. Immediately after the First World War came the South American Championships in Monte Video in 1919; the first Central American and Caribbean Games in Mexico City in 1926; the first British Empire and Commonwealth Games in 1930 in Hamilton, Canada, and the first Balkan Games in Sofia in 1931. Surprisingly, the first European championships were not held until 1934 in Turin. Others came later. The first Pan-American Games were held in Buenos Aires in 1951; the first Asian Games in New Delhi in 1951; the first Mediterranean Games in Alexandria in 1951 and the first Pan-African Games in Cairo in 1962. In all of these the amateur ethos was upheld. So, the IAAF and the Olympic movement were creating a GSO background for themselves and others that would follow. Athletics has been a significant element in promoting international and global events, now including the World Championships.

Concurrent with these developments, sport was becoming more professional and commercial but this was spread unevenly among sports. This occurred perhaps first and most radically in North America with the development of baseball especially after the Civil War. Basketball, of course appeared much later. The first professional game, apparently in Trenton, was played in New Jersey in 1896 and in 1898 a professional league of six teams was in operation (LaFeber, 2002, pp. 35–6). In European soccer the professionals were separating themselves from the amateur ethos as were sub-national sports such as rugby league. The Football League was formed in England in 1888. Yet only in soccer was regular international competition being created among the professional sports. International events were mainly amateur and the Olympics solidified this hold. The Olympics were of such power that in the very commercial sport arena of North America athletics stayed amateur for much longer than would otherwise have been the case. In some individual sports such as tennis and golf the amateur–professional split was accommodated with separate tournaments, and in tennis the dominance of the major tournaments as amateur carried into the latter half of the twentieth century.

Due to the political, economic and social forces at work in the late nineteenth and early twentieth centuries it seems that conditions were ready for the emergence of the GSOs, and for an amateur ethos to surround them. The movement towards internationalism created in part by European wars helped spawn the Olympic movement. In addition there was a long period of comparative peace in Europe with the end of the Franco-Prussian War. European colonisation had spread European sports across the globe, if somewhat haphazardly. The USA had followed a rather different path, but its colonisations after the Spanish–American War led to some international development of baseball. The speed, safety and certainty of international travel increased enormously allowing the greater development of international fixtures. And we venture to suggest that the creation of the electric telegraph in 1844 and its very rapid international expansion was critical. It provided news of sport in other nations that with an immediacy and freshness that was previously lacking. The telegraph went hand in hand with the development of the local and international sports pages in daily newspapers. These developments in sport were consciously followed if not fostered by the media. A local newspaper, The *Express and Star* based in the small industrial centre of Wolverhampton in England sent the son of the proprietor to Montreal to work in papers there for a year, the more advanced sports coverage in Canada influencing the reporting and treatment of news in that paper (www.expressandstar.com).

As we have suggested a necessary precursor for these developments was the formalisation of sport. In many countries the national federations associated with the creation and maintenance of that formalisation had already been in existence for several decades. In broad terms most GSOs emerged from specific sports that were already well on their way to their modern forms. Correspondingly, the GSOs, both individually and as a group, represent a late stage in the modernisation of sport. There have been dramatic differences in the way that GSOs developed. So each mainstream GSO, being concerned with a specific sport, is in some sense unique. In line with this not all sports that have become global have proceeded at the same pace.

Two games are chosen to indicate what can occur. The first is tennis. The evolutionary process was much slower in tennis, at least until the modern game arrived in the 1870s. In 1874 a new form of court was devised. Most importantly in 1877 the Wimbledon tournament began based at the All England Croquet Club located in that suburb. This was on the basis of a new set of rules that largely remain in force to the present. In adding a women's championship in 1884 the game of tennis became one of the least gender-specific major sports. By 1880 a national tennis championship was held in the USA; in 1881 the US Lawn Tennis Association was formed, followed by the Lawn Tennis Association in England in 1884. Since the 1870s the evolution of tennis into a global game has been rapid. In many ways that rapid evolution, almost entirely amateur until 1926 when a small group of professionals in the USA started their own tour, was influenced by what had already occurred in other sports. The evolution of modern sport is not therefore one of complete analogy with biological evolution. Imitation and adoption are potential evolutionary pathways not open to biological evolution.

The second of the sports is takraw and its associated forms. By global standards modern takraw has only a modest following. This is mostly in South East Asia where it originated. Known to be played in Melaka (Malacca) in the fifteenth century it was modernised in 1935 (www.takrawcanada.com/history_int.html; Trevithick, 1996, pp. 389–91). It is a ball game with similarities to badminton, and mostly played on badminton courts. The only ball contact allowed is with the foot or lower part of the leg. A wide variety of forms are recognised by ISTAF, the International Sepaktakraw Federation. Prior to ISTAF's formation in 1992 governance had been via the Asian Sepaktakraw Federation. This just did not have the clout of more Euro-centric sports in order to spread itself. The first official game only came in 1945, including teams from rural villages. After this it spread rapidly within South East Asia. The problem for takraw is that it is an Asian game, with no exposure in the formative years of the development of modern sports. Since then the development of takraw has in many ways been even more concentrated than that of tennis, but its original Asian location diminishes its chance to create a truly global game. A recent western adaptation of the game is footy bag, and it is not yet clear if this will either help or hinder the takraw's development. Much may depend upon a split or unity between ISTAF and the proponents of footy bag, including commerical developers. Unlike tennis here we have a sport that was not near the European heartland and so missed the conditions that might have led to an early formalisation and globalisation.

Species of GSOs

The vast majority of GSOs govern single sports, FIFA being the pre-eminent example. There are exceptions to this pattern, the first and most important being the IOC. The distinction between the IOC and the sport GSOs is that it is event oriented, that is, the Summer Olympics and, later, the Winter Olympics. As we have argued the IOC also arose from a different environment, its purpose, creation and structure marking it apart. For the originators of the IOC, sport was as much a means to an end as an end of itself. For a good number of global sporting events some purpose other than sport has often been the case, from the transplant Games (World Transplant Games Federation) to the Gay Games (Federation of Gay Games). If the IOC is a species of GSO with one member, these GSOs form a third species. As a group they represent a new species and indicate a potential for evolutionary divergence. The number of such sporting events/games is sufficient for an encyclopaedia to be dedicated to them (Bell, 2003). It has remained a singularity to the present. Its early start allowed the Olympics enormous power, along with the number of sports that it covered. The IAAF and other GSOs were in many ways founded because of the IOC and its example, along with the opportunities that it created. Its president, Rogge, announcing that nations that did not follow WADA's anti-drug guidelines would not be eligible to host the Olympic Games, signals the significance of the IOC. Similarly he pointed out that international sport federations that did not follow the same guidelines would be expunged from the list of sports in the Games.

The third and increasingly important exception is the set of specialist and support GSOs that have proliferated over the last fifty years. Function oriented, these GSOs are concerned with technical issues of sport medicine, the law and quasi-legal issues, adjudication, arbitration, doping and the use of performance drugs, and other technological developments increasingly affecting sport. Some are specific to a given sport, but the more important operate across a range of sports. Many of these are associated with the IOC, the exceptional history of the IOC again giving it pre-eminence. Evolution has now reached a stage that specialist organisations have appeared as a species of GSO. Why has this occurred? The reasons include: (1) the requirement for the independence of some of the functions that they perform from the individual sporting bodies; (2) the economies of specialisation, scope and scale that they provide and (3) the interests of client GSOs in divorcing themselves from some of the activities that may cause conflict between subordinate international federations and themselves.

Potentially forming a fourth group are the players' unions that are very small in number but in some sports are incredibly influential. There is a case for them to be regarded with individual sports GSOs but, equally, they may be regarded as something different. In the case of golf and tennis in particular the players' organisations are incredibly important.

Finally, noting that evolutionary processes continue we consider those groups that are not yet GSOs, and perhaps not even formal, but which create, develop and spread new sports. Important among these are skateboarding in various guises, competitive climbing, triathlons, beach and surf sports and collectively Xtreme sports and events. These sports are both culturally and commercially assailing the citadels of the old, and may even be moving towards new organisational forms. That many of these are largely a North American generated phenomenon is not a matter of chance.

This suggests a transition stage with the future of GSOs in their present form being uncertain. It may be that state intervention will occur or that some global body such as the UN will become involved, especially if sport migration between first and third world becomes an issue. This is a greatly problematic area. The increasingly globalised support industry of global sports manufacturers' associations, lawyers, marketing, management and promotional firms must also be considered although they themselves may not qualify as GSOs. However, there are private groups such as the NBA that have a global sports role. The potential for the species of GSOs to be driven to extinction in most cases cannot be dismissed. This prompts us to briefly examine the roles and functions of the GSOs.

GSOs: functions, roles and contradictions

Even though their constitutions are usually clear and explicit about their purposes and functions many GSOs do not seem sure how to interpret themselves, except in terms of rule making. Are they, for example, to behave as a forum, as a political assembly, a governing body (with varying degrees of authority and realms of governance), a development body, a commercial body or as an events body? Initially, the GSOs may have differed from each other in these respects but the forces of commercial development have meant that they have converged in form and function. But they are not equal. Some have gained massive revenue-raising power. Others have very little in the form of either wealth or income. But all may have changed in that where revenues were once the means to sporting ends, it is now sport that is the means to the financial success and survival that have become the de facto purpose of the organisation. In essence there has been an *inversion* of ends and means.

In the evolution of the functions of GSOs two of the most important of original functions are readily identified. These are (1) rules, governance and administration and (2) the development of greater participation.

1. Rules, governance and administration. For the great mass of GSOs, their rules deal with their sport as an abstract entity. The identity of the sport as an abstract entity is separate from those who play, especially as a set of rules. In the early evolution of modern sport – most often before the global level was achieved – this area was usually in the hands of a few individuals. In creating the rules that defined the sport they also formalised it. While this was often for their own ends they were in fact creating a public good that they could not entirely control as a played sport even under the governance of the GSO. These public goods (formalised sport) were usually created with little or no commercial interest. The interest in developing the sport was an end in itself. It is in carrying through this function that the GSOs are most clearly identifiable as INGOs and as playing a role in global civil society.

In identifying with this role the GSO had to emphasise its legitimacy (as the sole organisation to carry this out) and charitable aspects as an organisation. The public good aspects of the rules meant that no income could be derived from them. It is for this reason that the GSOs emerged as non-profit organisations, and often evolved from organisations in specific countries (rather than as international bodies *ab initio*) that had first undertaken the rule-making task at a more localised level. In a few cases these local organisations have remained as a governing body. For these organisations commercialisation and global competitions gave them embarrassingly large sources of revenue. It is quite reasonable to argue that this was not a function for which the GSOs had evolved to cope.

Through human agency the rules can respond to a degree to economic and other forces arising both inside and outside the organisation. Certainly the major evolutionary period of rule changes now appears to have ended for most sports that were formalised during the eighteenth and nineteenth centuries. These sports have reached a stable form, evolutionary developments now taking place elsewhere, that is, new sports being created or informal traditional sports taking on a modern form. This also means that this original and major function of the GSOs has largely disappeared, the evolution of the GSOs' functions and roles now occurring in other areas.

2. Participation development: mass and elite levels. One of the major functions of the GSOs has always been to develop sports in the level of participation at all levels of competitors and viewers. It is also about how these individuals are perceived, what the sport is to do for them and what they are to do for the sport. In the case of professional sport this spills over into other more active commercial functions. However, it relates very much to the public good aspects of a sport as its formalisation process develops. If it is a public good, the more who access it, the greater the level of welfare created. In that sense, this aspect of the GSOs is concerned with humans rather than the sport in abstract. The event GSOs are rather different in this context as they do not have the same requirements of the mainstream ones. These latter GSOs nevertheless also have a responsibility to develop the sport's audience, players and rules.

For some GSOs mass participation was important, but for others the form of the sport took precedence. In some cases, this involved internal conflict over objectives. One important example is the manner in which the early rule changes in soccer by the Football Association created the mass game by eliminating hacking from the game. It is considered unlikely the game would have developed if hacking had remained. Those dedicated to maintaining hacking can be regarded as placing the value of the first objective (mass participation) above that of the second (the form of the sport itself).

As commercialisation and professionalisation develop, so both objectives take on new meaning. Both rule changes and participation development push the GSO into becoming involved in the sport labour market and the development of global labour markets and labour market rules that can conflict with nation state prerogatives. This conflict between GSO and state is explored in Chapter 7. This brings into focus legitimacy and authority. And with the creation of commercial sport this brings into focus the adoption of values within the GSO that places the elite level above the mass participant. Tensions appear not only between the amateur and professional ranks, but also between the professionals if some players and/or clubs begin to enjoy superstar status.

The implication is that these two roles tend to lead if not lead inevitably to a third function, that of financial control and revenue creation on behalf of the sport or sport event. This is a step that helps the evolution of the inversion of end and means within GSOs.

Conclusion: the third role of the GSOs

Taking an evolutionary approach to the GSOs we have shown that sport existed as a commodity as early the seventeenth-century and quasi-professional athletes were in existence by that time. Because of environmental conditions obtaining in England in the following two centuries, that country saw sport beginning to be formalised by the codification of rules and the enormously important but previously ignored calendarisation of events. This was due to the existence of bodies willing and able to organise teams, increasing incomes throughout society and urbanisation creating classes willing and able to watch professional sport. Urbanisation concentrated these markets.

Sport became international with the spread of European colonisation and with the improvements in transport and communication resulting from the industrial revolution. As this occurred, some national bodies were created, grew and then between them began to form international organisations. These then took over the roles of law making, administration and development of the sports. As with all developing species, there were variants, so that some are single sport bodies, others are events bodies, and increasingly others that are progressively more specialised in their functions and roles. And in the future we can expect to see new variants based on new sports and novel commercial applications.

All of these bodies were and are known to each other and some overlap. They form a community that together control or influence a considerable part of global sports, both as economy and culture. And their functions are changing as they evolve. In particular, the GSOs are now very much occupied with a third function, marketing and revenue creation.

3 The economic approach to sport

There are many difficulties in approaching an understanding of the financial business of professional sport. These difficulties are the functions of two phenomena. The first such phenomenon – a point we have already made – is that professional sport is itself a relatively recent human activity. The second is that the academic disciplines that would seek to examine the business operations of sport are even more recent. Those disciplines, ranging from economics, accounting and marketing on the one hand, to sociology, political science and psychology on the other, are by and large the children of post-war education and research. That they are contemporaneous with the major growth period of professional sport is an accident, and one that has not been a necessary benefit. So while the two phenomena have grown at the same time and in great leaps, they have been more like two individuals growing in different countries than siblings in the one household. Only one of the disciplines mentioned above has any significant, long-term history in the examination of the sport business, and that is economics.

In this section of the book, we examine the business side of professional sport. That involves a discussion of the market forces involved, the handling of players, sponsorship of sport and its distribution (through either paid attendance or other media). In order to do this, we will draw on several of the business disciplines, including marketing, accounting, tourism and management. We also draw to a lesser extent on the sociology literature and the emerging discipline of media studies. We begin with an overview of the economic theory of sport.

Sport economics: an overview

The economics of sport has many achievements. Our examination of them leads us away from a direct concern with GSOs towards a more technical orientation. The main areas we will address are: (1) the economics of professional leagues, (2) competitive balance (wherein input is labour and output is a win/loss ratio) and, (3) the demand for attendance at regular sporting events and (4) the production function of teams. Omitted from this overview are discussions of the construction of stadia (and the related topic of sport tourism), and sport's relationship with the media. Each of these topics receives attention in separate chapters within this text.

The theory of professional sport leagues

Sport economics is primarily concerned with team sports and leagues of teams. Indeed, this has been the thrust of nearly all academic examinations of sport business for over a quarter of a century. As early as 1974, Noll made the centrality of this concern explicit:

> ... the subject of this book is confined to the business practices of teams and leagues in the four major professional team sports.
>
> (1974, p. 2)

And by so doing, he also made clear that the major theoretical bias of sport economics would be the analysis of North American sport. Similarly, the first behavioural equation in Quirk and El Hodiri's *A Mathematical Model of A Sports League* is not of a universal behaviour. Rather, it represents the '... drafting procedure in the model ... with greater team strength relative to the rest of the league reducing its access to new players' (1974, p. 59). Such drafts are almost uniquely a North American practice. More recently, Vrooman (2000) recognises this bias explicitly in the title of his review, *The Economics of American Sports Leagues*.

It is arguable, therefore, that much of what has been written on the topic of sport economics is culturally and theoretically biased to such an extent that it is either irrelevant or non-generalisable to other parts of the world. But, theoretical development is still development, and it is important to remember – and as we shall demonstrate – the USA has been the proving ground for professional sport and a great deal of the theoretical development we have seen is dependent on this earlier, ethnocentric work.

One major impetus for the development of the economics of professional sports leagues stems from antitrust concerns in the USA. For example, the implications of the National Baseball League's actions, through the reserve clause, were an explicit concern of a seminal article by Rottenberg (1956). This question of the status of antitrust exemptions has recently been brought back into the limelight (Flynn and Gilbert, 2001). From a theoretical and antitrust policy perspective, the major question which then arises is whether a league should be treated as a firm or a cartel. The antitrust aspect of sport leagues is not a concern here, but it has been a major impetus for developing theories of leagues. Following Rottenberg's initial attack, his model was formalised, modified and extended in a series of papers including El Hodiri and Quirk (1971); Quirk and El Hodiri (1974) and Vrooman (1995, 1997a,b).

What concerns us is how economics as a discipline has dealt with the dual competitive relationship of league teams, that is, sport competition and economic competition, combined with their need for cooperation.

Consequently, the major theoretical issue in sports league economics is the possibility of achieving and maintaining sporting competitive balance between teams with intrinsically different sizes of markets. In part this flows from the dual argument that (a) spectators are interested in uncertainty of outcome and evenly matched teams and that, (b) evenly matched teams and consequent uncertainty of match outcomes is financially healthy for all teams, as well as for leagues as entities.

This is what Vrooman (2000) describes as the application of 'conventional economic theory' to sports leagues. It also explains the idea that '. . . talent will gravitate toward large markets under unbridled free agency, and that constraints are necessary to defy gravity and maintain competition within a league' (Vrooman, 2000, p. 367). These constraints take the form of impositions on the more talented in order to retain them in certain teams or to redistribute them to weaker ones. The net result is to transfer wealth from players to team owners (p. 367).

Now this is the same argument as was put forward by Rottenburg in 1956, but with a rider attached by Vrooman (2000) that some of the initial premises no longer hold. This original argument has also been confirmed and developed by other writers including, more recently, Rosen and Sanderson (2001). What we can say then, is that there is a definite genealogy within the theory of sport leagues, beginning some fifty years ago in the USA and being tested and developed by researchers over time. This is important from the point of view of the development of a discipline of sport economics.

Competitive balance in sport

In analysing competitive balance between teams, that is, the proportion of wins that a team has, it is assumed – economically if not realistically – that success can be bought. This is done on a profit maximising basis in the player labour market. This model can also be extended to other inputs, including coaching and managerial talent and is consistent with the Dawson *et al.*'s (2000) estimation of managerial efficiency. The presentation of this model usually follows Quirk and Fort's (1992) simplification to a two-team league, where the two teams face different size revenue creating markets. It is assumed that they face exactly the same marginal costs of labour in a free agency market. In perfect competitive balance the winning season–losing season rates for the two teams will be fifty-fifty.

However, this is inefficient in terms of profit maximising: the marginal revenue (MR) curve of the larger market team will be higher than its marginal cost (MC) at that point. This larger market team will therefore be prepared to outbid the smaller market team to get more talent until MR = MC in both teams. Having gained more talent, the larger team will now enjoy greater than 50 per cent winning seasons. It will not benefit the smaller market team to outbid the larger market team to change this situation, as it will lose profits, making it even less able to buy talent in the longer term.

One important modification (Vrooman, 2000) is to relax the assumption of equal marginal costs. The general competitive balance result remains unchanged. Underlying the argument is a set of assumptions concerning the behaviour of fans with respect to the quality of games (higher uncertainty of outcome leads to higher quality of games). In this scenario, teams attract fans by winning. The problem is that a league depends upon a competitive balance. We therefore return to the essential problem of the theory of sport leagues: control of players as inputs in order to maintain the health of the league.

Again we see the development of a coherent body of thought. Its history is shorter, a little over ten years, but it is a beginning and points us again to the same problems of league management and the role of teams within that league.

Demand for attendance

The element that seems not to be addressed in these two preceding areas is the nature of fans and fandom. In the Quirk and El Hodiri (1974) model there is the assumption of a set of revenue functions based upon the size of markets and a sharing of total league broadcast rights plus local broadcast revenues (p. 60). Local broadcast revenues are determined by the local market size. An important point that is often overlooked is that the higher the percentage of the home team gate revenue that goes to the home team, the greater the tendency for smaller market teams to fail (p. 69). This is because they do not get as great a chance to share in the revenues from the larger markets when they are the away team.

Szymanski (2001a) has an argument based upon the collective utility of both committed and uncommitted fans. This is an interesting approach as it moves more readily and naturally to welfare effects, although the argument has distinct echoes of Quirk and El Hodiri. Szymanski argues that greatest benefit for those teams with large fan numbers is welfare enhancement. The major problem with both models from the viewpoint of this discussion is that the fan base is considered independent of sporting success, success only affecting either revenues or utility of fans.

A major success of the theory has been the overthrow of much of the folklore wisdom of how leagues operate and the impacts of the rules that they impose upon themselves, their teams and especially their players. Consequently it is argued here that the critical assumption is not the adoption of arrangements such as the draft or the reserve clause system, but the assumption that for each team there is only a limited and intrinsically local market available, although these will be of different sizes. Presaging our later argument, the critical assumption of limited local markets is increasingly invalid, with teams now competing in economic and sporting terms for an enormous non-local market, as well as enjoying the very small monopolistically competitive local market. Outside North America, the breakdown of this assumption is argued to be leading to the dominance of leagues by just a very few super teams. The Szymanski model perhaps moves closer to this possibility than the Quirk and El Hodiri model.

The production function of sport

While Rottenberg (1956) was the first to suggest the possibility of a production function (the relationship between inputs and outputs such that, Output = F (inputs)) approach to sports teams, Scully (1974) was the first to provide empirical estimates of such a function. Scully's methodology observed the marginal product of players in baseball. This is interesting because in baseball each player plays more individually than in other team sports, especially when batting. Only one player is in charge of the system at each moment in time. Consequently it is very easy to see the inputs to production. Estimated during the reserve clause era Scully's study showed a deep discount of wages on the Marginal Revenue Product (MRP) of individual players. Not surprisingly later studies have followed this methodology, and have generally agreed that the removal of the clause has led to the theoretically justified situation of Wage = MRP (Rosen and Sanderson, 2001, p. F56). This provides not only a policy impetus with respect to such rules but also has provided an enormous level of support for the conclusions of the theory of professional team sports.

While inputs are relatively visible and measurable it is not so clear how the output of sports teams should be measured. Usually this is treated as the ratio of wins to losses by the team over some period of time, especially a full season. In many ways, however, the output is also a joint product with the opposing team, that is, a contest, but this can be taken as a constant and not dependent upon production effort beyond the supply of a team to play. Rottenberg chose total revenue as an output measure but this is a lead that has not been followed as it is not only at odds with conventional production theory but also depends upon factors other than team performance such as pricing policy. Scully used a two-equation approach that circumvented most of the problems of the Rottenberg approach and allowed an individual player's contribution to revenues to be estimated. Scully's methodology has been repeated many times with increasing sophistication and to a variety of team sports beyond North America and baseball (e.g. Zech, 1981; Schofield, 1988; Carmichael and Thomas, 1995; Carmichael *et al.*, 1999). These studies use average production functions rather than production frontier estimation as is strictly implied in the theory. Production frontier estimation in sports begins with Zak *et al.* (1979). According to Dawson *et al.* (2001), with the exception of their own estimation of coaching efficiency in English soccer, all such studies have been restricted to North American major leagues. But these have allowed the individual impacts and efficiencies of team coaches to be estimated. An important study is that of Ruggiero *et al.* (1996) who compare several estimation models and procedures using the same data set and demonstrate considerable differences occur with different model specifications and procedures.

Production and re-production of sports

If there is difficulty with the commodity then we necessarily have a problem with the firm as the production unit. This is because the firm will not always be sure what it is producing. In essence there will be a continued shift from the sport being an output (an end in itself) to being an input (to other production), and this will result from and also cause, sporting teams to become the subsidiaries of other companies with related but diversified interests.

The general attributes of sport production correspond to those of craft production. While the demise of craft production in many industries is attributed to the ability to break down the pattern of work into easily imitable and repeatable practices, this strategy is not possible in sport. Equally the nature of sport consumption is strikingly different to that of most commodities or services. Even at the local level sports commodities have many of the attributes of public goods, especially non-rivalrousness. In many ways the political economy of global sport is the history of the privatisation of ownership of production and a concurrent push to diminish the status of sport as a public good. The transformation of the nature of sport consumption, using mass re-production as opposed to mass production, is crucial in this history. This has especial impacts for the GSOs in several areas. Directly affecting the GSOs are attempts to change viewing from public-good attributes (broadcast – free-to-air) to private-good consumption (cable – pay-for-view); from local to global market and the creation of the electronic event and its distribution. This dramatically alters the potential sites of profit realisation.

Given the possibility of the mass market, how could this be catered for if on-field production was necessarily retained as craft production? In the pre-electronic media period the answer lay in the re-invention of the mass stadium. This meant that changing inputs other than labour and capital could directly influence the size of the market. For some sports this translation was less easy, for example, archery, bowls and darts, which remained at the village level until the introduction of methods of mass re-production, distribution or transmission away from the point of production. In this respect the sport product, as with other entertainment, is capable of faithful re-production. Certainly the video is not the same as the live game but it has many of its essential qualities, plus the advantages of convenience and cheapness.

Craft production requires immanent skills. Only an individual person can possess such skills but they are not innate, and neither are they teachable in the abstract – they are only achieved through practice. Consequently they cannot reside in a corporate memory, which dramatically affects the property relations they engender. As a consequence training has to be 'on the job' or some simulation thereof, that is, by practice. This is enormously expensive for individual firms especially when they cannot retain the property, but they require the skills. While mass production is not possible in the normal use of the term, this does not mean that productive capabilities cannot be enhanced. In the case of soccer, for example, this means that the production of matches per unit of input is increased, so that each player plays a very high number of matches.

In the period of the super-team, the market extends beyond national leagues. The playing time this requires implies a very high demand for labour input and superstars can only play so many games each season. Thus, these teams keep rosters of players of an extraordinarily high calibre far beyond what is required of normal national league play. In this sense the organisation of soccer especially has gone far beyond that of North American sports. Soccer has a first-mover advantage that will take a lot to overcome, especially given that it is an incredibly simple game to play at the street level.

Stardom, increasing returns and super teams

While superstar is a term that is often used loosely in relation to sport, economics has created a very specific and useful definition of the term, but more importantly has a theory of this phenomenon (Rosen, 1981). A small but distinct economics of superstardom literature has grown up for sport and other industries, also largely in entertainment (de Vany, 2004). This section unites the superstar model with the idea of increasing returns (Arthur, 1989, 1996). This is applied to teams in order to understand some of the forces creating dominant super-clubs in a variety of leagues. By combining the two models, we attempt an explanation of the potential for growing competitive imbalance in leagues outside North America. This relies on the existence of global markets for what were once purely national leagues and the technology to exploit them. North American teams have much more limited markets for sport so the standard theory of leagues remains more applicable. For individual sports such as golf and tennis, a rather different approach is required where superstar theory is analysed separately in the following section of this chapter.

In essence the model suggests that teams in major leagues are no longer constrained by the size of their local markets and can have a far greater reach. Fort (2000) for example suggests that 50 per cent of all committed fans in the UK are supporters of Manchester United. This is a phenomenon repeated at the global level for Manchester and at the 2002 World Cup it was clear that David Beckham had become a global star. In North America, only the NBA appears to have this kind of global presence thanks to successful basketball leagues outside the USA. Super teams consequently have more affinity with each other than with their nation-based league opponents. A good example is the desire of Celtic and Rangers, the two peak

Scottish teams, to join the English league in order to exploit the greater global market available to the English Premier League. It is highly unlikely this move would be favoured by FIFA or by authorities in the UK but the EU rules may make it difficult to stop. Certainly some Super Teams have even attempted to move into re-production, thereby challenging their leagues on property rights.

Superstars

Rosen's superstar theory flows from the observation that there are practitioners in a great variety of fields (especially performers such as musicians, singers, sports players, film actors, artists) whose earnings are dramatically greater than the great mass of their fellow artists (Adler, 1985; MacDonald, 1988; Hamlen, 1994 for a contrary view). Because there is a need for variety and there are differences in characteristics there can be more than one superstar in a given field. Empirical tests of the model rely on the argument that earnings increase more than proportionately in relation to measures of talent. These measures of talent have to be capable of being made completely independently of the superstardom (Figure 3.1). The diagram shows the convexity of the relationship between talent and earnings that gives rise to the superstardom phenomenon. In the case of a relatively small percentage rise in talent, that is, from T1 to T2, towards the top of the performance level, the rise in revenues that this generates, that is, from R1 to R2, is extraordinarily large. Note that the convexity of relationship between revenues and talent does not necessarily arise from the superstar mechanism, as there can be

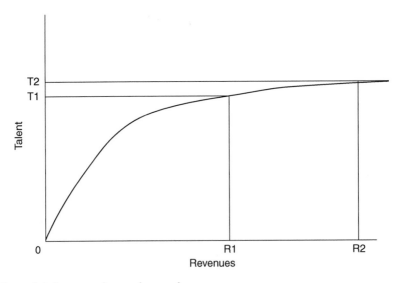

Figure 3.1 Superstardom: talent and revenues.

other explanations. In this diagram the intersection of the two axes rules out those amateurs with talent who play for nothing, many of whom may be more talented than lower level professionals. It does not have to be assumed that individuals of very high talent are a rarity, although this reinforces the model's effects. The reason is that it is not the absolute level of talent that is important but the relative level (of the superstars) compared to that of others.

Those with inferior talent are not necessarily substitutes for those with superior talent, but Rosen points out that this alone does not explain the disproportionate revenues of the most talented. The ability to create those disproportionate revenues depends upon the performer's ability to create the performance for many at the same time. The highest talented craftsperson can only work on one part of one item at a time, while a boxer can perform to several hundred in an auditorium, or a more talented boxer to several thousand in a large stadium. At an even higher level, a TV broadcast of the boxing match allows this to be seen by many millions simultaneously around the globe. In the case of the most talented boxers this translates into millions of dollars for the performance.

Super teams

In the case of the superstar in a team such as soccer or ice hockey the situation becomes more problematic because the team has to support this performance. On these grounds alone there is revenue complementarity between top teams and superstar players. Technology also plays an important role, as does the potential size of the market. Additionally, a superstar player receives remuneration from the team not just for playing skills and contributions to the team production function but also to audience generation. The implication is that a player might be employed as much for revenue generation possibilities as for on-field playing ability.

We now need to ask how leagues can generate increasing returns for clubs that could turn them into super clubs with virtually unassailable positions? They are able to do this by retaining interest via a fan base. This does not mean that these clubs will always win competitions. Instead, they can recover from two or three years of losses by having a large fan base to supply revenues in order to buy superstars who will guarantee a victory.

It is not possible to predict which team(s) will dominate a league. However, it is clear that there is a deliberate policy by the top premiership clubs in the UK to: (a) create the Premiership apart from the league, (b) create specific deals for the Premiership as a whole with TV and (c) within the Premiership create even better deals for the top teams (Arthur, 1996). The super teams will be able to buy the talent to enable them to stay at the top and over a period of failures to recover their position. It is predictable that some will continue with this status for long periods and that others will come and go. What can happen, however, is that a fall from grace can be rapid as revenues are lost but costs stay high. Bankruptcy, failure in economic terms, will be a potential threat even with moderate success.

Following from this, increasing returns in leagues to super teams will mean competitive imbalance over the long period, because the returns to victory increasingly favour the team(s) that gets ahead. They will have a huge fan base and therefore very high revenues. This implies the means on the part of the super teams 'to lock in a market, the possible predominance of an inferior product, and fat profits for the winner' (Arthur, 1996). Essentially this means that super teams lock in their dominance in both economic and sporting terms. It also means that, even if other teams win, the returns to those teams will still be lower than wins to the super teams. This will give the super teams the ability to rejuvenate their sporting success. The large profits will arise from global marketing and creation of a team brand name. Manchester United is case in point.

If we have superstardom of teams then the quality and talent of the team becomes an endogenous variable rather than the exogenous one as assumed in Rosen's original superstardom model. Consequently this model of league domination cannot rely on the superstardom model for both the team and the player. This is also different from most superstar models in that the player is an input to a team rather than a solo performer. Thus superstar teams become increasingly composed of superstars, with the possibility that superstars do not exist outside the super teams. There is a need to protect these investments, both individual and team, given a stochastic event that can throw a team away from the top while it has enormous wage bills. This may also be a problem should the sport industry undergo a downturn in fortunes. In that scenario, the best teams may be most liable to financial failure, unless they can claim an increasing proportion of the sport's revenues.

A critique of sport economics

The major problem with the standard economic analysis of sport described above is that there are so many lacunae in the analysis as a whole. These important lacunae can be argued to include a theory of the optimal forms of leagues and tournaments – there are nevertheless signs that this is beginning. There also needs to be an empirical examination of the different forms of leagues and interactions between leagues in order to overcome the bias arising from North American-based models. In its turn this suggests an analysis of the conditions for the existence of leagues. There may also be a need for an analysis of when tournaments and tours take over from leagues as competition structures. All of these areas have impacts upon the GSOs and their ability to control and influence the direction of the sport under their wings.

Perhaps most of all there is a need to understand how the competitive balance of leagues is affected in the long term by the onset of the electronic media. This is because the old assumptions used in league models no longer hold good. We need models that tell us something of the optimal size and number of matches within a league season. We need models that explain why some leagues then go on to a knockout competition to decide the top clubs while others use separate league and knockout competitions. Why do just one or two teams dominate some leagues over very long periods of time and why do fans still go when uncertainty of outcome is apparently highly desirable?

There is an even greater and pressing need to develop analyses of individual sports such as golf and tennis, especially as these are global in their nature. These problems can be addressed within the standard framework to at least some degree but solo sports have been almost entirely ignored. The economics of superstardom, coming from outside sports economics offers some hope of a fruitful analysis.

Perhaps most pressing, however, is the fact that there is no economic theory of amateur sport, perhaps on the basis that it is of little importance. The argument made here is that it is of extraordinary importance and that it now often merges into the professional ranks. Thus most competitions are open but in practice this means the top teams are professional. This may help explain why the English FA Amateur Cup which in the 1957 final attracted 90,000 spectators to Wembley, was abandoned in 1974. Amateur sport also allows the greater intervention of the GSOs.

There also needs to be some explanation of the reason for the change to open competitions and the end of the amateur–professional distinction in several sports, most of which occurred in the 1960s and very early 1970s. These included the opening of Wimbledon, the end of the player–gentleman distinction in cricket and the professionalisation of the IAAF. This requires a book-length treatment in its own right, although we can suggest that this is in part because of the dynamics of the GSOs, as well as globalisation as a background force for nation states, economies and GSOs. This also flows from the specific intent to create global markets by the marketing companies. It is argued that much of sport remains at the 'village' level. These are a hierarchy of markets for spectacle and for participation and for labour. It is this hierarchy that the GSOs partially but not wholly control. One of the major elements that seems to be determining sport at the moment is a battle between competitive balance and superstardom. This has impacts that run right through to the amateur and grass roots local leagues versions of every sport with elite professionals and elite teams. This is most clearly expressed in the organisational and institutional shifts in soccer that are attributing greater and greater proportions of the revenues to a few dominant clubs and their players. The potentially perpetual existence of clubs provides an added dimension to superstardom in that it is perpetuated by the greater proportions of the total revenues that a sport achieves. They can buy their future success. In addition they organise themselves such that new entrants can never challenge them. This may be one of the greatest challenges for the GSOs and governments if sport is to retain a social and cultural relevance.

4   Sources of sport revenue

In the previous chapter we examined the various economic theories pertaining to sport, with particular emphasis on the areas of professional leagues, competitive balance, demand for attendance and the production function. We now turn our attention to the demand for the product and in so doing adopt a marketing stance. To understand the demand for a product we need to understand the nature of the commodity as much as its production. There are innumerable demand studies in sport but they are almost entirely limited to attendance as the measure. The vast majority is of the single equation type examining the demand for attendance at specific stadia, that is, for a given team, or for a given type of sport, relative to their sports. These include Schofield (1983) cricket; Bird (1982) Rugby League Football; Hart *et al.* (1975) Association Football and so on. Empirical work is consistent with the uncertainty of outcome being an important factor in demand (Noll, 1974; Jennett, 1984; Janssens and Kesenne, 1987; Knowles *et al.*, 1992).

Our approach to the problem is once again evolutionary. In essence, we examine the relationship between sport and its delivery – in marketing terms, its distribution. We also discuss the revenues attaching to professional sport with an emphasis on the role of the media – in particular TV – and the symbiotic nature of these two industries. In identifying the natural consequences of that relationship we also examine the nature of sport sponsorship. We begin with a discussion of the nature of sport as an industry and as a marketing phenomenon.

Sport as a marketing phenomenon

Professional sport as we know requires paid viewing, either by physical presence, reporting or electronic delivery. As such – and as we have observed earlier – it has a fairly limited history. In 1719, James Figg founded his London amphitheatre which was used for animal baiting and bare-knuckle fighting, an early example of professional sport delivery. In the USA Richard Jyle Fox was the first major fight promoter in the 1880s (Cashmore, 1996). From these modest beginnings professional sport has grown into a major international industry. In the USA, for example, the sport industry was estimated in 1996 to be worth US$100 bn, and projected to reach US$139 bn by 2000 (Pitts and Stotlar, 1996). In Europe soccer alone was considered to be a US$10 bn business in 1997 (Giulianotti, 1999). This may be a gross underestimate when every year a select few clubs generate close to US$100 mn each. Each of these examples is completely dependent on the spectator viewing it – to marketers, the consumer.

In addition to a means of distribution and a paying spectator, professional sport also needs performers or players. The professional athlete is also a recent phenomenon. It was only in the second half of the nineteenth century that sports were able to pay or subsidise competitors. Those that were able to do so included cricket, golf, walking, soccer, rugby league and boxing (Cashmore, 1996). But despite such a late start, player payments at the elite level would rise staggeringly. For example, John L. Sullivan was able to command $25,000.00 per fight in the 1890s. By the 1930s Babe Ruth was earning $80,000.00 per annum (Cashmore, 1996). In 1976, the average major league baseball salary was $51,500.00, by 1987 it was $412,454.00 and by 1992 it had reached $1 mn (Gorman and Calhoun 1994). And the phenomenon is not confined to the USA. In European soccer in 1996 the transfer fee for Alan Shearer of the UK was £15 mn (US$24.8 mn). In 1997 Denilson of Spain cost £21.4 mn and Ronaldo of Italy, £18 mn (Dobson and Gerrard, 1999).

All of these examples, of course, can be accounted for in terms of the theory of superstardom discussed in the previous chapter, as can the response of teams and leagues in light of the theory of sport production. Not surprisingly, when professional league soccer started in 1888 in the UK, one of its first acts was to reduce the expense of players. In 1891 a restriction was imposed on the transfer of players between clubs (Dobson and Gerrard, 1999). This accounts for the large sums now involved and the fact that most transfers can be demonstrated to be club-motivated. The inflation rate of transfers is about 11.6 per cent per annum over the period 1972–96 which is consistent with the growth of the soccer industry itself (Dobson and Gerrard, 1999).

This rise of professionalism has been fought by various bodies, particularly in the UK, where, Dunning and Sheard (1979) suggest, sport needed to remain amateur because it was directly related to a gentleman's activity, at least conceptually. The concept of training and being paid for it would prevent it from being leisure and allow the working classes to participate. Preventing this was an early role for governing bodies. While this situation no longer obtains, major differences in structure remain evident between the USA and the UK. For example, most professional sport teams in Britain were (until recently at least) run by an elected committee, while in the USA they are individually owned and those owners have a commercial background and (therefore) orientation (Brower, 1976; Coakley, 1978). In both areas, though, they tend to gather together to form leagues that operate as a cartel, or monopoly (Leonard, 1997).

The situation in Britain is rapidly changing to match that in the USA. In 1983, Tottenham Hotspur was the first soccer club to list on the stock exchange. By 2000, fourteen were listed (de Ruyter and Wetzels, 2000). Much of this has been fan induced, as these shares are not necessarily attractive to serious investors (Woodford *et al.*, 1998; de Ruyter and Wetzels, 2000). It seems that fans will buy shares in a soccer club out of a sense of personal obligation if the club is in financial distress. This will also occur if there is no financial distress out of a sense of indebtedness to the club. There also appears to be a sense of reciprocal altruism as a result of feelings of group membership. However, this needs to be done in a way that will be noticed by other members of the group. This is consistent with the research of Fishbein and Ajzen (1975) and Fisher and Price (1992) into decision-making paradigms (de Ruyter and Wetzels, 2000).

While these changes have been occurring in the administration of the club and game, and while the fan has become a more important player in the industry, something has happened to the player. It appears that as athletes proceed through the process of playing for the pleasure of the game to later seeking extrinsic rewards (money or adulation), so they lose control of the game to a bureaucracy that will need to cater to the increasingly important fan (Crone, 1999). The reason for this is the need for revenue generated by the fan to be spent on the costs of administration. In this way, while players have seen rapid increases in salary, we can also observe a massive increase in the pursuit of various means of raising revenue for the sporting body itself. Again, in light of the theoretical development we described in Chapter 3, none of this is surprising. We now turn our attention to the sources of revenue for sporting organisations.

Now while we have emphasised the importance of viewing a game, we have not as yet sought to distinguish between different means of viewing. Interestingly, there have been major changes in the form that this takes over time. For example, in USA National Football League (NFL) in 1974, ticket sales provide 55 per cent of the whole League's revenue, 34.5 per cent came from broadcasting rights, 3.4 per cent from programmes and concessions and so on (Demmert, 1976). Twenty years later this had been turned on its head, with ticket sales providing 24 per cent, broadcast rights 62 per cent, and concessions 9 per cent (cf. Leonard, 1997). So in the last quarter of the twentieth century we see the complete dominance of broadcasting rights in providing revenue streams for the NFL. Also noteworthy is the doubling of the contribution from concessions (sales of food and beverage etc.) which now includes programmes.

As we suggested in the last chapter, the need to develop these revenues is partly due to the need of the teams that form the league (in particular those that are dominant) to afford the rising salary costs of maintaining their superior position. Additionally, we suggested that it would be the teams themselves that would be the major financial beneficiaries of competitive balance, despite increased player costs. This is amply demonstrated by the case of the NFL over the period we are discussing. In 1974 player costs were less than about one-and-a-half times that of a non-player. In 1994 they were double (cf. Leonard, 1997). At the same time, so did the market value of the franchises in the league. Looking at the total value of franchises in the four major US sports (football, baseball, basketball and hockey), in 1995 it was $11 bn and increasing at a rate of 15 per cent per annum (Worsnop, 1995). So as player costs go up, so does dependence on non-ticket revenue and so does the value of the franchises or individual teams that control the league.

Having therefore established that the theories discussed in the previous chapter apply in at least one case, we now proceed to examine each of the individual methods of raising revenue available to teams. We begin with ticket sales, concessions and what is something of a 'new kid on the block': merchandising.

Ticket sales, concessions and merchandising

Charging for team sport – as opposed to individual contests such as boxing – only began in the UK in soccer and rugby in the 1880s, and in baseball in the USA (the Cincinnati Red Stockings) in 1868 (Cashmore, 1996). But boxing remained the king for a considerable time. In 1922 gate receipts in New York alone for boxing were $5 mn (Sammons, 1988). One fight in Philadelphia (Dempsey vs Tunney) in 1926 gained $1.9 mn from a staggering 120,757 people (Cashmore, 1996). This figure can only be matched by the English FA Cup Final of 1923 at Wembley Stadium, where 200,000 people paid for admission (Cashmore, 1996).

By 1950, 92 per cent of team revenues in US professional sport came from attendance and concessions (Gorman and Calhoun, 1994). As we have shown earlier, the majority of that derives from tickets. The numbers attending are impressive. Before the First World War, baseball averaged 3,000–5,000 visitors per game and after it 8,200 per game. Despite a drop during the Great Depression, numbers have always risen at the various US sporting events so that by 1990 football, for example, was averaging 62,000 attendees per game (Gorman and Calhoun, 1994).

So ticketing has been a major source of revenue for sport bodies and most of that revenue has been distributed amongst league members. The reason for that distribution is to overcome the possibility of weaker teams being completely driven out and to maintain at least the semblance of competitive balance (see Chapter 3). However, one source of ticket revenue – which is attractive to teams alone – is that from corporate boxes which is generally exempted from sharing with the governing body (Gorman and Calhoun, 1994). This dates back to 1883 when A.G. Spalding built eighteen luxury boxes at his stadium in Chicago for use by guests and friends. Its first commercial use was by the Dallas Cowboys in the 1960s (Gorman and Calhoun, 1994). It actually does not form a huge percentage of income but we note its existence here. Its importance lies in the fact that it is not shared income so there is a clear incentive for team owners to develop this area as much as possible. Since, as we shall see in Chapter 5, most stadia are built at public expense, corporate box income is essentially provided to teams by the taxpayer.

Another small source of sport revenue is the concession, and it has been observed that not even '...half the cost of taking your family to a baseball game goes to tickets...' (Gorman and Calhoun, 1994, p. 116). This also has an interesting history. In 1887, Harry Stevens bought the right to print and sell baseball scorecards in Columbus, Ohio. By 1894, he had food and drink concessions in New York. He also invented the hot dog's name (Sugar, 1978). By 1991, the income of the Harry M. Stevens' company had reached $190 mn and it was the largest concessionaire in the USA (Gorman and Calhoun, 1994).

Similarly, licensing agreements for the use of team images or logos generates some income for sport organisations. Such merchandise earned $5.5 bn in the USA in 1985 and by 1992 had reached $12.2 bn (Gorman and Calhoun, 1994). It was the Leagues who first seized on these revenues, for example, in 1963 with the NFL's marketing arm, NFL Properties. Up to 1982 all of this division's profits were donated to charities, but not any more (Gorman and Calhoun, 1994). In 1981, the Professional Golfers' Association (PGA) of America created PGA Tour Properties to conduct joint merchandising ventures (PGA, 2000) (http://www.pga.com/FAQ/History/chronolgy_8.html).

Sport and the media

But while these sources of sport revenue have impressive histories and figures, they pale into insignificance when compared to the broadcasting incomes involved in sport. The relationship between TV and sport is characterised by grandiose sums, intensive bidding processes and staggering losses. For example, in the USA the major sport leagues earn billions of dollars in TV rights alone. Between 1990 and 1993, the NFL took TV revenue of US$3.6 bn, Major League Baseball earned in excess of US$1.5 bn and the National Basketball Association US$0.9 bn. The rate of increase in these figures is impressive also: between 1980 and 1992 the cost of purchasing TV rights for the Olympic Games in the USA alone rose from US$85 mn to US$400 mn (Gorman and Calhoun, 1994).

But why would this be the case? In order to understand this we need to look at the nature of the sport fan, an individual that we noted in Chapter 3 as being understudied. As we have seen, most economic examinations of sport treat it as a production function: players and coaches forming inputs and the game being an output consumed by spectators (see e.g. Dobson and Gerrard, 1999; Vrooman, 1995; Szymanski and Smith, 1997). An important element in this lies in the nature of sport consumption, which acts directly on the relationship between sport and the media.

As observed by McPherson (1975), consumption of sport is either direct (attendance) or indirect (broadcast and reading). This is the core product of sport and involves the consumer (often a fan) in costs that may or may not be monetary. The act of watching a free-to-air football game involves opportunity cost rather than monetary. However, financial transaction still occurs within the distribution channel through the sale of advertising directed at the fan or the witnessing of sponsorship images. (Harris (1988) estimated a total of 1,233 advertising messages associated with the telecast of a single day of cricket.) Such components of the market constitute – in marketing terms – the non-core product of sport and it is this element that forms the basis of the relationship between sport and TV.

Since these non-core elements are aimed at the indirect sport consumer, we make a brief mention of what is known about this individual. The propensity to be a sport fan has been demonstrated to cross ages and income levels and all forms of marital status. Only in gender does there appear to be any difference (Shank and Beasley, 1998). This difference may be related to women seeing sport viewing and attendance as a social outing rather than an informational activity (Dietz-Uhler *et al.*, 2000). Given this large body of potential fans then, it is not surprising that there has developed a strong competition to acquire access to this market through the medium of sport. The first of the media to use sport to access these sport consumers was print.

Sport and the print media

Newspaper coverage of sport has long been a factor in press sales. Sports sections were found in *Bell's Life in London* (founded in 1822) and later a dedicated sport broadsheet, *Sporting Life*, appeared in 1865. Similar and contemporary papers in the USA were *American Farmer* and *Spirit of the Times* (Cashmore, 1996). In this century sport coverage in newspapers has increased in response to public demand, with that demand being responsible for as much as 30 per cent of newspaper sales (Edwards, 1973). So popular has sport become as a news item that newspaper sports stories increased by 79 per cent in the Chicago Tribune from 1900 to 1975 (Lever and Wheeler, 1989). It has even been argued that some of this demand was stimulated by TV access to sport (Snyder and Spreitzer, 1983). The same researchers suggest that more news is devoted to sport than any other single topic.

There are several reasons for this. While the propensity to be a fan is generalised across society, by definition it requires the individual to be involved with the activity. The construct of involvement contains both interest and importance. So to be a fan requires more than just finding something entertaining, it also requires the individual to attach importance to the outcome, an importance that sees its most extreme manifestations in such activities as football riots. This involved fan requires regular 'fixes' of information to maintain a happy level of interest. So the media, in particular daily media become important sources. But as the supply increases, so too does the need for information, very much like a narcotic. In this sense, the media interact with each other to promote each other's news services in sport.

Sport and radio

Radio also has had a long history of association with sport. The first radio telecast of a game was on 5 August, 1921 at Forbes Field in Pittsburgh. It was called by Harold Arlin who broadcast a tennis match the next day (on Radio KDKA) (Smith, 1992). By 1927, there were live broadcasts of Rugby Union, Henley Regatta and Wimbledon on BBC (Cashmore, 1996). The sale of broadcast sponsorship rights followed quickly. In the 1930s Buick paid $27,500.00 for the broadcast naming rights of the Dempsey–Tunney fight (Cashmore, 1996) and in 1934 Ford paid US$400,000 for the rights to the World Series which was to be aired on all major networks simultaneously (Gorman and Calhoun, 1994).

Radio still retains a major foothold in sport, though the sums are not as dizzying as those in TV agreements. In 1992, radio broadcast rights payments to US pro-football teams were US$49 mn and to baseball teams US$13 mn (Smith, 1992). Radio's access to the sport fan has shown good returns on these investments. In 1987 Jeff Smulyan founded the all sport radio station WFAN in New York. By 1990 he had accumulated 10 per cent of the New York radio advertising market (Gorman and Calhoun, 1994).

TV's involvement with sport then, followed a history of media use of sport's attractiveness to the public and therefore advertisers. Oddly, the first sport telecast was by a free-to-air broadcaster that did not gain advertising revenue. In 1937 the BBC showed twenty-five minutes of Wimbledon as an experiment, and by 1939 was showing boxing and the FA Cup Final (Cashmore, 1996). Across the Atlantic at Baker Field the Princeton vs Columbia baseball game was telecast (Gorman and Calhoun, 1994). But to understand TV's relationship with sport is to understand the history of TV itself.

Sport and television

Uptake of TV was dramatic after the Second World War. In 1946, USA had only 5,000 sets (Cashmore, 1996). In 1949, still less than 12 per cent of US households had one, but by 1955 that figure was 67 per cent and by 1990, 98 per cent (Zimbalist, 1992). This penetration of the household by TV has seen a concomitant increase in the cost of TV rights to sporting events. In 1946 the rights to broadcast a Yankees game was $75,000.00 (Gorman and Calhoun, 1994). By the late 1980s, CBS was prepared to pay – and did – US$1.1 bn for major league baseball for the years 1990–94, knowing that they would take a loss of US$450 mn (Cashmore, 1996). This is completely due to the power of sport in attracting audience to TV.

It has been observed that sport on TV was '. . . a key element in launching the TV industry' (Goldlust, 1988, p. 8). But not only did it help to launch it, it has also shaped the industry structure. In USA in 1959, ABC created the first network sports division. In 1960 ABC was third in the ratings, and by 1976 the first. This was done in partnership with Gillette who gave US$8.5 mn in TV advertising during sport programmes. In 1960 ABC purchased the rights to NCAA football and started *Wide World of Sports*. They followed with the rights to PGA, the US Open, track and field and the Olympics. In 1970 they started Monday Night Football. The impetus for all of this was early market research that showed that mostly men – at that stage the major household purchase decision-makers – watched sport (Rader, 1984).

Additional evidence for the powerful effect that sport has on the structure of the TV industry can be found in TV ratings for sport events. Superbowl is the biggest single event in US sport, and: 'Of the 30 most popular shows ever to air, half are Super Bowl games.' By 1991, it cost US$875,000 for a 30-second spot in the telecast (Gorman and Calhoun, 1994, p. 68).

The value of a TV network as reflected in share price is also affected by its involvement in sport. In the mid-1990s two media empires fought for control of the Rugby League football code. This game, predominantly played in Australasia and the North of England is the major winter TV sport shown in two of the most populous states of Australia. Its TV rights were held by the company Publishing and Broadcasting Ltd. (PBL). In 1995, News Corp sought to secure the pay-TV rights and was rebuffed. In order to secure the game, News decided to create a rival league, known as Super League and set about signing players from the existing teams (Forster and Pope, 2002). Throughout the year of intense battling, the share prices of both parties showed consistent rises and falls along with the media index. At one point however, from the 6th to the 10th of April 1995, PBL's shares dropped from $3.80 to less than $3.60. At the same time, News Corp's share value rose from about $6.30 to $6.75. The reason for these changes lies in the manoeuvring for control of Rugby League. On the 5th of April it was announced that PBL was spending $21 mn to retain players within the existing league (Prichard, 1995a). The very next day – when the share movements began – News Corp announced it would spend $300 mn on the same process (Crawley, 1995). The share prices did not move back into common movement and equilibrium until the announcement that talks would begin between the two corporations on the weekend of the 8th and 9th of April when the markets were closed (Prichard, 1995b).

Similar stock market effects have been observed in sponsorship arrangements. For example, Cornwell *et al.* (2001) found that sponsorship of a winning vehicle and driver in auto racing had a positive stock price effect and Olympic Games sponsorship has been found to do the same merely by announcement (Miyazaki and Morgan, 2001). We now turn our attention to sponsorship of sport.

Sport sponsorship

Commentators have found various historical contexts for the origins of sport sponsorship: the wealthy of ancient Greece supported athletic and arts festivals in order to enhance social standing and gladiators could be supported (or owned) by members of the Roman aristocracy for the same purpose (Sandler and Shani, 1993; Cornwell, 1995). But the first modern, commercial use of this promotional activity has been traced by some commentators to the placement of advertisements in the official programme of the 1896 Olympic Games and the product sampling rights purchased by Coca Cola for the 1928 Olympics (Sandler and Shani, 1993; Stotlar, 1993). It would seem, however, that Australia may be the first nation to have been involved in sport sponsorship when, in 1861, Spiers and Pond sponsored the first tour of Australia by the Marylebone Cricket Club, claiming a profit from the activity of £AUS11,000 (Sleight, 1989; McCarville and Copeland, 1994). The first recorded use of the sponsorship of sport in the United Kingdom occurred in 1898, when the Nottingham Forest soccer team (that year's League champions) endorsed the beverage company Bovril (Marshall and Cook, 1992).

Despite this early history, researchers in the area argue that corporate sponsorship of sport, as it is understood today, is a phenomenon of the period from 1975 to the present (Meenaghan, 1991; Sandler and Shani, 1993). They observe that the largest increase in sponsorship of sport occurred between the 1976 Montreal Olympic Games and the 1984 Los Angeles Olympics, partly as a reaction to the losses incurred by the city of Montreal (Stotlar, 1993). Which brings us to the situation of the GSOs.

The GSOs and sport marketing

In Chapter 3, we argued that much of the theoretical development occurring in sport economics is derived from the North American situation. That body of theory suggests that: (1) wealth will be transferred to team owners, (2) player standards will be equalised between teams in order to maintain competitive balance and (3) super teams will come to dominate sports through the employment of highly paid superstars and will fund that investment through sale of extraneous product to or through the fan base. Importantly, there will be active seeking of an expanded geographic market in order to secure that fan base.

It is logical to argue that the North American theoretical model can only apply to the GSOs if we can show that they conform to these suggestions. In this chapter it will be noted that we have also drawn heavily on the North American situation. What we have shown is an increasing dependence on non-attendance based funding, principally deriving from broadcast rights and sponsorship. Again, we need to demonstrate that this occurs in the situation of the GSOs in order for our theories to prove correct.

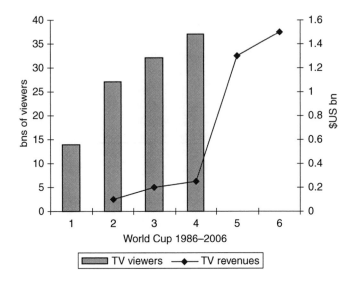

Figure 4.1 World Cup TV viewers and rights revenues, 1986–2006 (projected).

First, we look at broadcast rights. We can demonstrate that currently the GSOs derive enormous income from these. For example, the International Rugby Board (IRB) increased its revenue from broadcasting of the World Cup to £45 mn in 1999 from a mere £1 mn in 1987. FIFA claims that for the World Cup in 1998 they had 33.5 bn viewers and generated 135 mn Swiss francs in broadcast revenue. Ambitiously, they projected that they would earn ten times that sum in TV rights for the 2002 World Cup (FIFA, 2001) (see Figure 4.1).

Figure 4.1 shows that the growth of TV audience is gradual but slowing. Broadcast fees, by contrast, have been quite stable but are tipped by FIFA to increase massively. Why would they make such a prediction? The answer can be seen in figures for other GSOs.

In Figure 4.2, we see the broadcast revenues obtained for the Olympic Games. We see that the growth presents as a concave graph indicating greater rates of increase in the future. Part of this is the result of inflation and part can be attributed to the rise of pay TV. But there is another cause. In Figure 4.3, we show the same information broken down by USA and other markets. Note that the trend has been, and is anticipated to be, greater penetration of the non-US markets. This is the anticipated source of the growth in broadcast rights. What is interesting then, is that not only do we see the same sort of growth pattern in broadcast income as we did in the North American experience, but we are also seeing the search for newer and bigger geographic markets as we would theoretically expect.

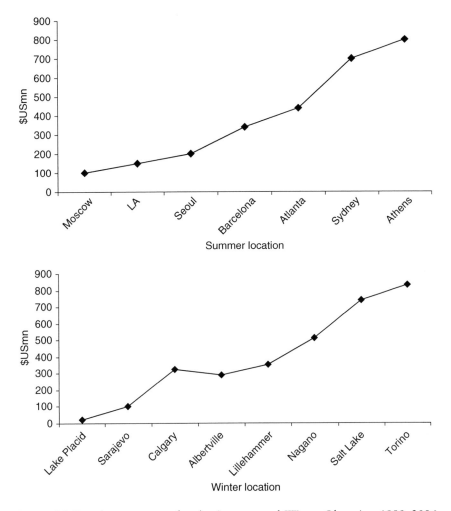

Figure 4.2 Broadcast revenues for the Summer and Winter Olympics, 1980–2006 (projected).

That said, if we were to fully replicate the North American experience into the GSOs, we would also anticipate a growing dependence on broadcasting and non-core revenues to be exhibited by the GSOs. This would also reflect the theoretical perspective of the need for super teams (in this case national bodies) to finance increasingly expensive labour inputs. In fact, this is happening. At Figure 4.4 we show the sources of income for the IOC. We see that half comes from broadcasting, 40 per cent from sponsorship and only 8 per cent from ticketing. The remaining 2 per cent derived from

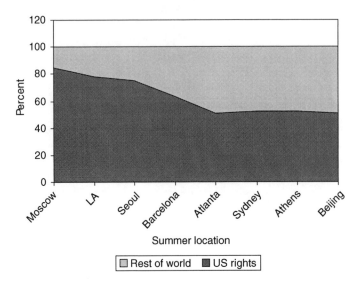

Figure 4.3 Olympic broadcast revenue by region, projected.

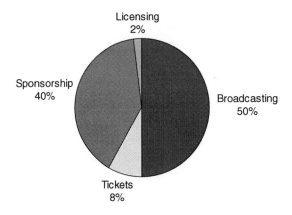

Figure 4.4 Sources of income for the IOC.

licensed merchandising. This is very similar to the figures we presented for North America.

To sum up, what we are seeing with the GSOs is the same growing reliance on broadcast and non-core revenues as we have seen in the US sporting bodies. We are also seeing an active pursuit of wider geographic market to meet costs. But are we seeing the league members, national bodies in this case as opposed to teams, becoming wealthier? Where in fact is

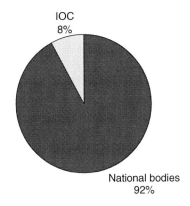

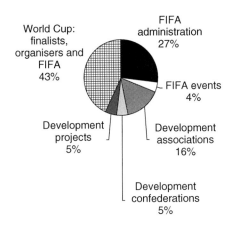

Figure 4.5 Expenditure distribution of IOC and FIFA.

the money going? Again, we are seeing this. At Figure 4.5 we show the income distributions of FIFA and the IOC.

In both cases we see that the majority of funds are re-distributed to the national bodies. But the case of FIFA illustrates two other points in our theory. Granted, the league members are major beneficiaries of the funding, but we see that the finalists – the strongest teams – reap a considerable share that is not distributed to the 'also-rans', thereby strengthening the position of the super teams. However, in order to maintain competitive balance, development funds are distributed to enable these to remain in the competition. A similar situation obtains in F1 where, as we write, the Formula One Constructors' Association (FOCA) is negotiating a $30 mn fund to assist smaller teams to remain in the sport but which is insufficient to make them a threat.

We might therefore accept that the model developed in Chapter 3, drawing heavily on the North American experience, is applicable to the GSOs. That is to say, the tendency among the GSOs is for teams to become the dominant elements within the sporting organism. While support will be directed to the teams from the governing body in order to maintain quality and parity of competition, a few super teams will develop that will dominate the sport both competitively and financially. We have seen this with both, the Olympics and soccer in particular. Funds are provided for the development of the sport in new and developing nations, but the bulk of attention is provided for the benefit of the few who dominate. Additionally, this trend is now leading to the need for the GSOs and the dominant teams to move into new geographic and demographic markets. In the following chapter we examine the means to that end: the global event and its surrounding media delivery.

The figures now involved in this area are impressive, as they are for TV rights. What is more important is the dependence that has developed in sporting organisations, in particular GSOs, on income from both broadcast and sponsorship revenue. FIFA claims that for the World Cup in 1998 they had 33.5 bn viewers and generated 135 mn Swiss francs in broadcast revenue. They projected that they would earn ten times that sum in TV rights for the 2002 World Cup (FIFA, 2001). The IOC reports that from its marketing arm it received for broadcasting, sponsorships, licensing and so on the sum of US$3.5 bn overall between 1997 and 2000 (IOC, 2001). And this dependence is increasing. For example, the IRFB increased its revenue from broadcasting of the World Cup to £45 mn in 1999 from a mere £1 mn in 1987. For the same period sponsorship income increased from £2 mn to £17 mn (IRB, 2001).

5   Going for gold
Global sports events

The relationship between the media – in particular TV – and sport with emphasis on the development of globalised broadcasting and the parallel growth of the GSO is critical. We have noted that the majority of the income derived by GSOs from events comes from (1) broadcast rights and (2) the ensuing sponsorship payments made by corporations seeking to exploit the global TV coverage offered. In that sense, we have identified major sources of revenue for the GSOs. A crucial element in understanding these events is that they are the sole means that most GSOs have available with which to raise revenues. As such the GSOs are anxious to avoid competition with other global sports events. Anything less than a global hallmark event has the potential to impinge upon the more localised revenues of the GSOs' member national federations. In this chapter, we examine the means used by GSOs to gain those revenues and also to offset their costs. While discussing only a limited amount of theory in this chapter (little has been developed), we base a large part of our argument on three particular case studies. These are the Sydney Olympics of 2000, the Rugby World Cup (RWC) of 1999 and, the structure of F1 motor sport.

The GSOs secure substantial revenues from events yet incur very few of the costs. In addition, we will show that the revenues often go to a very small group of individuals or groups within the GSOs. These events tend to occur on a no more than annual basis and often in the four-yearly cycle established as the model by the Olympic Games. Different nations bid for the right to host these events. They are broadcast and reported internationally by networks that have bid for these rights. The host nations take care of the costs and the networks provide the revenues and publicity. All of this stems from the monopoly control position of the GSOs over their individual sports or sporting events. Our discussion considers the hosting of these events and the means by which the GSOs have come to negotiate with government in such a way that the taxpayer subsidises GSO activities. We examine the motives for governments and their publics to host such events, the benefits associated with these events and the evidence for and against the realisation of those benefits. One of the interesting elements in this area is that nation states have to court the GSOs whereas the normal role for INGOs is that they will court nations. This is one of the crucial distinctions in the political economy of the INGOs. We conclude with an examination of two four-yearly events: the last of the twentieth century and the first of the twenty-first, the 1999 RWC and the 2000 Sydney Olympics. This is followed by an examination of an unusual structure (F1) wherein a series of annual national events constitute an annual championship of competitors who do not represent their countries but commercial entities. In case it is thought this is a unique structure it is noted that both motorbike racing and cycling have commercial teams and similar structures.

The events that we consider in this chapter are known either as a hall-mark or a mega-event (Hinch and Higham, 2001). When run by a GSO these are global in scope. In this text we refer to them as global hallmarks. The archetypal type of global hallmark event is that which is based on athletes representing nations (or perhaps more strictly their national federations) in a tournament of some kind. This includes activities such as the Olympics, World Cup Soccer and test cricket but there are many others whose numbers are increasing. Often, these are paraded as world championships of various types, for example, swimming, athletics and chess. Others however, are of a far more specific nature. Gay and lesbian sectors, firemen, policemen, organ transplant survivors and a host of others all have specific games events that culminate in a global meet often depicted as a world championship. For some events the financial return to the sport is small and the emphasis is on sport-for-sport's sake. For the more commercial sports this has become the major avenue for not just play but for exposure of the sport to an audience and the corresponding revenues.

Types of event that are offered by the GSOs tend to fall into distinct categories. We discuss them here:

1   *Bilateral internationals* between national federation teams on an *ad hoc* basis are often termed 'friendlies' but increasingly have to be systematically organised and sanctioned by GSOs to avoid interfering with domestic competitions and the increasingly complex and disturbingly numerous championship events on the international calendar. They do not count towards any championship. They make some money but not much by comparison with the hallmarks. GSOs provide adjudication in case of (1) disputes both before and after the event over eligibility of individuals to play for a nation, (2) punishment of rough play and cheating, (3) timing of the games and suitability of venues, (4) security and (5) provision of officials. These kind of small events, largely for sport's sake are under pressure and may disappear in intensely commercial sports. The global sport economy has evolved away from them as a vehicle for matches.

2   *Olympics*, both winter and summer, are the archetypal global hallmark event and under the IOC has enormous influence on the style, calendar and commerciality of other global sports events and their GSOs. There

is also now a World Games that is allied to the Olympics and provides an outlet for several sports including some not in the Olympic Games but whose GSOs are recognised by the IOC. We separate these because of their influence and the structure of the GSOs, as will become apparent in Chapter 6.

3 *World championships* are organised as one event on a regular calendar basis but may involve several individual sports as in athletics or just one as in soccer or cricket. A major division exists here – some are immense while others are small and peripheral except to the GSO and the sport. As we go down the global sport chain, so the GSOs and individual federations and athletes have to pay to compete. Some were created in the amateur period for sport's sake and some were created to take advantage of commercial opportunities.

4 *Tournament Circuits in highly commercial solo or quasi-solo sports* as in golf and tennis hold local tournaments at relatively fixed locations but some tournaments have a global significance. Generically we might call them the Grand Slam events. These do not necessarily make great calls on the taxpayer/host as there are well-established facilities but they are a quasi-monopoly. Here the events are explicitly graded as to their worth to world standing and this often involves the prize money offered (men and women's tours have these and are shown on their websites). The Grand Slams are the apex of this pyramid. We include in this the international motor sports, including F1 and MotoGP.

5 *New Amateur Events* such as the gay games are a new development in sport, largely ignored, but they are creating new opportunities and competition for the GSOs. They are globally based in some ways (e.g. gays, transplants and firefighters). These are the ones that best fit directly into global civil society's normative ideas. It is possible that these events will eventually determine the shape of amateur sport into the foreseeable future. The question then becomes how far can they resist any commercial pressures that they may generate and buy their own success?

Off-field rivalries

Rivalries between the national sporting bodies that constitute a global organisation are not unusual. Indeed, a case can be made that the raison d'être of these national sport federations, most of the major GSOs having come into being in the late nineteenth or early twentieth centuries, was a sense of nationalistic athletic superiority. One would therefore expect rivalries to exist between these member federations of the GSO. This rivalry can be seen at its most benign in competitive bidding for the hosting of events and reach its apotheosis in activities such as the undertaking and breaching of so-called 'gentlemen's agreements' to gain advantage.

One example of this was the English Football Association's bid for the 2006 World Cup. In 1993, the English FA Chairman and his German counterpart entered into an agreement whereby Germany would back England to host Euro 96 and in return England would support Germany's 2006 World Cup campaign. Having gained and enjoyed Euro 96, the English FA thereafter reneged on the arrangement and entered its own bid for the 2006 World Cup (Ingle, 2000). On the part of each we see rivalry between national federations within the sport seeking advantage over other national federations.

In order to convince the taxpayer and the government to pay them subsidies, both the GSOs and their member national federations mount arguments of national economic benefit. Three arguments are common to these campaigns (Noll and Zimbalist, 1997a). They are: one, the generation of new jobs through visitor spending; two, the publicity and image benefits which – it is suggested – attract both tourism and new businesses into a re-generated urban area and; three, offset of government and community investment in facilities and stadia through community use, tax and lease revenue (Ashworth and Goodall, 1988; Crompton, 1995; Babin, 1996; Gratton and Dobson, 1999; Fredline and Faulkner, 2000; Jones, 2001). In other words, governments and publics are offered a sort of miracle cure for urban decay. They can have new sport facilities, increased business investment, greater tourist income, regenerated living areas and be 'on the map' internationally. Best of all, in the long run they would not have to pay for it. It pays for itself! This is a very simple argument to mount and one that has worked many times.

In return for these benefits, GSOs require certain commitments of the host country and city. For example, in selection of Olympic venues, the requirements for even being considered are government guarantees of finance and obligations, and certain legal rights and obligations being placed on the host city. Thereafter, major considerations include the infrastructure of the Olympic village, transport logistics, stadia, finance and a media centre (Persson, 2002). Similarly, requirements in motor sport often include transport costs and provision of public utilities such as roads, hospital and security (Pope and Ransley, 1995). This last item, by the way, is becoming increasingly expensive with, for example, the Japanese security budget for the 2006 World Cup in Soccer being estimated at £14 mn (Chaudhary, 2001). Increasingly however, there is evidence that most of the public subsidy tends to go to the monopoly league rather than to the subsidised event (Noll and Zimbalist, 1997b) as we shall demonstrate in our discussion and cases, later.

Yet the expense of hosting an event – and indeed bidding for the event – is either largely or totally borne by the taxpayer of the national body's home country. This is essentially a government industry subsidy to the sport for them to locate in a specific region. The argument used is always one of economic benefit. So there is no reason that an argument applied to industry in general should not apply to sport. The only question that arises is as to whether or not the promoted benefited eventuates – a question that is asked more and more.

Given this, one needs to ask the questions: what is the motivation for governments to commit taxpayer funding to support global hallmark events for GSOs and are the suggested benefits real? To get the answers to these questions we need to understand the economics of public expenditure. An investment of public funding can be justified in any one of the three ways:

1   unused resources are being used in a way that is the most productive use of those resources;
2   if all resources are already in use, this re-allocation will generate future, higher revenues and;
3   the productivity of the public investment exceeds all other alternative investments (Noll and Zimbalist, 1997b).

Clearly, the first of these is not applicable to expenditure on a sporting event. Few, if any, governments are in possession of unused resources. Equally, the third can be rejected: no government would be unwise enough to argue that investment in a global hallmark event was more productive than investment in other areas such as education, health, welfare or defence. Only the second justification is viable: that such a re-allocation of resources will generate future, higher return. Interestingly, it also gels with the arguments put forward by GSOs when suggesting that governments bid for the rights to host an event: and governments are not slow to bid, often paying for the privilege of so doing. For example, the English FA bid for the 2006 World Cup cost £10 mn, of which £3 mn was taxpayer-provided money from the National Lottery (Chaudhary, 2000). Nor are there extremely high levels of government reluctance to become involved in the process. British Sports Minister, Richard Caborn, was quick to offer support to both the British Racing Drivers Club and Octagon Motorsports, joint owners of the Silverstone race circuit, for their improvements to traffic flow rather than allow the British Grand Prix to lose its F1 status (Rookwood, 2001). This occurred after personal phone calls from the British Prime Minister, Tony Blair, and the Chief Constables of Thames Valley and Northamptonshire, to the head of the FIA, Max Mosley, offering undisclosed assurances (Henry, 2001). That this level of government is willing to become involved in such decisions is astounding, particularly given the difficulty that heads of third world states have in obtaining an audience with the same individuals.

Not surprisingly then, the decision to bid for and host a global hallmark event is a political one most often made by an incumbent government (Pope and Ransley, 1995; Gamage and Higgs, 1997). But whether or not the decision was correct depends on how well it satisfies the criteria of generating future, higher revenues, as discussed earlier. Unfortunately, it is very rare to find proper post hoc analyses being conducted (Roche, 1992). It is the government that generally carries out or commissions such an evaluation and therefore any such evaluations tend to come from an unbalanced viewpoint

(Pope and Ransley, 1995; Boyle, 1997). It is not in the interests of an incumbent government to admit an error or the wasting of public funding on a major sporting event. Instead it is in the interests of an incumbent government to claim a success by using measures that are either flawed or based on false premises.

Additionally, quite often the bidding process has involved expenditure of public monies that are not debated or accountable. The processes may even have involved corruption (Hall, 1993; Gamage and Higgs, 1997) a claim that has dogged the Olympic movement and its associates over the last decade. We now examine the various claims of economic benefits to host communities and the rather limited international research into those benefits.

Looking good on TV: the proposed benefits of global hallmark events

One of the most common means used for establishing the benefits of a global hallmark event is the Event Economic Impact Study. Typically, these will involve a survey of an event's attendees. The process involves four steps:

1   identifying those who are not locals (i.e. tourists);
2   calculating the average expenditure of a tourist during any type of visit (not just to an event);
3   estimating a multiplier effect based on 'industry experience' (usually between 1.5 and 2);
4   multiplying the average expenditure by the multiplier to provide an overall economic benefit (Noll and Zimbalist, 1997b).

Each of these steps is seriously flawed. The major flaw is the assumption that a visitor to a sporting event will spend in the same way as an ordinary tourist. There is no evidence to support this contention. In fact, it has been demonstrated that sport tourists appear not to engage in tourist activities aside from the event itself. This is due to time or financial constraints, or both (Nogowa *et al.*, 1996). Indeed, when speaking of global hallmark events, there is a general assumption that a large number of international tourists will be attracted. Again, what evidence there is seems to indicate that this is a very minor part of the event's audience. For example, of those who visited the 1996 Olympic Games in Atlanta, nearly 80 per cent were Americans and of those 15 per cent were from Atlanta itself. The major reason for attending was an interest in sport (51 per cent) while tourism accounted for only 17 per cent of those who visited. While many of these had attended other mega-events, in nearly all cases those were within the USA itself (Neirotti *et al.*, 2001).

All this tends to make a mockery of the multiplier that is used, and many commentators have suggested that it should, in fact be reduced to below 1.0

in order to allow for costs as well as benefits (Crompton, 1995; Pope and Ransley, 1995; Coates and Humphreys, 1999, 2000). Since global hallmark events generally attract members of the host community or nation, it is arguable that any such spending is diverted away from other alternative activities, often within one's own entertainment sector (Baade and Sanderson, 1997; Noll and Zimbalist, 1997b). Additionally, when examining the tourism effect, it is also necessary to consider the possibility of tourism switching. This is the situation wherein an individual will elect not to visit an area because of the event. It is likely that this is substantial in the case of global hallmark events and this has certainly been suggested as an effect of the World Athletics Championships in 1995 at Goteborg (Hultkrantz, 1998).

Lastly, with regard to tourism, it has been suggested that even if the sport tourists are from the same country and even if they do not indulge in other forms of tourist activity, their expenditure at the event will still boost the local economy of the host city. Unfortunately this appears not to be the case. Most concession profits (e.g. food, merchandising etc.) go to external manufacturers (Noll and Zimbalist, 1997b). With regard to employment, it has been observed that any jobs created tend to be low-paying and that the real economic impacts of sport franchise and event subsidy are that (1) there is no effect on economic growth and (2) there is an actual decline in per capita income, largely through volunteerism and low pay (Baade and Sanderson, 1997; Coates and Humphreys, 1999, 2000).

Two other claims are made regarding economic benefits in hosting global hallmark events: (1) awareness of the host as a tourist destination is increased and (2) the image of the host is improved. Again, the available evidence suggests that these are not real. It has been demonstrated that awareness of a host-city as a result of the Olympics shows an increase that decays after about one year while there is no evidence to show a long-term increase in tourist visitations as a result of such awareness (Ritchie and Smith, 1991). Where such an increase has occurred it has been shown that the increase resulted from improved tourist infrastructure and did not recoup the original outlay in hosting the event (Spilling, 1998).

Improvement to the image of a host is extremely difficult to quantify and can produce quite ridiculous results. A very common method used to provide a dollar value for an event is media exposure. The technique includes equating the time a host region is displayed on TV or measuring the column inches of print in a newspaper report mentioning the country to paid-for advertising exposure, sometimes discounted but often not (Pope and Ransley, 1995). This is extremely misleading. First, paid-for advertising is designed for a specific message delivered to a specific audience. The hosts of either the Atlanta or Munich Olympics most certainly did not intend the message of their cities as terrorism destinations to be delivered. Second, the concept of mere exposure is highly debatable as a communication technique and without proper messaging becomes meaningless.

This leaves the last possibility of benefit to a host nation or city, urban regeneration and development of sport facilities that can be re-used. There is significant evidence that the hosting of global hallmark events can result in forced evictions of poorer residents (Olds, 1998) and small businesses (Jones, 2001). Furthermore, use of the infrastructure after the event has been found to be minimal, particularly when compared to the infrastructure left after a more minimalist event (Hiller, 1998). This last point is interesting. Because of the competition between members of a sport league (in this case, a GSO), there is a need for those members to have facilities at least as good – and preferably better – than their fellow members. The end result of this is that stadia have a commercial use-by date, imposed not through functionality but by intra-league rivalry. Currently the life of a professional sport stadium in the USA is about five to eight years (Baade, 1996) and Europe and other countries are not far behind. The problem for a host city left with a stadium is that new users will either want a new one in that time period, or that they will leave for a new host who will provide one. That is why purpose-built professional stadia tend to be empty quite soon after a global hallmark event.

It would seem, then, that hosting a global hallmark event is an unwise investment on the part of a nation or city. Yet, governments persist in doing it. It must be remembered that the arguments presented to governments – and thereafter their publics – are based on the premise of economic benefit. After the event, it is generally the government that made the decision that evaluates the success of achieving the stated goals. It is not in their interests to admit failure and by establishing suitable criteria they can ensure demonstration of success. The end result of this is to continue a fiction of benefit in hosting global hallmark events, a fiction that perpetuates the practice. We turn our attention now to two particular global hallmark events in order to demonstrate how this works. The two events we examine are arguably the last of the twentieth century and the first of the twenty-first century: the 1999 RWC and the 2000 Sydney Olympics.

The 1999 Rugby World Cup

The RWC is a four-yearly, international event, usually held in the year between the Soccer World Cup and the Summer Olympics. Whether deliberate or not, this has the effect of avoiding TV and crowd dilution through competition with other major hallmarks. The bid to host the 1999 event was led by the Welsh Rugby Union (WRU) (a member of the IRB who are the owners of RWC Ltd) with the support of Cardiff County Council. The County Council also pledged infrastructure support including a new stadium. However, the RWC held in Cardiff was only partial, as five Unions altogether hosted the Cup, a result of intra-league rivalry and the negative effect it can have on GSO cooperation.

The sales pitch to the Welsh public was successful. When surveyed, 90 per cent of the Cardiff community favoured the event (Jones, 2001) quoting the usual perceived benefits of international recognition, future tourism and improved city image (Ouillon, 1999). Further, a profit figure was projected of £78 mn. The event was to be run by a special office (RWC Tournament Office) with the assistance of a new consultancy firm (Rugby Solutions Ltd). The consultancy would be paid a percentage for their several weeks' work. The impression then is one of great benefit for little or no outlay.

Support from the taxpayer consisted of a three-year advertising campaign which resulted directly in about 40,000 visitor inquiries for 1999 (WTB, 2000). They also mounted a major campaign in the USA, Germany, France, Ireland and Holland. Note that three of these countries (the USA, Germany and Holland) are not famous for being rugby union nations. The stadium, which cost £130 mn, was financed by the UK National Lottery (40 per cent) and the WRU, which made only an initial outlay of £3.5 mn. The remaining WRU portion was to be paid off through gate receipts up to 2003 (Jones, 2001). The WRU was also presented with a £3 mn bill for '...media management, team travel and accommodation and transport for VIPs' (Jones, 2001, p. 246). Of the £78 mn projected profit, £48 mn was to be given to RWC Ltd with the remainder to be split between the five hosts. As we noted earlier, of the £6 mn due to the WRU, £3.5 mn was advanced towards stadium construction. Effectively, therefore, the WRU ran the event at a loss of £500,000 while RWC Ltd made £48 mn profit.

The event was deemed to be a success after an evaluation was performed. The Wales Tourist board commissioned an independent review of its economic impact, finding an £83.2 mn net benefit. They additionally claimed that only £4.8 mn of public sector funding had been expended, and suggested that the event had '... supported 2,000 part time jobs and increased hours for 4,000 full time jobs...' (WTB, 2000). The net benefit is calculated from tourist expenditures greater than would have otherwise occurred. Whether or not it also included image benefits we cannot say.

What is interesting is that there appears to have been no allowance made for expenditure on advertising prior to 1999 (WTB, 2000). Additionally, we have some problem with understanding the suggestion that public sector expenditure was only £4.8 mn. What then of the £46 mn spent on the stadium? Even if that amount were recouped through gate receipts – we have been unable to establish if this is the case – there is still a heavy opportunity and interest cost involved. And what also of the costs of policing and other services provided?

Were the event to have been a success in generating tourist income, one might reasonably expect that it would be reflected in the government's own tourism figures. There is some evidence for this. Bedspace occupancy figures in South Wales for October and November 1999, when the event was run, show an increase whereas in north- and mid-Wales there was no change. This resulted in an overall very slight change for those months in Wales (up by 1 per cent for each month over the previous year). However, the proportion of overseas visitors occupying beds for those months showed virtually no change, up from 8 to 9 per cent for October and down from 9 to 7 per cent for November as compared to the previous year. There was, however, an increase in UK tourism to Wales for 1999 from 9.8 mn trips in 1998 to 10.9 mn. This was still less, though, than in 1996 (WTB, 2001).

The most frequently used accommodation by these visitors was 'staying with friends or relatives' (37 per cent) (WTB, 2001), and it is difficult to see that this would generate the significant amounts of revenue claimed. So while we accept that there may have been some income derived by the community from hosting the event, it is doubtful that it was anywhere near the amount claimed. It would seem, in fact, that the event was almost certainly run at a very large loss to the British taxpayer, and if that is the case, where did the revenue go?

The reader will note that in the preceding section we have used published and publicly available figures. Where possible, we have used the government's own figures. We now turn to the public accounts of the IRB. As a result of the 1999 World Cup, RWC Ltd was able to pay £35 mn in dividend to the IRB Trust. This was after a net result in excess of £47 mn. Interestingly, the RWC Tournament Office that managed the event was effectively the consultancy company Rugby Solutions Ltd. This was paid 2 per cent of the expenditure and profit overall, or £1.4 mn.

This company has an interesting composition. It was chaired by Mr Glanmor Griffiths, the then-chairman of the WRU and had as its CEO Mr Keith Rowlands, former Chair of the IRB A director was Mr Tom Kiernan, Honorary Treasurer of the IRB and Chair of the IRB Policy Committee (IRB, 2001). It appears that, on their own figures, the IRB made a considerable profit on the 1999 RWC. It also seems that this profit was generated by a consultancy company that was comprised of IRB's own former and current senior executives.

In sum, the cost to the taxpayer for hosting the event was at least the £4.8 mn outlay claimed, plus: the interest on £47 mn over three years; the cost of policing and other ancillary services; any of the £47 mn outlay not recovered; and, the consultancy fee paid to the firm conducting the event economic impact study. The outcomes were a minor increase in visitor numbers that was still not as high as three years earlier (which was when the advertising campaign started) no profit from the event itself, no increase in international visitors and a marginal increase in domestic visitors who stayed with friends or relatives.

Perhaps there were positive image benefits accruing to Wales for hosting this event. The IRB thinks not:

> Although the Welsh Tourist Board, the Welsh Development Authority and the Cardiff Bay Re-development Authority did magnificent jobs for Wales and for RWC '99, and although Cardiff City Council promoted the city and decked it out in a most worthy manner, there was no

overall awareness throughout the Five Nations that a major sporting
event was taking place...

... the 'feel good factor' was lacking, leading to a poor impression of
the tournament in the minds of some commentators ...

(IRB, 2001)

If the IRB is correct, it would appear that any image benefit was actually
negative. This is a serious matter. Since, as we have shown, there was considerable public investment and little or no financial return (our opinion is
that there was a loss, but the figures are not clear enough to establish this
beyond a doubt) one would at least expect some form of other benefit to be
present. Unfortunately, this does not present itself. If indeed the image benefit was negative, as the IRB suggests, then one must seriously question the
wisdom of Wales' involvement in the RWC.

The situation of Wales and the RWC raises several important issues
regarding the way that some GSOs deal with nation states and the hosting
of hallmark events. First, the bid to host the event requires competitive bidding between nation states as well as between national sporting bodies. This
is important. While there is understandable rivalry between the national
bodies, it is through the influence of senior individuals in those bodies that
governments are convinced to compete for host rights. Second, the GSO
exists as a representative of many national bodies and these bodies appoint
executive authorities from their own ranks. Usually, these people are also
senior members of their own national bodies. Three, the potential for these
individuals to coerce their own national bodies, influence their own governments and then negotiate terms with themselves as representatives of the
GSO leaves extraordinary scope for unethical behaviour. We are not suggesting that this was the case in Wales, but are instead making the point that
this is a possibility that must exist within the structure of this type of GSO.
It is a subject we return to in the following chapter.

The 2000 Sydney Olympics

We have observed already that governments are keen to become involved in
global hallmark events. This is peculiarly so of the Olympic movement, and
the willingness to pay for the privilege is extreme. The Australian Federal
Government was as keen as any other to be involved in the Olympics when
the opportunity came to host the 2000 Games. They had already contributed $5 mn to the bid and they further pledged $150 mn for facilities.
(All figures are presented in Australian dollars.)

However, as is common with major infrastructure projects, costs
escalated dramatically. Total cost of the games to the Federal taxpayer
would eventually be $1.1 bn (DPMC, 2001), while venues alone would cost
the New South Wales taxpayer $1.6 bn (NSW Treasury, 2000). There may

be some overlap in these figures, but certainly government investment in the Sydney Olympics exceeded $2 bn, on their own figures.

Again tourism was – and is – one of the major benefits claimed. Visitor arrivals to Australia in 2000 showed a 10.9 per cent increase on the previous year. But this is still less than the 15 per cent increase achieved in 1993 and the 12 per cent increases in 1994 and 1996 (Tourism Forecasting Council, 2001). Those years did not have Olympics. More importantly, for the same year, the growth in world travel and tourism demand rose from US$3,500 bn to US$4,000 bn, or by about 14 per cent (WTTC, 2001).

So in a year when international tourism rose by 14 per cent, Australia experienced a rise of only 11 per cent. We suggest that it is possible that the Olympics were responsible for Australia falling below the world average. Indeed, it is probable that a good deal of switching occurred. A breakdown of September arrivals for the year 2000 show that US tourism increased by nearly 100 per cent over September 1999 to about 53,600, a major achievement that we agree was likely due to the Olympics. However, significant others went down (DISR, 2000):

- People's Republic of China (down 33 per cent)
- UK (down 15 per cent)
- Taiwan (down 30 per cent)
- Malaysia (down 25 per cent) and
- Singapore (down 30 per cent).

While there was undoubtedly some increase in tourism, it was offset by switching and still not meet the level experienced worldwide for the same period. That is not to say that there was not a tourism benefit, in fact it seems that this was a case where there was, but we must ask: (1) was that benefit sufficient to justify the more than $2 bn spent and (2) was the increase due to the Olympics or did the Olympics suppress what would otherwise have been a higher figure for tourism?

Again, we examine the image benefit that was claimed. The Australian government states that:

> ... alliances with Olympic sponsors generated additional publicity for Australia in 1999–2000 alone, which at commercial rates would have cost over $100 mn ... and, ... the $12 mn allocated by the Commonwealth Government to the ATC [Australian Tourist Commission] for Games-related promotional activity delivered the equivalent of $3.8 bn in publicity for Australia.

> (DPMC, 2001)

This is a rather extreme case of misusing media audit. Note the use of the words 'would have cost' and 'the equivalent of'. Clearly the dollar values ascribed are not income: nor are they a saving. The Australian government never intended to purchase that airtime or to deliver messages in that way.

There is no measure of the effectiveness of that communication. This is a pity, because it is now too late – in all probability – to examine what impact the Olympics did have on visitor intentions and behaviour. That could have been measured and a proper analysis of the value of this investment established. Unfortunately, if it has occurred, it has not been reported.

With regards to other costs, the Federal Government has been very open about real spending. The figures given above included policing and ancillaries. Interestingly, of the facilities built for the Olympics, we see that the New South Wales government has now established an Olympic Authority that is charged with development and management of the area (Sydney Olympic Park Authority, 2001). This again is at taxpayers expense on top of the initial $2 bn outlay.

But did anyone make a profit from the Olympics? In our discussion of the RWC, we observed that the IRB certainly did from the 1999 World Cup. One group who expended on the 2000 Sydney Olympics was the Australian Olympic Foundation, who expended $3.3 mn in that year. Not surprisingly, they recorded a surplus in that year of $90.9 mn (AOF, 2001).

In sum, the Australian and New South Wales taxpayer expended in excess of $2 bn and the state government has an ongoing expense in managing the Games area. There was a possible tourism boost – mainly from North America – but this was offset by declines from other countries. The rise in tourism was lower than the rise generally reported internationally. The only body that has reported a profit from the event is the Australian Olympic foundation. They outlaid $3.3 mn and received a return of 2,755 per cent on that investment.

What makes the 2000 Olympiad different from the situation obtaining in Wales in 1999 is the structure of the GSO involved. In Wales, the IRB was a governing body formed from and representing a group of national bodies. In the case of the IOC, the national bodies are essentially approved by the GSO. They are effectively its agents and derive any funding from the top down, as opposed to the IRB, which is funded largely from the national bodies. This gives the GSO much more power in negotiations because the national bodies are acting for their own survival in competing for hosting rights. Additionally, the IOC itself has ensured that its own, self-appointed membership is strongly represented in the influential circles of power. It is an extremely effective lobby group. Consequently, it is well able to negotiate with and draw extreme concessions from governments that are negotiating from a position of weak influence.

And then there was one: Bernie Ecclestone and modern F1

What we have seen in the two cases above is a situation wherein governments commit to hosting and funding activities on behalf of the GSOs. The profit from the activity goes to the GSO or one of its members with other fees sometimes being paid to individuals within the GSO for consultancy purposes. We now move on to discuss an extreme case of this type of activity (F1 motor sport) and show how this situation can develop. We continue with the evolutionary approach that we established earlier in the book and demonstrate how an organisation is capable of changing from purely sporting to purely commercial. Before we begin that discussion we make a brief mention of the nature of cartels and how they function.

We have already established that GSOs operate as cartels for the benefit of all members. As such, they increase individual members' profits by acting as the sole bargaining agent for output and pricing decisions. The effect of such monopoly leagues in sport generally is to create an inflated price for a host city in subsidies. This takes effect through the need to move teams or events (enforcing control over league members) and in controlling host communities (Fort, 1997; Noll and Zimbalist, 1997a).

But cartels are conceived on the basis of economic situations that obtain at the time of creation and these situations can change. It is of the nature of these agreements that it can be very difficult to change the rules thereafter, largely because of the need for either unanimous or majority support among members. It is therefore in the interests of individuals to break rules and agreements in order to increase income, sometimes at the expense of other members. Where no prohibition exists on rule breaking, it will tend to occur (Baade, 1996). Hence it is natural to expect that in sport, as in other cartels, some rivalry will occur between members and this may include breach of agreements and sometimes rules. We now show how this occurs and the effect it has, through our discussion of F1.

Modern F1 began with the first world championship in 1950. Although claiming the title 'world' it was – and has remained – essentially a European sport. In its first decade, the races were conducted on the continent in spite of a short period in which the Indianapolis 500 in the USA was included: none of the European teams attended that event. In this period Italian manufacturers dominated the sport. Alfa Romeo, Maserati and Ferrari between them would win eight of the first ten world championships. Of the other two, one was won by Mercedes Benz and the other, in 1959, by a British Cooper Climax.

The winners of these championships also show a geographic bias. From 1950 to 1959, Italians won three times, an Argentinian resident in Italy five times, an Englishman once and an Australian resident in Britain once. Significantly, the native English speakers won the last two championships of that decade.

During this period, the sport was available to the (albeit well off) amateur. Aspiring champions could – and did – purchase second-hand race vehicles from the manufacturers and participate in events. Famous names such as Jack Brabham, Stirling Moss and the American Masten Gregory all followed this route. The sport was administered by the International Motor Sport Federation (FISA), an arm of the FIA in Paris. Subsidiary bodies in the European nations, for example, the Royal Automobile Club in the UK, administered the national interests and rules. FISA itself was amateur as was the FIA. Indeed, even now the President of the FIA is an unpaid official.

The second decade of the sport marked great changes in the nature of F1. The victory in the world championship of a British driver (the Australian born but England resident and British licensed Brabham) in a British car occurred in the first Grand Prix held on American soil, the US Grand Prix at Watkins Glen in 1959. It marked the beginning of a period of British domination of the sport. From 1960 to 1969, the world championship was won by: an American resident in Italy once, an Australian resident in Britain twice, a New Zealander resident in Britain once, and Britons six times. Each of these individuals was a native English speaker. With only three exceptions (Ferrari in 1961 and 1964; Matra in 1969), the vehicles used were of English design and construction, and with the exception only of Ferrari (1961, 1964) and Brabham in 1966 and 1967, the engines were of British manufacture. The teams, including Honda in a brief foray, were based in the UK, with the notable exception of Ferrari in Italy.

In this second decade, the sport was still available to amateur entrants, but becoming less so. Instead, the trend became toward the ownership of teams by wealthy amateurs with employed professional drivers to steer them. For example, Rob Walker of the whisky family was an entrant in the sport during this period with vehicles from manufacturers Cooper, Lotus and Brabham. Frank Williams was a racing car dealer who entered Brabham cars with Cosworth engines. Ken Tyrrell, a timber merchant, would win a driver's championship through the former Olympian Jackie Stewart in a French Matra with a Cosworth engine.

To a very large extent, it was the development of that particular engine which allowed the development and creation of the British based teams that would enter the following decade. Prior to 1965, British teams had been reliant either on the BRM engine, designed for use in the BRM chassis, or could buy an off-the-shelf Coventry Climax engine (from the manufacturer of fire pumps). In 1966, this company returned to its core business. The gap was filled by Cosworth Engineering who developed – with the assistance of the Ford Motor Company – what was essentially two Ford Cortina engines joined at the bottom to form a V8 racing engine. The engines were relatively cheap, reliable and very powerful. Most racing engines of this time were essentially highly modified versions of road-going engines. For example, the Repco engine used by Brabham in 1966 and 1967 was an American Oldsmobile fitted with Daimler connecting rods and pistons. The availability of the Cosworth engine led to the creation of several new teams. Tyrrell we have already referred to. Also there was McLaren who manufactured their own vehicles. A former driver, Bruce McLaren, ran this company.

By the early 1970s a situation had developed wherein the teams were being run by former drivers (e.g. Brabham and McLaren) or by engineers (e.g. Enzo Ferrari, Colin Chapman at Lotus and Ron Tauranac, who took over from Brabham) or by wealthy amateurs (e.g. Ken Tyrrell and Frank

Williams) using a common engine with the exception of Ferrari. At the same time, sponsorship was entering the sport, having been first allowed in 1969. The teams derived their incomes either from the limited amount of sponsorship available or from other sources. Those other sources in most cases derived from the sale of racing cars to other formulae and the growing North American market. Only Ferrari and Lotus sold road-going vehicles. The teams of the wealthy amateurs could not derive any income from these sources, and remained dependent on the owner's wealth, sponsorship and appearance and prize money. Individual teams negotiated appearance money with individual track owners. If the money was insufficient, then the team could always choose not to attend.

The situation changed dramatically with a single occurrence in late 1970. In that year, a man with a background in second-hand cars and motorcycles as well as in land development purchased the Brabham F1 team. By the end of the century, Bernie Ecclestone would have a road in Hungary named after him, own the travel company that moves the F1 teams around the world, negotiate with Sylvester Stallone over the rights to make a film about F1, have the London finance world's slang for £1 mn named after him and even have the rights to pay-toilet money at a European racing circuit (Frank, 1998). It was an extraordinary achievement borne out of the evolution of a GSO.

One of Ecclestone's first moves on becoming a team owner was to realise the value of F1 as a commercial product. He negotiated the first £1 mn sponsorship for his team: with Martini for the 1971 season. Most importantly, in the mid-1970s, he became the President of the FOCA. This was a body that represented all of the team owners, as opposed to the FIA. The FIA itself is an administering body whose function is to: '... approve every circuit wishing to stage a grand prix; it subjects every F1 racing car to technical scrutiny...' (*The Economist*, 2000, p. 97). It is essentially a rule maker and scrutineer.

It must be remembered that Ecclestone was a businessman among amateurs, former drivers and engineers. His task was to deal with a voluntary, unpaid officiating body. It was natural that the other members of FOCA would look to him for leadership in an increasingly expensive sport and allow him to begin negotiating on their behalf with organisers. They also allowed him to handle their transport arrangements. By 1977, Ecclestone had also started using the services of an in-house lawyer, Max Mosley, in his negotiations.

By 1980, with sponsorship and broadcasting becoming major revenue sources, a great deal of bargaining power had been vested in FOCA. Ecclestone and Mosley succeeded in negotiating an arrangement with the FIA that would eventually see TV revenues divided so that 47 per cent would go to the teams, 30 per cent to the FIA and 23 per cent to a company, Formula One Promotions and Administration (FOPA), which would pay the prize money thenceforward. Mr Ecclestone was the owner of FOPA.

Significantly, the agreement also leased the FIA's commercial rights to F1 to FOCA. These would eventually be leased on to FOPA and Mr Ecclestone.

The agreement, known as the Concorde agreement after the Place de la Concorde where the FIA sits, is renewed every four or five years. It had a major effect on the structure of the sport and placed a great deal of power in the hands of the cartel members (FOCA). But it was established in one economic situation and rivalries would naturally occur as that situation changed.

Interestingly, FOCA members also infiltrated the FIA, the other party to the agreement. In 1987, Ecclestone became vice president of promotional affairs with the FIA and Mosley was on the senate. Also on the senate was Marco Piccinini, a Director of Ferrari. Also in 1987, under a renewed Concorde agreement, the FIA leased its TV rights to a company called Allsopp, Parker and Marsh. This company had two directors: one '...a close business associate of Mr Ecclestone since 1984...' and the other '...a trustee of an offshore trust set up by Mr Ecclestone's Croatian second wife...' (*The Economist*, 2000, p. 99).

Mosley became President of the FIA in 1991, a position he still holds. In the same decade, Mr Ecclestone became a circuit owner (Spa Francorchamps), which put him in the unusual position of having to negotiate fees with himself. In 1995, an astounding thing occurred: the FIA senate approved a deal granting Mr Ecclestone an exclusive lease on the commercial rights to F1. The vice president of FOCA claimed not to have been informed prior to its announcement (*The Economist*, 2000, p. 98).

In 2000, the FIA voted to give the commercial rights to F1 to Ecclestone's Formula One Management Ltd until 2110 – more than a hundred years – in return for US$360 mn. This was inclusive of TV and promoter fees. This was an astounding deal considering that in 1997

- the combined F1 TV audience including news and repeats was eight times the world population;
- the cost of putting the teams on the grid was US$1 bn;
- the F1 brought in US$750 mn in sponsorship (five times the amount brought in by American NFL);

and in 2000

- the rights to NASCAR for one year were US$400 mn and;
- the rights to Premier League Soccer were US$2.4 bn for three years (*The Economist*, 1997, 2000b; Frank, 1998).

At the time of writing, the commercial rights are vested in a company named Slec Holdings (Mr Ecclestone's wife is Slavica Ecclestone) in the Channel Islands. It is 75 per cent owned by three banks that took over shares in Kirch and EMTV when they collapsed. Mr Ecclestone had sold those shares for £950 mn (Griffiths, 2003). He retains managerial control of the company.

A new development in the cartel has occurred over the period of Mr Ecclestone's involvement. The large car manufacturers have become team owners. Toyota, Ford (through Jaguar), Daimler Benz (through McLaren), Fiat (through Ferrari) and BMW (through Williams) have become partial or complete team owners and members of FOCA. They see themselves as valid members of the cartel and would like their share of the commercial rights held by Mr Ecclestone. To that end, with the support of teams they partially or outrightly control, they are moving to establish a new company Grand Prix World Championship (GPWC). This may be a threat to address perceived financial and power imbalances in the cartel, but it goes to show the changing nature of cartels and the jockeying for power within them.

F1 represents yet another type of organisational structure in GSOs. While we have seen national bodies creating a GSO (IRB) and a GSO creating national bodies (IOC), F1 is different: it is the situation of individual players (the race teams) creating a cartel, then taking over the GSO and vesting all its power in a single individual. In this power structure they become very similar to the IOC in some ways. The major difference is that with the power in F1 went virtually all of the revenue. It is quintessential capitalism and completely based on TV rights. It may even be the future of sport.

Commentary

This case especially indicates that while the GSOs exist for the benefit and enrichment of the member bodies, control can become vested in the few superteams among them. In order to maintain competitive balance, the weaker members will be propped up but not to the extent wherein they become a threat to the more powerful. Their main sources of income are increasingly dependent on TV and sponsorship rights and that increase is dependent on the growth of newer and more dispersed geographic markets. In order to minimise operating costs they will encourage nations to compete for the purported benefits of hosting their events.

But despite having an aura of presenting a general economic theory of (professional) sport the basis of current sport economics is profoundly historically specific. The background to this specificity is that over hundreds of years sport has changed from being largely a pastime to being a market commodity. Yet sport economics is concerned only with sport as a commodity, and within a highly specific set of firms, inter-firm structures, that is, professional leagues, and customers. The largely amateur sports organisations and institutions that facilitated this change are largely ignored by standard economic analyses of sport. In the economic analysis of sport it is as if national sports organisations, and the great mass of GSOs such as FIFA, the IAAF, FIA and the IOC, did not exist. Within this historical specificity, centred on the latter middle half of the twentieth century, theory still has to come to terms with the new markets and media approaches that have been applied to sport and to which sport has applied itself. Certainly the electronic media are represented in most models in a manner that is closest to the practices of the 1960s–1970s.

One of the few exceptions to this is Cave and Crandall (2001). They not only analyse the impacts of the media but also give an historical overview of US sports leagues and European soccer as an introduction to their analysis. They then presage in a rather different form one of the arguments of this chapter – that property rights in sport are of enormous importance. Unfortunately their paper is largely descriptive and so stands outside the major analytical and reductionist framework of economics. These new media approaches cannot be divorced from the global nature of sports markets, the largely North American theoretical bias notwithstanding. Just one more aspect of this is mentioned here. This is that both inside and outside North America the electronic media presence of leagues and competitions has already given rise to the development of teams that are superstars in their own right. Ultimately, and notwithstanding their necessity for organised competition such as they find in their leagues, these teams have the ability to challenge those leagues and the associations and organisations to which they belong. Again this ignores the emphasis that there is now upon global events.

The organisation of sport, and sport competition in less than two centuries has moved from the 'village' to the national level, making a crucial move from 'community' based organisation and institutions to organisation at the level of the polity. Moves to supra-national and global competition still continue and are probably intensifying. As it moved away from the village, from being pastime to commodity, so sport has also moved from the amateur to the professional. Yet sports economics yields little or no sense of the evolution of sport, let alone its history. What economics ignores is that the move to global sport took place in the amateur mode. Most spectacularly this happened in the Olympics; but the evolution of the Grand Slam in tennis, Test matches in rugby union and cricket, and international athletics meets also took place in the amateur mode. And certainly this happened before most sports became fully fledged commodity producing industries. This has had two extraordinarily important consequences that should not be ignored in the economics of sport.

The first of the consequences is that for most sports, their organisation at all levels from village to globe, has evolved and essentially been controlled by non-profit organisations. This remains the case as virtually without exception the GSOs remain non-profit organisations in a thoroughly professional world. This is perhaps most strikingly carried through in the present IAAF, which is the controller of professional athletics and, despite its title, now apparently decries its own amateur past. Of course the GSOs cannot interfere too much in the affairs of professional leagues and tournament sports without provoking a reaction. Yet there are some areas where they still assert an economic authority. A recent simple case was a FIFA ruling on soccer transfers. FIFA is able to assert authority here, as the soccer labour market is global with leagues wary of each other, especially after the Bosman case. The new rules proposed by FIFA, as they apply limit transfers to Britain, to the close season (i.e. off-season) and to January and August. Moxey, the CEO of the English first division club Wolverhampton Wanderers is reported as saying, 'If FIFA get their way it's going to make every manager's job a lot more difficult. We know for definite that the window is in place for international transfers, but we want to maintain the "status quo" here. It has worked and served English clubs very well so far' (Moxey, 2002).

While it has often been claimed that the era of the amateurs, the 'gentleman-administrators', such as Brundage, Kilannin and so on, is past, few have critically examined the organisations within which they operated as a group. It is as if these organisations were cypress, entirely taking on the hue of the individuals that inhabited them. Yet their non-profit status and structure remains the case even though the sports and events involved are now entirely professional. So sports economics has no sense of organisation and evolution and is entirely without any concept of time.

The second consequence is concerned with time as future as the move to the supra-national and global has the potential to bring the various levels of any sport's organisational hierarchy into conflict. Already there appear to be conflicts of jurisdiction between FIFA (global), EUFA (supra-national regional) and national soccer associations. In a purely amateur and pre-commodity period this would be a battle purely over control. Increasingly, however, the market for sport is a global one so that these battles are both broadened and intensified into ones that also concern profits, profit distribution and property rights to profit-generating events within sport. Consequently the GSOs are increasingly likely to be a party involved in long-term disputes (with their constituent members) over ownership of the rights to various events. In the shorter-term, before ownership is resolved, these moves increasingly involve negotiation over the distribution of the proceeds of those events. These arguments flow from the previous chapters.

The absence of history is central to our argument for taking a political economy approach in this book. Yet there are major methodological stances of the economic approach that have to be acknowledged as extraordinarily important. The first and foremost of these is the consistency and openness of its methodological stance. Within this are a series of other points. In summary these are (a) the clarity, consistency and crispness of its theoretical assumptions, especially that of individual rationality and (b) the ability to derive unexpected and insightful theoretical conclusions from those clear assumptions.

But economists have shown a deep ambivalence to sport as subject matter. They highlight the universality and significance of sport on the one hand and then immediately reduce it to tractability and illustration on the other. For example, Rosen and Sanderson (2001) seem aware of this when they say:

> Perhaps one day Political Economy will sort out how franchise owners have managed to impose reserve option restrictions in the past and salary limitation treaties today. The main intellectual interest in the topic currently does not so much stress the political struggle for property rights as the problem of externalities among teams.
>
> (F65)

In many ways this comment reflects the position taken in this chapter and in the book as a whole.

Given this ambivalence, a possible key to simultaneously understanding the strengths and the weaknesses of the approach is that conventional economics operates in a reductionist manner. In the sport context this means holding as fixed organisational and institutional structures such as the GSOs. The analysis is almost invariably conducted at a single level, usually team or league but rarely at the sport or industry level. In particular it ignores the interactions of the actors/agents at each level with those at other levels. The strength of this approach is that it allows concentration in detail on processes at one specific level by treating them in isolation. This analysis is usually at the elite level, but being almost entirely concerned with the team and league level of analysis – what can be called 'stadia economics' – current sports economics neglects the interactions between the electronic media and sport. Nevertheless recent works give extraordinary prominence to professional leagues and team sports. Consequently there is no coherent or over-arching theory of sports business or the sports industry. The economics of sport is a very incomplete patchwork. Ironically one of the greatest achievements of standard sports economics, describing how *teams* operate within a *league* and what impact this has upon the league as a whole, does span two levels of organisation. Indeed there appears to be a synthesis emerging in the sports economics literature that will unify production, demand and league theory into a whole.

The GSOs have moved from being purely governance mechanisms to being production mechanisms. The IOC was the one GSO that from its inception was a producer, albeit of an amateur event that brought in little revenue. FIFA was very quickly a producer in the World Cup. So there is a tendency for GSOs, small and large to create events out of the sport that they control in order to raise revenue that lessens their reliance on the national organisations that are their members. Another means of doing this involves the use of Third World labour, which gives more power to the GSOs who are represented there. For example, the USA both imports and exports sport labour. It exports from baseball, basketball and ice hockey. It imports in the same areas, usually importing higher quality because it offers higher returns.

The critical assumptions lying behind the analysis of leagues – that there are naturally limited markets for individual teams – needs to be overturned. Once this happens the economics of leagues will become much closer to the reality outside North America. In many ways the markets for North American league sports are limited, having little weight beyond North America. Avoiding the limited markets assumption allows the idea of increasing returns and the returns to stardom to be used. This then suggests that teams can and will become economically dominant and simultaneously virtually unassailable on the sport field except by other superstar teams. They may suffer reverses in specific seasons and even over two or three seasons, but they will retain a global following that will allow them to re-create themselves professionally. The ability to raise capital because the return to talent employed is global will be highly significant.

This suggests that individual professional leagues and teams will challenge the GSOs for dominance in their specific sports and that an international coalition of such teams can dictate terms not only to national associations but also to their GSOs. Some leagues, as they have done in the past may declare independence and operate autonomously. The commercial pressures that drive this are restricted by the need for a global market. In both cricket and rugby league in Australia the GSO could not protect its own leagues and teams against the interlopers. In other sports, such as chess and tennis, there have been similar moves. The level of power that a GSO can bring to bear may be crucial in deciding outcomes. For the GSOs the most important of these weapons in both symbolic and economic terms is their possession of a world championship or some other global hallmark event.

The GSOs have an extraordinary number of strengths and weaknesses and these cannot be balanced in any rational manner. These result from a series of forces that they initiated but over which they may now have little control.

6 Architectures of control
Structure and process in the GSOs

Examining decisions

Having examined the history, development and external environment of the GSOs we turn our attention to their internal processes. The GSOs are reticent about disclosing their internal affairs. Very few expose their accounts to conventionally accepted audit standards. FIDE (chess) and the International Triathlon Union (ITU) are two which do, while the unaudited figures previously provided by the IOC leave much to be desired (Brewer, 2001, pp. 2–3). Only recently have FIFA and the IOC begun to release audited accounts. Given the absence of full disclosure, analysis of these organisations becomes detective work. For example, when *The Economist's* Intelligence Unit examined F1, Bernie Ecclestone and their relationship with the FIA (*The Economist*, 2000a,b), it was forced to rely on clues and hints that were either unavoidably or fortuitously available rather than clear open statements. Nevertheless these sometime glimpses through the opaque exteriors of the GSOs are quite telling. When they occur, the observer has to piece together a puzzle of what has happened and deduce its meaning by a combination of evidence, logic and surmise.

An example of this approach relates to three far-reaching decisions for many sports. These were taken at the IOC's 114th session in November 2002 in Mexico City. The first limited the Summer Olympic Games to 28 sports. The two other – closely related – decisions (1) confined the Summer Games to 300 events within those 28 sports and, (2) limited participation to no more than 10,500 athletes and a corresponding number of administrators and coaches. The decisions were made on the basis of proposals put forward by the IOC Executive Committee, including the President, Jacques Rogge. The three proposals were adopted unanimously by the 117 members present. Coming less than two years after Rogge became its President in a contested ballot, it seemed a ringing endorsement of proposals that he was backing. And all the more so as the decisions represented a reversal of the expansionist policies that the IOC had followed during the Samaranch presidency.

The question must arise of how such an apparently fundamental change in direction and philosophy could take place so rapidly. Perhaps the decisions had a rational basis – evidence that the limit of expansion had been finally reached. But if this is so, it is surprising that all members should have been of the same mind. Consequently, how the decisions were made is as important as the grounds on which they were made. Having been made in one of the most powerful (if not the most powerful) of the GSOs, these decisions have ramifications for many sports and the professional and amateur athletes who compete within them. For some sports not receiving the potential media coverage of the Olympics – and not being able to offer the prospect of gold to aspiring elite athletes – means they will remain or become marginal. For athletes already committed to a sport by virtue of their specialist training it can wipe out any pathway to a financially viable professional career.

Despite their significance, we know little about how such decisions are made inside the GSOs. In this chapter we present an empirical framework for more theoretically oriented interpretations of what happens inside the GSOs. This is further developed in the following chapter. In most discussions of GSOs and the emphasis on the personal politics the absence of reference to organisational elements is striking. This is strangely akin to the economic analyses of sport that almost completely ignore organisations (Chapter 3). We now rectify and examine the formal organisational structures and processes of the GSOs – namely the internal elements that both organise and affect decisions such as those made in Mexico. In doing so, and despite the vast differences in the sports, events, constituencies and traditions that each of the GSOs represents, we find some striking similarities in the ways the GSOs are structured and operate. This goes towards resolving the contradictions inherent in a sudden shift away from the previously expansionist philosophy of the IOC. At the same time it helps explain why a related decision to be made at Mexico City was postponed, rather than being passed or defeated by the session in what would have been a damaging and divisive vote. It also suggests limits to the power of the new President.

The postponed decision of the 114th session flowed from a proposal to delete three sports currently in the Olympics programme: baseball, softball and the modern pentathlon. In part this was proposed to allow new sports into the Games given that numbers would now be restricted to twenty-eight. This proposal was a more difficult prospect as existing sports and their constituencies were affected, including those IOC members associated with these sports. One of these was Prince Albert of Monaco who belongs to the modern pentathlon movement. The pentathlon has other significant supporters and immense lobbying efforts were mobilised on behalf of the sport.

There are apparent sound commercial reasons for the deletion of modern pentathlon:

> At the 2000 Games in Sydney, Australia, NBC and its two cable networks showed exactly one minute of pentathlon – out of more than 441 hours of coverage.
>
> (Fatsis, 2002)

As much as economic causation, it is the process of the decision that concerns us here. Given that unanimity or near unanimity of the IOC was impossible to obtain, making the decision was postponed, and any potentially damaging splits in the IOC avoided. So while the decisions made can be interpreted as the end of the expansionist philosophy, they can also be viewed as representing 'business as usual' at the IOC. It is the President who wields power and has control, except where well-defined interests may be threatened.

This is not simply a matter of the personal authority of Samaranch and Rogge. The IOC is structured internally in ways that enhance presidential power. None of the recommendations upon which the decisions were made or postponed came directly from the President, allowing the President some distance if they became problematic. Samaranch was a master of this approach. President of FIFA Sepp Blatter used a similar device in distancing himself from FIFA's executive committee's decision not to grant the Oceania confederation direct qualification to the World Cup finals. Within the IOC's formal structure such recommendations first come through Franco Carraro, the Chairman of the Olympic Programme Commission (Carraro, 2002). Nevertheless the Programme Commission does not operate autonomously but reports to the Executive Board of the IOC through Carraro as Chairman. It is then the Executive Board, headed by the IOC President and including the Programme Commission Chairman, that decides to take any recommendations or not to the IOC in session. That the exclusion decision was postponed simply indicates limits to the power of a new president, especially where the interests of individual IOC members are directly affected.

Understanding the organisations

Most examinations of sport structures concentrate on individual organisations. A problem with this is that a different perception of the ways in which decisions are made is found when organisations are viewed in isolation. Necessarily missed in individual studies are the structures and imperatives that similar organisations, such as GSOs, have in common. These commonalities organise and direct the decision-making process of these organisations. This is why the IOC example is pertinent. It is an individual example of the GSOs' overwhelming concern with personal politics. In the broader context, it is explained by the simple but vital observation that the GSOs as a group do not have political parties. While they are political assemblies, in the absence of political parties there is little ideological as opposed to personal basis for their internal politics. Furthermore mainstream political parties provide organisational infrastructure, as well as officers (party headquarters, party president and secretariat and so on), that are separate from governmental offices and structures. This parallel structure does not appear within the GSOs. In addition the permanent administrative bureaucracies of the GSOs have generally remained very small (Union of International Associations, 1993/94). This reduces the potential contribution of large bureaucracies to the internal stabilisation of the organisations. Consequently permanent staff cannot consciously or unconsciously act to mitigate the personal element of GSO internal politics.

Another reason that personal politics play such a dominant role in the analysis of GSOs is the absence of alternative models other than the GSOs themselves. As Chapter 3 indicated there is little organisational modelling in conventional economic analysis of sports. This is because organisational economics was still a new and underdeveloped area when the major economic models of sport were conceived in the 1960s and early 1970s. While the *A Behavioral Theory of the Firm* appeared in the early 1960s (Cyert and March, 1963), its impact was relatively limited and since that time organisational economics has remained theoretically rather than empirically oriented. The empirical analyses that have been conducted have been outside sport, the absence of data covering the internal workings of the GSOs and other sports organisations being a contributing factor. Furthermore, organisational economics takes the firm as its paradigmatic organisation. That the GSOs and many other sports organisations are most emphatically not firms contributes to their neglect.

Similarly, political economy has offered little to understand the organisational arrangements of sport. The primary interest has been in explaining capitalist production and hence explaining the workings of organisations that directly relate to production. In a classic contribution Marglin is concerned with explaining organisational internal hierarchy. In his terms:

> ...it is asked why, in the course of capitalist development, the actual producer lost control of production. What circumstances gave rise to the boss-worker pyramid that characterizes capitalist production?
>
> (1974, p. 34)

In dealing with these questions in capitalist firms, other types of organisations including the GSOs are left unexplored. Nevertheless, Marglin's question is an interesting one in the context of sport organisations. In particular how did the amateurs as organisers (as well as being consumers and producers of sport) lose control of sport given that it was not initially a surplus producing activity? One argument is that the gradual commodification of sport created a network of hierarchies to control the producers (professional athletes), but within the organisational framework (including the GSOs) formed when sport was an amateur consumption activity. The objectives and internal structures of the GSOs can be expected to reflect this evolution. We have seen how the IAAF changed its objectives and generally repudiated its amateur past in this context.

Others around that time were taking a more general view of organisations and hierarchies than the purely private firm. Etzioni (1961) pointed out that:

> The Weberian model, for example, applies particularly to business and governmental bureaucracies and in part to hierarchical churches and some military organisations as well. But when we consider prison, universities, hospitals, research organisations, egalitarian churches, schools, political parties and labor unions, many propositions must be modified or specified considerably before they hold true.
>
> (pp. xii–xiii)

Etzioni offers compliance as vital to the operation of the organisation, with power lying at the root of that compliance (Etzioni, pp. 3–6). Somewhat later Hechter (1987) follows up this approach with an emphasis upon group solidarity, rather than compliance imposed solely by power. He emphasises willingness to conform, which is a relatively small part of Etzioni's analysis. Both treatments seem relevant to the GSOs. Later still Gambetta (1993) dealt with specific forms of creating and maintaining compliance such as violence and patronage. Hirschman (1970) discussed concepts of exit, voice and loyalty. This has specific relevance to the GSOs in that individual federations have great difficulty in exiting from their relevant GSO without significant loss, that is, the inability to play in GSO legitimised tournaments and even friendly internationals.

Formal structures and memberships

Both the type of sport and the function of the GSO lead to different structures within GSOs. We divide the GSOs into four categories to examine this issue. The first group consists of those GSOs that are the supreme governing bodies for team sports. A generic or idealised structure for such GSOs is outlined, while specific GSOs are used to illustrate this form in operation. The second group of GSOs is concerned with solo sports, most notably golf and tennis. The considerable differences between the organisational structures of the team and solo sports we explain in terms of some of the commercial aspects of the two types. The third group of GSOs contains just one member, the IOC. This special treatment relates to its enormous power within the entire set of GSOs as much as the fact that it is a sport event GSO rather than sport GSO. It is shown that although superficially similar to that of other GSOs in terms of its hierarchical structure, the IOC in fact has a very different formal structure. A generalisation flows from these types: GSOs with different functions have modified their operational and governance structures accordingly. The prominence of the sport also affects GSO structure; the more economically important the sport, the more complex and formally structured is its GSO. The fourth type of GSO comprises the specialist bodies, exemplified by those covering drugs and doping, arbitration, and sport medicine. In addition, sport event governing bodies other than the IOC, such as those covering the Masters games, the now defunct Goodwill Games, the Firefighters, Police Games and Gay Games are covered: indeed they might be considered a fifth group. North American based sports such as basketball, baseball and ice hockey are also briefly considered. Their associated GSOs are much less powerful than their corresponding commercial leagues. One such GSO is FIBA (Le Federation Internationale de Basketball): there is little doubt that FIBA is far less powerful than the NBA.

Team sport GSOs

Team sport GSOs generally have memberships comprised of national sporting federations as opposed to having individual human beings as members. The team sport GSOs, therefore, are most often organisations composed of other organisations.

As we have discussed, the desire for standardisation of rules and coherent governance of competition led to the formation of national associations and federations. A desire for stable bilateral international competition led to the need for internationally agreed standardisation. The lack of interest and laissez faire attitudes of late nineteenth- and early twentieth-century governments allowed the national non-government organisations to claim the privilege of selecting those that would represent their country in the early bilateral international competitions. When multilateral international competitions came to be established on a regular basis, the international federations came into being as the creation of the established national federations. The privileges have remained to this day with occasional national government interference in some nations. That the national organisations with this privilege formed the GSOs gave them the power to organise the multilateral contests. The mutual legitimation of national associations and the GSO are seen in their membership structures.

For team sports GSOs this structure is shown in a composite or archetypal form in Figure 6.1. Representing no specific GSO it is derived from the structures of a variety of team sports GSOs, with a heavy reliance on the structure of FIFA given its pre-eminence in team sports. Needless to say there are innumerable versions of this archetypal form. For example, the smaller the sport in terms of its overall audience, the simpler is the structure. The GSOs have the job of governing the sport and these structures are designed to ensure that this is done on behalf of the sport's constituency as a whole rather than some smaller group.

In Figure 6.1, the arrows represent the direction of formal control as represented in GSO constitutions. It is the individual clubs that have ultimate, formal control of a GSO in that they vote for representatives in their national associations that are members of the GSO. It is nominated representatives of

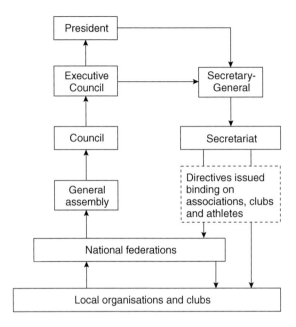

Figure 6.1 Structure and control of an archetype sport GSO.

the national federations or associations of the sport that form the member-ship of the general assembly. The basic deliberative and policy-approving ele-ment within the GSO is the general assembly (or congress, similar terms are used) of the national federations. These generally meet annually. The purpose of this assembly is to discuss, debate and put forward motions for vote. These may or may not be binding upon the executive. In virtually all GSOs there is some form of secret ballot for membership of the council and for the President, Vice-President(s) and other office-holders. The ways in which indi-vidual athletes or grass roots clubs exercise formal control is, therefore, diluted. Even the national federations have little formal say in the operations of the GSO when there are potentially over one hundred national associa-tions represented (e.g. the International Hockey Federation (IHF), where there are 112 such associations).

The Council is the supreme decision-making body of most GSOs, although it is not a full-time body. Thus within that body there is always a smaller appointed or elected group that meets more frequently to make operational decisions that are impossible for the Council to make. Executive Council membership for most GSOs is, therefore, in part a sub-set of the Council membership. However, it can also include the Secretary-General, the head of the administrative arm of the GSO. The President in the archetypal GSO is shown as formally controlled by the electorate of the

GSO. While this may be the direction of formal control, the power and actual control may be very different. The GSO then has some formal control over the national associations and clubs through the directives that they issue. These will be binding upon those organisations if they wish to be regarded as part of the sport and be represented both on the international field of play and within the GSO.

A specific but fairly standard structure is that of the IHF (Figure 6.2). Hockey developed in its modern form in the eighteenth century in England, especially in schools. In 1909 the hockey associations of Belgium and England came together to 'regulate' their international relations, and were soon joined by the French association. It has had considerable representation at the Olympics but has not been a permanent fixture there. Indeed, the IHF was founded in Paris in 1924 in response to the dropping of hockey from the Olympics of that year held in Paris (www.fihockey.org). The International Federation of Women's Hockey Associations (IFWHA) was founded in 1927, the two bodies amalgamating in 1982. Most players remain amateurs. This GSO, headquartered in Brussels, might be considered

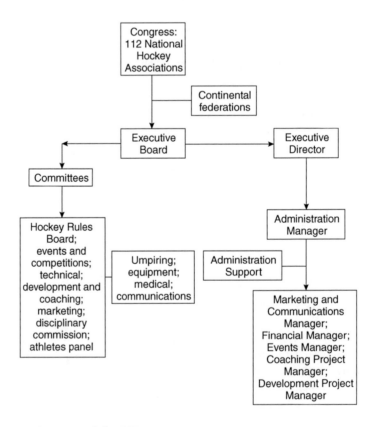

Figure 6.2 Structure of the IHF.

a mid-level GSO in that it governs a team sport with a considerable following, but which does not have the commercial standing or size of soccer and FIFA.

One differing feature of its structure is that there are specific continental group representatives (Africa, Athletes', Pan-America, Europe, Asia and Oceania) although this form is not restricted to hockey and the IHF. FIFA has such continental groupings and Chapter 8 considers some of the dealings between FIFA and its most powerful continental groups. That such groups are represented is an indication that the Executive Group is closer to a policy discussion forum rather than a true executive group. There are references to an IHF Council but it is not indicated in the official formal structure. In addition the IHF refers to its Executive Board, listing twenty-three Board members including a President, as well as an honorary treasurer, two Vice-Presidents and an Honorary Secretary-General, whereas a Secretary-General is normally the most senior paid employee. The indications are that only the President has a paid position other than the administrative staff, up to and including the Administration Manager. Essentially, the IHF shows a relatively complex structure with considerable numbers of supporting committees (e.g. concerned with umpiring, rules, etc.). Nevertheless, the IHF does not have anywhere near the formal structures and paid employees of FIFA.

Clearly some nations have more power than others do in the operations of a GSO, especially if they have predominance and/or traditions in the sport. This leads to a problem that vexes the UN in that one nation-one vote ignores not only world power structures but also sheer numbers represented by each nation, be it as member of the UN or as member of a GSO. In the ICC this has become formalised in that national cricket associations are graded in their membership of the ICC according to their recognised historical playing strengths. We present the structure of the ICC at Figure 6.3.

Like the ICC, the International Lacrosse Federation (ILF) also recognises different grades of membership of its national associations. The ILF Constitution is one of the clearest and we use it to illustrate this point:

4. MEMBERSHIP

    4.1 The national governing body for lacrosse in any country or territory shall be eligible for membership of the Federation. Only one Association from each country or territory may be affiliated, and such Full Member, Associate Member or Affiliate Member shall be recognised by the Federation as the only national governing body for all lacrosse in such country or territory. (Refer Bylaws Appendix 4.)

    4.2 Membership may only be conferred by a resolution passed by a majority of at least two thirds of those present and voting (by ballot) at a general meeting of the Federation.

4.3   Membership categories shall be:

    4.3.1   Full Member. This entitles the Full Member to two voting delegates at the Federation Meetings and nomination of persons as officers and committee personnel.

    4.3.2   Associate Member. This entitles the Associate Member to one voting delegate at the Federation Meetings and nomination of persons as committee personnel.

    4.3.3   Affiliate Member. This has no voting entitlement.

               (ILF Constitution, May 2001, p. 2, www.intlaxfed.org)

Other organisations deal with what is essentially the same sport. These are the International Federation of Women's Lacrosse Associations (IFWLA) and the Federation Internationale d'Intercrosse (FIIC). Lacrosse is of interest in that it developed from a game indigenous to North America, the modern game having been created in 1856 with the foundation of the Montreal Lacrosse Club. The sport achieved Olympic status in 1904 and 1908 but has not been a full Olympic sport since then. The world championship was first held in 1967 and has been held at four-yearly intervals since 1974 (www.lacrosse.ca). The Lacrosse GSOs' structures are necessarily simpler and more informal given their small playing and commercial bases. Only ten national associations belong to the IFLWA.

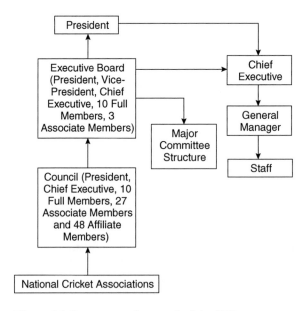

Figure 6.3 Structure and control of the ICC.

The numbers of officers and the structures of the ten associations are more complex and numerous than for the international body, suggesting that power does not lie in the international association. This leaves it with some coordination and rule-making functions, as well as a global event that has little commercial vigour. The IFLWA has a President and three vice-presidents (Administration, Rules, and Umpiring and Competition). In addition the IFLWA president, Fiona Clark, is also an office bearer (Director of Special Projects) in Women's Lacrosse Australia, while Sue Redfern, Vice-President Administration is President of the English Lacrosse Association. Such crossover office bearing is less usual in the larger sports although individuals coming through the national association ranks tend to be like those chosen as national representatives in the GSOs.

Several versions of lacrosse are played one of which, Intercrosse, now has a GSO. In Intercrosse men and women play together what is a modified and much less ferocious version of box lacrosse, neither body contact nor lacrosse stick, that is, 'cross', contact being allowed. The FIIC was formed which holds world games annually. Significantly for its philosophy, no national teams are allowed. In this sport, the essence of its culture appears light years away from commercialisation and professionalisation.

Virtually all of the larger GSOs have structures with permanent committees, as well as allowance for ad hoc or additional permanent committees as the sport develops or conditions change. In the case of the ICC the main elements of their relatively simple permanent committee structure is shown in Figure 6.3. A formalised committee structure provides, in part, an intersection between the operational tasks carried out by administrative staff (see Figures 6.3 and 6.4 for the position of the administrative staff within the ICC) and the policy and executive decision-making of the officers of the GSO. This is especially important for the GSOs in that their officers are, in the main, part-time and not professional managers. The ICC now has a large part of its efforts devoted to a nevertheless relatively autonomous commission on corruption in cricket with investigative staff around the world. These are largely retired senior police officers. The committee structure varies enormously in complexity according to the GSO and the size of the sport or event.

In virtually every GSO there are (a) rules and conditions of play and, (b) development committees. The significance of the rules committees dates back to the discussions held by the FA in 1864 which disallowed 'hacking' as part of games, thereby creating the modern game with its first professional league in England only twenty years later. In most established sports such committees are now engaged in more minor adjustments, although these are often considered at the behest of commercial interests, usually television. The development committees are concerned with the spread of the sport and as many of the GSOs are European in origin this is a point of contact with Third World nations. They provide an avenue for the use of any funds generated by their activities, such as World Championship revenues

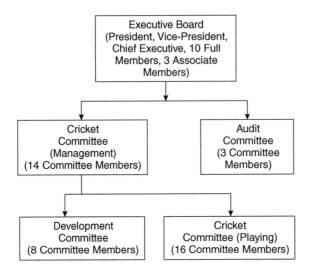

Figure 6.4 Committee structure – ICC. (Each committee has a staff manager associated with the function of the committee.)

and sponsorship deals, that the non-profit GSOs might otherwise distribute to shareholders.

Solo sports

Sports competed in by individuals rather than by teams are as diverse as boxing, chess, golf and surfing. In most such sports the athlete's sporting autonomy goes hand-in-hand with commercial autonomy. We find that this commercial autonomy of the athlete seems to have had a significant impact upon the structure and organisation of the associated GSO. Certainly, there is a much greater variety of organisational forms in solo sports that makes generalisation difficult. It also makes an examination of the internal workings of the controlling bodies difficult for a variety of reasons. The sheer number of these GSOs is one major reason. Also, what can best be termed quasi-GSOs remain private clubs. A more fundamental reason is that they act as networks rather than the single hierarchical organisations that we observed as prevalent in team sports. Supporting the argument that commercial autonomy is of importance in determining the structures, the GSOs in amateur and commercially weak solo sports have arrangements close to those in team sports.

As opposed to this, the commercially important solo sports operate through networks of GSOs rather than a single, unified body. Indeed, in some solo sports there is a superfluity of mutually antagonistic GSOs. This is especially true in boxing and the martial arts. In boxing commercial antagonism is a driving force behind this while in other martial arts it is also a stylistic matter. Continuing the theme of competing GSOs in some sports such as tennis and chess, there have been recent attempts to form new GSOs. In the past in almost all of these solo sports, there is a history of breakaway movements and organisations. Given this fluidity we first indicate some of the relevant differences between individual and team sports.

Solo sports are those for which one-against-one competition is intrinsic to the nature of the game. These sports cannot be re-formulated as team sports without changing their nature. Such a demarcation is necessarily blurred but the commercial, organisational and governance implications of the distinction are critical. Tellingly, even when adaptations to teams are highly successful (as in doubles tennis) the commercial rewards are much lower than in the solo version. Rather different are those sports where athletes still play the game one-on-one but where individual results are merely aggregated to create a team score. Chess has teams from the national level right down to local club teams. Tennis as well as doubles has national teams in the Hopman and Davis Cups, while golf has team play in the Ryder Cup. Unlike tennis doubles, where true teamwork operates, team scores are simply an aggregate of the individual scores. As a consequence both individual and team titles are awarded in many individual sports. A pertinent example is F1. It has both a drivers' world (individual) championship and a constructor's (team) championship. In F1 it is not clear if it is an individual or team sport or even what or who composes the team. The 'team' in this case comprises an enormous supply chain of logistical and technical support, research and development. The same is true of the individual riders and the teams in the Tour de France.

Notwithstanding this blurring of boundaries between individuals, teams and logistical appendages, the more commercialised a solo sport, the less there seems to be any adaptation of the sport to team play. The reason is quite simple. Team formats are economically much less attractive to both sponsors and superstars of individual sports. If the stars are absent from the teams there is little chance that the teams will be attractive to sponsors and tournament organisers, regardless of their success on the field. In professional tennis and golf, the occasional nation-based team events such as the Ryder Cup and Davis Cup rely on the stars playing for prestige, commitment to fellow players and to the game, as well as patriotism. In all of these sports, membership of such teams is transitory.

While economic analysis is oriented towards team sports a fundamental exception to this is the analysis of superstars (see Chapter 3). Such analysis is especially appropriate for solo sports and their organisational forms. Yet even the players in the lowliest of fringe and satellite circuits of solo sports, in common with the superstars of their sports, operate as individual firms rather than as labour inputs to a firm. It is an autonomy they have in common with Andre Agassi and Tiger Woods, whereas even Michael Jordan (basketball and baseball) and David Beckham (soccer) are classified as employees. Tennis players, golfers and chess players are not employees. Rather they are the employers: of coaches, trainers, physiotherapists, caddies, seconds and equipment technicians. Nigel Short, for example, refers to fellow grand master John Nunn acting as his second in his chess world championship qualifiers (Short, 1989, p. 108). All this means that their political economic situation is playing for profit, fundamentally different from playing for wages.

Further emphasising the organisational differences between commercial solo and team sports, solo sports tend to be played within tournaments while team sports operate within league frameworks. As a consequence teams have a fixed home stadium location. In these they play on a regular home–away basis. Conversely, solo athletes roam layers of tournaments around the globe, with tennis and golf again the exemplars. Tennis has its Grand Slam tournaments, the ATP tour as well as other satellites.

Unlike professional solo sports, those that remain largely amateur have GSO structures virtually identical to team sports. This may be mandated by the IOC (for those sports involved in the Olympics), even though the athletes so 'represented' are essentially professionals. This effectively requires the existence of national associations and an associated GSO covering both the amateurs and the professionals. For most of these sports the lack of commercial success when compared to tennis and golf implies less strict distinction between the two groups. The most important of these are almost certainly IAAF and FINA, athletics and swimming being mainstays of the Summer Olympics and composed of intrinsically individualistic sports such as the discus, 1,500 m and Marathon; the range of swimming events and others such as archery. This means that the fundamental organisational differences between individual and team sports exist when the commercial sport is of global commercial significance. In pursuing this theme we examine two such sports in more detail, first golf and then tennis.

Any examination of golf begins with St Andrews. Celebrating 250 years of existence in 2004 it remains a private club (www.randa.org). Founded to provide recreation for its local members its early inception has helped give it an almost unprecedented global legitimacy in both amateur and professional golf, even though the economic realities of golf have caused it to yield some of its authority to North America. Nevertheless, while remaining a private club it has some of the functional attributes of a GSO. Most importantly, outside the USA and Mexico, it determines the rules of golf, a function it shares overall with the United States Golf Association (USGA) (www.usga.org/rules/). St Andrews also owns and runs the British Open. While this seems anachronistic it is completely explicable in terms of the evolutionary schema presented in Chapter 2. It is consistent with the start of the modern formalisation of sport occurring in the British Isles at the same time as the advent of the capitalist period.

Also consistent with this evolutionary perspective golf and tennis and some other solo sports such as cycling have no widely recognised world championship, the need for this development never appearing. The International Tennis Federation (ITF) runs a world championship but this is completely overshadowed by the Grand slam events and the ATP Tour and WTA tour rankings. Some tournaments became pre-eminent early in the modern development of the sport. They have then remained localised in name, such as the British Open Championship in squash, but have attained a global reach and are recognised as the de facto world championships. This has not saved the British Open Squash Championship from coming close to not occurring for the first time in its eighty-one-year history due to commercial pressures. It is now privately owned by promoters John Nimick and John Beddington '...who plan to restore the competition's status as the sport's blue riband event' (Ananova, 2003). This pre-eminence can be shared among events. These include the US Open and British Open among other events in golf; Wimbledon and the three other Grand Slam events in tennis. There is no dispute that the Tour de France is pre-eminent in cycling. That it is often referred to as just 'The Tour' indicates its pre-eminence and while it also serves as a team event, it is the individual titles (represented by the Yellow, Green, Polka Dot and White jerseys) that are important. An indication of its solo nature is that it is he who wins the Yellow Jersey, 'Le Maillot Jaune', that is probably of greater concern than which team wins the team championship. This is as true for the team sponsors as much as the fans – the US Postal team is more interested in Lance Armstrong as the individual winner than in winning the team trophy.

While these events or tournaments are potential money-spinners for their owners (see Chapter 5), in the case of St Andrews it is deemed inappropriate for a private member's club to be the sole beneficiary of the returns from such an event. Consequently St Andrews uses the Open's profits towards golf development as a whole (www.randa.org). As opposed to private ownership for profit, this allows the club to retain its status within golf. That these are non-profit makes it more difficult for any challenger to its position of owning and administering the premier British golf competition. The matter of trust is extraordinarily important in the club's ability to operate in this way. Nonetheless the importance of North America, as the heartland of both amateur and professional golf, dictates the sharing of the St Andrews rule-making function.

As opposed to this, there also exist other global golfing bodies such as the World Amateur Golf Council (WAGC), headquartered in the USA. Its function as the name implies is promoting amateur golf worldwide. The PGA of America, however, despite its power is not a full GSO. This is because other national PGAs exist around the world, such as the PGA of Australia and the Canadian PGA. There also exists the PGA European Tour, which operates at a supra-national level but remains less important than the PGA of America. This means that the PGAs are a network rather than a single organisation. They have monopolies in their own backyards but both cooperate and compete at the global level, operating with objectives rather than just profit. The PGAs are often companies limited by guarantee within their respective national legal systems. This allows them to more readily trade with the public than adopting some other form of legal governance structure. The women's game maintains a completely separate structure and this reflects both the commercial and performance differences between the male and female professional players.

In tennis the situation is similar but not identical to golf. The nearest equivalent to the network of PGAs are the Women's Tennis Association (WTA) and the Association of Tennis Professionals (ATP) for men. As opposed to the PGAs, both operate globally as single organisations rather than as a network. The four grand slam tournaments (i.e. the French, Australian, Wimbledon and USA) operate as separate entities but with the tour overall perform part of the function of a GSO. In the case of Wimbledon, its championship is administered by the club itself and the Lawn Tennis Association (LTA). The LTA is the governing body for lawn tennis in England, providing an example of a private club and a national association administering what is considered a global event. Nonetheless, in individual sports such as tennis and golf, the situation is rather different. In these sports the player acts as an independent enterprise rather than as an employee and the players associations are understandably far stronger.

The ATP, which began as its name implies as a player organisation, now acts less as a form of trade union than as a tour governing body and promoter. The ATP claims that:

> As the governing body of the men's professional tennis circuit, the ATP is committed to creatively and professionally leading the worldwide growth of the game, building on the rich traditions of tennis and innovating to ensure it is always vibrant and relevant.
>
> (www.atptennis.com)

The ATP was founded in 1972 solely as a players' collective organisation but in 1988 it used the commercial muscle of its members to take over the men's commercial tennis circuit. The structure of the ATP is shown in Figure 6.5. Highly commercially oriented it is headed by a CEO rather than a President or Secretary-General. The CEO is both a member of and reports to the Board of Directors. The Board members, other than the CEO appoint the CEO to a contract with the terms decided between the Board and the CEO. This has similarities to the boards of directors of companies but it is not a Board in the sense of being shareholder elected. Rather the six Directors other than the CEO are constituency based. Three are player representatives and three are tournament representatives other than the representatives of the four Grand Slams. The two groups of directors are in turn determined by a Player Council and a Tournament Council (Figure 6.4).

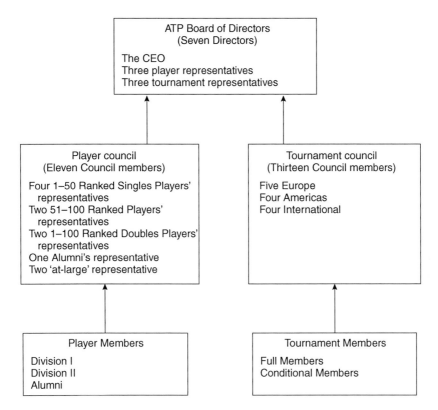

Figure 6.5 Basic governance structure of the ATP.

Source: www.atptennis.com/en/insidetheatp/theorganisation/default.asp

These two councils are in turn selected from the player and tournament members of the ATP. The ATP is a money-making venture through a variety of means including sponsorships, fees and merchandising. Like the WTA it contracts with the tournaments to provide them with players of suitable stature for their tournaments.

The Women's Tennis Association, known as the WTA Tour, is the governing body for professional women's tennis (www.wtatour.com). The WTA grew out of the Virginia Slims female professional circuit founded in 1970 just before the founding of the ATP and only very shortly after open tennis began in the late 1960s. Being tobacco related, that sponsorship was ultimately doomed but it laid the foundation for the WTA. The structures and functions of the WTA and the ATP are virtually identical even though their histories are different. The WTA has a ten member Board of Directors composed of the CEO, three player appointed directors, three tournament appointed directors, a federation director and two non-affiliated directors. The CEO is appointed by the Board and (s)he reports to it. Despite the similarities between the WTA and the ATP the WTA emphasise its links to other tennis organisations, notably the ITF, one of the directors representing the ITF tour component of the circuit. It also has a closer relationship to the four Grand Slams than the ATP including a Grand Slam observer able to attend meetings of the WTA Board of Directors.

This chapter began by pointing out the lack of openness among the GSOs but the WTA Tour appears to be among the most open. The evidence for this lies in several areas but the most telling is the comprehensive (340 pages) nature of its rules and their public availability (WTA Tour Inc., 2002). The Rulebook is extraordinarily detailed in outlining not only playing rules beyond the standard rules of tennis, but spells out the obligations of the WTA Tour as an organisation, its player and tournament members, sponsors, their financial responsibilities and rules of conduct and the penalties for breaking those rules.

In the case of solo sports the picture is much more complex than for team sports. Decisions regarding a specific sport are not internal to a given GSO but shared and internalised within a network of sport organisations. Each of these organisations bears some but not all of the functions of the more centralised organised team sport GSO. This means that such decisions need not be made on a single conscious basis but emerge from the reactions of each organisation to the decisions and actions of the others. This is not the only way in which these solo sports are governed. In the case of a number of the solo sport GSOs they have organisational structures similar to the team sport GSOs. This is partly a result of history. However, if it was history alone that created the situation we would expect to see the more networked forms eventually appear.

What we see in golf and tennis as examples of individual sports is a shared and decentralised set of GSOs, rather than the central, single GSO of team sports. In the case of golf the pattern that exists globally is almost certainly due to its unique transatlantic and then global evolution. Also the idea of tours and circuits is somewhere between the event and sport distinction. Here we see something of the nature of the individual sport governance and its GSOs. It operates as a network rather than single GSO, although for each network specifics may be different, the underlying reasons for development appear similar. Worthy of note is the potential for disintegration being much higher than within a single GSO as witness what is currently happening in tennis, has happened in chess, and has happened in boxing to the ultimate degree.

The IOC and the Olympic family

There are other event organisations that are global but none has the impact of the IOC. As a GSO, the IOC deserves its own treatment on several counts. First it is an event GSO as opposed to a sport GSO. A second major reason is the concept of the Olympic family, a set of affiliations that gives

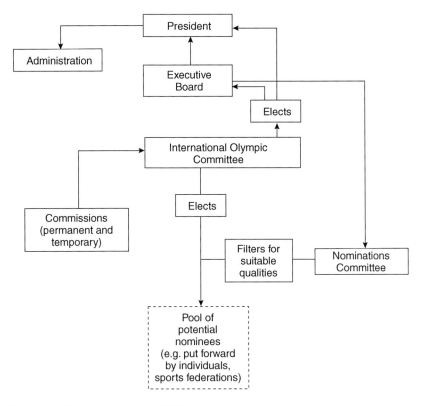

Figure 6.6 Elective structure – IOC.

it extraordinary power and makes it a legitimising force in the eyes of many both inside and outside the sports movements. A third and enormously important difference is also apparent. The IOC does not exist at the behest of the Olympic committees of various nations but exactly the reverse. And so it is with the individuals that belong to the IOC as members.

The structure of the IOC is given in Figure 6.6 based upon the highly detailed information available on the IOC website (www.olympic.org). The members meet annually in 'session' as the supreme body of the Olympic Movement but the real power lies with the Executive Board and especially with the President of the IOC. Unlike most other GSOs, they are not nominated by national sporting associations to the position, but are voted onto the IOC by its existing members. The IOC states that:

> The members of the IOC are individuals who act as the IOC's representatives in their respective countries, not as delegates of their country within the IOC.
>
> (www.olympic.org/uk/organisation/ioc/index_uk.asp)

Thus the IOC is a self-perpetuating body. The IOC in session elects the Executive Board, each board member being elected for a four-year term. The fifteen person board consists of ten ordinary members, four Vice-Presidents of the IOC and the President. Members elect the President for a term of eight years, renewable for four years. This difference in periods for which office can be held provides distinct power to the President compared to other members. The IOC reinforces this with a nominations committee ensuring they are 'qualified' before the Executive Board presents candidates for election in session (www.olympic.org/uk/organisation/ioc/index_uk.asp). Presumably this is only after further consideration of the candidates by the Executive Board.

This process has led to an extraordinary set of biases in the IOC membership, including an unexpectedly high proportion of IOC members belonging to European and Arab aristocratic and royal families. In addition, the election of Juan Antonio Samaranch Junior in 2001 appears lucky given the numbers of other exceptionally well-qualified individuals. Overall there is an extraordinarily high percentage of European nationals in the IOC, with very small European nations extraordinarily well represented as a group. One aspect that appears not to be commented upon in this respect is the bias that the Winter Olympic Games promotes. The inclusion of Winter sports creates a situation in which the IOC is firmly bound to a North Atlantic view of sport.

The hegemony of the Olympic movement among global sports is partly ensured by a series of structures that constitute the 'Olympic Family'. While the current Olympic Games has well over thirty sports (twenty-nine Summer sports including softball, pentathlon and baseball and seven Winter sports) and nearly 400 events, the IOC strives to impose standards upon even those sports that are not current in the Olympic programme. The IOC also 'recognises' other activities as sports and this is a necessary condition to be considered for inclusion. Croci (Chapter 8) examines the attempts of DanceSport to become an Olympic sport but there are many others that are recognised in some way as part of the Olympic family. To be eligible to become an Olympic sport it must have an International Federation (IF) that among other functions, 'governs its sport at world level and ensures its promotion and development' (www.olympic.org/uk/organisation/if/index_uk.asp).

Those IFs that gain inclusion in the Olympic programme become International Olympic Federations, a state they wish to preserve for their sport and which means that they are – to a degree – supplicants to the IOC. Thus 'international sports federations seeking IOC recognition must ensure that their statutes, practice and activities conform with the Olympic Charter'. This has led to the formation of another layer of GSOs, these IFs. They are: 'the Association of Summer Olympic International Federations (ASOIF), the Association of International Winter Sports Federations (AIOWF), the Association of IOC Recognised International

Sports federations (ARISF), and the General Association of International Sports Federations (GAISF), which also includes other sports federations' (www.olympic.org/uk/organisation/if/index_uk.asp). The GAISF was founded in 1967 while the others were formed in the early 1980s. While having laudable stated aims these GSOs of GSOs can also operate as cartels to protect the commercial aspects of their sports against others.

The Commission and Committee structure of the IOC is one of considerable complexity. It ranges from the fundamental commissions dealing with the programme to those that deal with peripheral issues such as the IOC Museum and philately. Conversely the IOC has helped create some of the most important specialist GSOs.

Specialist GSOs

The specialist GSOs operate in a derivative role when compared with the other GSOs that we have analysed. However, they have taken increasingly significant roles. Three are of note and have similar structures: WADA; the International Council for the Arbitration of Sport (ICAS) which governs the Court of Arbitration for Sport (CAS) and Federation Internationale de Medicine du Sport (FIMS). This is partly because the stakes have become so high that anything that can be done to protect commercial interests should be done. Thus the specialist medical GSO(s) are designed to protect the individual and corporate investments in human capital that are bound up in sport.

The oldest of these is FIMS. Its precursor, the Association Medico-Sportive (AIMS) was founded in 1920 at the St Moritz Winter Olympics, heralding a long association of FIMS with the IOC (www.fims.org/fims/general/history.asp). At a conference/congress held at the Amsterdam Summer Olympics in 1928, AIMS became the Federation Internationale Medico-Sportive et Cientifique in 1933, changing to the present title at the Chamonix Conference of 1934. The present structure of FIMS consists of:

- Council of Delegates – one representative each from National Member Associations.
- Executive Committee – President, four Vice-Presidents, Secretary-General, Treasurer, eight elected members.
- Bureau – President, a Vice-President, Secretary-General and Treasurer.

In addition there is the

- General Assembly – comprising representatives of the Council of Delegates, The Executive Committee, representatives of FIMS multinational associations (e.g. Europe, North America etc) and individual and associate members.

The General Assembly has little or no role in the active running or governance of the organisation but is a discussion forum. This makes it clearer that the FIMS is an organisation of organisations. The Council of Delegates is the voting establishment for the officers of the organisation. The problem of drugs has passed into specialist hands but the importance of the FIMS may increase in future years as the question of other forms of medical perform-ance enhancement appear, especially genetic modification to individual ath-letes. In addition to such external parametric changes it is also to be noted that FIMS by virtue of its expertise has a source of power that allows it independence. It is not immediately dependent upon the other GSOs for funds. It has alternative associations notably with the scientific and medical communities that provide it with protection but its members also have individual commercial values that make them less prone to pressure.

There is plenty of room: conclusions

A primary motivation for any examination of the GSOs as a group must be that global sport is intermediated by a host of organisations. As a conse-quence, it is one of the most highly institutionalised sectors of the global economy. The GSOs, when seen as INGOs, recreate global sport as part of global civil society and one of the most important manifestations of global culture. Thus the 'democratic' elements of GSO structure are of extraordi-nary importance. In practice, however, the GSOs have largely become the creatures of their executives and of commercial imperatives. The structures of the GSOs relate very much to their non-profit status but this line becomes blurred in their processes and very much in their structures in the case of solo sports. Here we have argued that the background to the structures is complex and related not only to types of sport but to the non-profit status of the GSOs. The evolution of the various sports has had a considerable influence as has the degree to which they have become com-mercialised. Some sports operate with single structures while others operate with networks and there is a strong tendency for these organisations to come together to form new overarching organisations. This has not prevented the creation of new organisations that threaten the quasi-monopolistic positions of GSOs within the very sports that they claim to govern. As sport commercialisation intensifies and broadens, this will cre-ate new structural forms where private enterprise will increasingly demand a share in the governance mechanisms or create its own. One way in which this can occur is through the vehicle of joint ventures between private enterprise and the GSOs. The North American model is likely to become a feature of global sports structures. Rather than the political assembly structures seen here the private corporation may become the dominant organisational form. Ownership of sports may then become private rather than public.

7 For the good of the game
GSO opacity as public interest organisations

The GSOs lay claim to being public interest organisations. They lay claim to an important place in global civil society. FIFA explicitly points itself in this direction. Just prior to the Second Gulf War it claimed that:

> As the world stands on the brink of war, football's role as a force for reconciliation has yet again been demonstrated in the nomination of FIFA President Joseph S. Blatter for the American Global Award for Peace...in recognition of the active part he played in bringing together the co-hosts of the 2002 FIFA World Cup Korea/Japan.™
>
> (www.fifa.com)

The Olympic movement in particular has always made strong claims in this area but with no more demonstrable success than FIFA. And as we shall see later, apart from governing swimming around the world, FINA claims among its objectives the promotion of international relations. These three GSOs are not alone in this, several of the major GSOs claim a higher calling than mere commerce or even sport. Yet as we saw in the previous chapter one of the paradoxes of the GSOs as public interest, non-profit organisations is their opacity. They offer the public less financial information than the listing requirements of the world's stock exchanges. At the same time the amateur and professional athletes who can lay claim to being major stakeholders in sport are little represented in the GSOs. Claiming to be democratic organisations they are more accurately described as oligarchies.

It is in this context that in order to explain the behaviour of the GSOs we turn to the literatures concerned with corporate governance and especially with the control of organisations and resources. This is especially appropriate as the GSOs operate as governance bodies. In particular we examine principal–agent theory, stakeholder theory as well as Hirschman's examination of exit, voice and loyalty in organisations, especially those in decline. While largely outside the political economy literature it is certainly appropriate for examining governance bodies. The possible reason that this literature lies outside political economy is that although it does sometimes have a critical tone it is generally supportive of corporate activity.

We also examine concepts of clientism, patronage and corruption. Certainly these appear appropriate for the GSOs judging from some of their behaviours. This indicates a methodological thread that runs through this analysis. In the absence of substantive empirical evidence of the internal workings of the GSOs we have to rely to a great extent upon the evidence of the external actions of the GSOs. We then make inferences from these actions to the internal mechanisms.

Our interpretation of GSO behaviour begins with an examination of the stated objectives of the GSOs. In particular we try to understand the unavoidable imperatives of a highly commercial world upon a group of non-profit organisations virtually all of which have control of potentially valuable assets – the global control of a sport or event.

Ends and means

While the mass of their actions is directed towards sport a shift in objectives has occurred in these organisations. That shift allows the statement of an *ends–means inversion* hypothesis. This states that non-profit organisations have a tendency for: (1) their original ends or objectives and (2) their financial means of achieving those ends to become inverted. In the case of the GSOs their original end purpose was to support and promote a sport, sporting event or function. To that end they used and hence sought financial support. For the GSOs this was initially drawn from areas such as membership fees and other contributions from member national federations. As the GSOs gradually asserted independence from and then domination over the member federations, they required independent sources of funding. We have pointed out that this came from the commercial exploitation – if not the creation – of global hallmark events. As these events developed, they changed the relationship of the GSO to its members. From dependency it moved towards independency if the sport had a commerical following at the global level. Ultimately in important cases this makes the national federations dependent on the GSOs. As this continued, the GSOs' relationship to sport was also changing. Sport was now required to contribute to the GSO. As a result, the member federations found themselves the servants of the GSOs. Finally the sport – via the global event controlled and owned by the GSO – became the means by which the GSO attained its financial goals and asserted its dominance.

Appropriate to the political economy approach is the dual nature of these organisations as being both cultural/not-for-profit and being intensely commercial. It also involves an analysis of the bi-directional channelling of power within the economic relationships established. First, power leads to economic opportunities for the GSO, and as a consequence, individuals or groups of individuals within the GSO. Second, control of the sporting means to financial success helps lead to power. Third, this creates new needs for management, marketing and finance specialists within these organisations. They will not have the same sporting sensitivities as many of those who came to the GSO via sporting affiliations. In this argument, we see the mechanisms through which the ends–means inversion can take place. In part it takes place within the individuals who are already there and wish to see the organisation survive. It also takes place because new individuals within the GSO at all levels represent a different ethos to the sporting types. That success leaves them with the problem of the accumulation of a surplus, sometimes extraordinarily large, which they then have to manage. The distribution of the surplus throughout the sport is an even more difficult problem. And the more successful they are commercially, the greater this problem becomes.

A crucial aspect of the ends–means inversion is that the GSOs have general and abstract objectives. This is as opposed to private enterprise corporations where the overriding objective is to make profits. When corporations make profits these can be quantified and benchmarked against all other corporations in similar markets. Their share price is a reflection of this, the capital and stock markets playing highly visible and immediate if indirect roles in their corporate governance. For the GSOs there is relatively little market visibility, despite their involvement in highly commercial and highly profitable ventures. As we have seen in Chapter 5 the major GSOs have a demonstrated ability to pass on costs to others, especially public authorities. It is this ability to engage in commerce as a central element of their operations that sets them apart from most other non-profit organisations, especially INGOs such as Oxfam, Medecins sans Frontieres and Amnesty International.

GSO objectives are usually defined in terms of the furtherance and development of a specific sport or event as the examples illustrate. The ITF claims that with the WTA and the ATP it forms a triumvirate of the 'main bodies involved in tennis' and that it is the 'world governing body of tennis' (www.itftennis.com/html/big/struct.html). It is directed towards

- the administering and regulation of tennis;
- organising international competitions;
- structuring tennis by sanctioning international circuits and events;
- developing the sport through the worldwide Development Programme;
- promoting the game.

While the ITF statement appears quite specific at first sight, it nevertheless makes it difficult to identify specific stakeholders – except, perhaps, those 'international competitions' and the 'international circuits and events' it has already organised or sanctioned. Other than these groups the sole beneficiary is apparently the game itself. The statement makes no mention of players, organisations or national federations all of whom might be regarded as the servants of the game. In its Mission Statement The ATP is even less precise, stating that:

> As the governing body of the men's professional tennis circuit the ATP is committed to creatively and professionally leading the worldwide growth of the game, building on the rich traditions of tennis and innovating to ensure it is always vibrant and relevant.
>
> (www.atptennis.com)

The commitment again is to an abstraction, the 'worldwide growth of the game'. At face value the implication is that 'the men's professional tennis circuit' is the means through which tennis is promoted.

In the case of FINA there is greater specificity in its Constitution where it states the Objectives:

> C.5.1 to promote and encourage the development of Swimming in all possible manifestations throughout the world
> C.5.2 to provide drug free sport
> C.5.3 to promote and encourage the development of international relations
> C.5.4 to adopt necessary uniform rules and regulations to competitions in Swimming, Open Water Swimming, Diving, Water polo, Synchronised swimming, and Masters,
> C.5.5 to organise World Championships and other FINA competitions, and
> C.5.6 to increase the number of facilities for Swimming throughout the world
> C.5.7 to carry out such other activities as may be desirable to promote the sport.
>
> (www.fina.org/const.html)

Here the appeal is to the sport of swimming, but there is a much more specific commitment to the sport, including providing a drug free sport. As opposed to this increasing facilities can mean almost anything. The other aim that is specific is to organise a world championship and to this FINA could find itself accountable. But again the World championships have become a commercial means as much as a sporting end in itself.

In hockey the IHF (or FIH) has a very clear set of objectives but again they are a mixture of the operational combined with the abstract (International Hockey Federation Statutes and Bye-Laws). 'Article 4. Objects' state to:

> 4.1 Encourage, promote, develop and control hockey at all levels throughout the world;
> 4.2 Support and maintain the ideals and objects of the Olympic movement and in particular the fight against doping by means of appropriate tests;

4.3 Exercise jurisdiction over and to determine disputes or disagreements between Members, between CF's, between members and CF's, between athletes and a CF;

4.4 Establish and maintain an efficient administration;

4.5 Preserve the independence of the FIH in all matters directly or indirectly concerning Hockey without the intervention of any outside authority; and

4.6 Conduct itself and take such administrative, financial or other actions as are necessary and in conformity with and in furtherance of its objectives.

(www.fihockey.org)

This is one of the most intriguing in the various elements it contains as well as the amount of detail. Also interesting is the very legalistic framing of the FIH document compared to the simpler language of other GSOs.

The ILF Constitution resides in relatively plain English but has a similar tone to it. The Objects of the Federation shall be:

3.1 To promote and develop the game of lacrosse throughout the world.

3.2 To establish and maintain rules and regulations governing international competitions.

3.3 To arrange international competition between members.

3.4 To decide any dispute that may arise between members, if called upon to do so.

3.5 To acquire such property, assets and rights as the federation deems necessary for the purpose of carrying out the aforesaid objects.

(International Lacrosse Federation Constitution, www.ilf.org)

We saw in the previous chapter that inter-crosse, a close sporting relative of Lacrosse, was committed to a specific set of ideals that run counter both to elitism in the sport and to elements such as national teams that have been important in international competition since the late nineteenth century (see Chapter 2). There is an inkling of this in its goals as stated in its constitution, which states the goals of the federation are as follows:

1. To promote inter-crosse throughout the world;

2. To increase the number of inter-crosse players;

3. To establish and promote a philosophy of inter-crosse as well as research and discussion of teaching methods;

4. To organize and govern meets and competitions between inter-crosse players.

(constitution, by-laws, www.intercrosse.tk)

It is important to indicate that we are not claiming that the generalities in these statements, be they constitutional, mission statements or preambles to regulations, are designed to allow the organisations to escape obligations. It is, in fact, difficult to see how they could have been formulated in any strikingly different way. The result is that the GSOs have general rather than specific obligations and these are open to a variety of interpretations allowing the GSOs flexibility of action while still being able to claim that they are in pursuit of these ends. While it is certain that the objectives and goals have changed over time, such as the inclusion of anti-doping, it is clear that these are not intended as profit-making organisations. This is despite the massive commercialisation of sport that has taken place. This places all of the GSOs open to commercial pressures but for only a few, such as FIFA, do the riches of a global event become a reality.

The more abstract the objectives or ends of the organisation the fewer the number of specific individuals, groups or organisations that are directly and adversely affected by the shift to commercialism. It is easier for the organisation to claim any action that it undertakes is consistent with its objectives. This does not mean that the shift is without dissent or that it is ever complete. In some organisations there have been those that have argued that the move to commercialism is inimical to the ethos of the GSO. For some the move towards commercial ends came slowly while for others it meant a rapid change, and could take on different forms. An example is Wimbledon, which moved as a global hallmark event of the amateur game to perhaps even greater status as an open, that is, professional, event in the late 1960s. It almost certainly had little choice if it wished to retain any major status at all. In the case of the IAAF it meant a repudiation of their status as an amateur as opposed to open federation while the descriptive title remained. Unlike Wimbledon and the IAAF for most organisations with abstract ends, the level of the abstraction entails that they do not have a commercial property to sell. In the case of the GSOs, however, this is decidedly not the case given the attention paid to sport. There is, therefore, both (1) a strong opportunity to move towards commercial exploitation of the sport and (2) relatively little opposition. This implies that the explanatory models and theoretical frameworks that we use in this chapter have to be considered in the light of this unstated objective.

Principals, agents, stakeholders and members

Whether they have a membership composed of individuals or of national sports federations it is the assembly or congress of these members that is the formal supreme authority within the GSO. As in the case of FIFA and many other GSOs it is the national federations that brought the GSO into existence. Despite this we have seen that the constitutionally stated objective of the GSOs is not to act in the interests of the sport rather than to act directly in the interests of its members. A possible implication is that the GSO's major stakeholder is not the body of its members. Its members are only indirectly served by the GSO, and often a GSO's decisions can go against individual members. In this section we examine a variety of models as potential analytical devices for understanding GSO governance, particularly in terms of its relationship to its members.

Agency theory is mainly concerned with the analysis of owner–manager relationships. Beyond this, it analyses more general principal–agent relationships. These concerns date from the work of Adam Smith (1776). Smith argued that the managers of assets cannot be expected to look after them as diligently as their owner. The seminal paper on principal–agent relationships appeared two hundred years later (Jensen and Meckling, 1976). In their work, the manager again acts as the agent of an owner and as such, is contracted to act solely in the principal's interests. In general the agent receives compensation for undertaking the task. Unfortunately for the principal, often quite simply by virtue of the knowledge gained in being the asset's manager the agent is better informed about the state of the world in relation to these assets than the principal. This allows exploitation of the principal by the agent. As a consequence the mutual problem for putative principals and agents is to design a system of monitoring and incentives to govern their fundamentally dyadic relationship. This design is intended to align the agent's interests with those of the principal while compensating the agent, who is induced to act in the interests of the principal. Experience indicates that such design is difficult both in theory and practice. Certainly we do not appear to see such binding behaviour on the part of the GSOs and their apparent principals. One possibility is that the design is poor while another is that the relationship between GSO and member(s) is not that of a principal and agent.

The ambiguity of ownership of sport codes raises questions with respect to the principal–agent model. In the sports context the principal will be either a person or an entity such as an organisation or a group of national sports federations that contracts and instructs an individual or organisation (the GSO) to act as their agent, and to make decisions and take actions on their behalf. This implies the principal relinquishing a large degree of control over their own affairs or assets because they believe it to be in their interest to do so. In this light and given that they created the GSOs, national sport federations might be seen as the principals of the GSO, and the GSO as their agent. But does such an interpretation succeed?

As a realistic illustration we take a major jurisdictional function of the GSOs. A GSO has a much greater ability to perform international control and adjudication tasks than any national federation. This flows from the national federations limited neutrality in the detection and punishment of cheating by its own athletes at international levels. This is especially the case with respect to performance enhancing drugs. Certainly national federations have colluded in this with their athletes, perhaps the most notorious example being the East German regime. In addition, the ACB has concealed the guilt of some of its players. If the agency model is to apply, the GSO has to be the agent of the national sports federations in a collective sense. It may be more appropriate and consistent with this example to regard the GSO as operating independently of the national federations and not as their agent. If the national federations are the principals of their GSO it appears as it is in the sense of being the collective owners of the sport, the GSO managing it on their behalf and for their benefit. In fact, the constitutional arrangements are more consistent with the idea that it is the sport itself that is the GSO's principal. This means that an abstraction is the principal and it is, therefore, the abstraction's interests that the GSO is deemed to further.

This interpretation has two complications. First, any agent must know what the principal's wishes are. In the simplest situations the principal unambiguously informs the agent of these wishes. This is difficult in the case of a collective of national federations and impossible in the case of the sport itself. Second, the agent must have a specified degree of control over some part of the principal's resources in order that action can be taken in order to achieve the principal's aims. Sport as an abstract entity has no such resources and arguably neither does the collective of federations. These arguments render untenable an implicit basis of the principal–agent model in that the principal and the agent are unambiguously identifiable. A lack of ambiguity is clearly not the situation in sport. Consequently the principal–agent model fits sport governance only with difficulty. Nevertheless its potential relevance cannot be entirely ruled out. This is especially so for solo athlete organisations where the athletes are interpreted as being the principals. Yet even there we have seen that the WTA and the ATP do not act solely as the players' agent and this is the contention of the International Men's Tennis Association (IMTA). If the GSOs are to be interpreted as the agents of the national federations it seems that the agents have seized control from their principals.

Given problems with principal–agent theory, the stakeholder model may be more appropriate. Its advantage is that it provides a highly flexible framework within which to analyse individual cases. The cost of this flexibility is methodological in that it provides less definitive theoretical predictions than the principal–agent model. These two models deal with different but related governance issues rather than being entirely in conflict.

Stakeholder analysis is a strong and increasing component of the organisational governance literature but has been largely absent from the analysis of sport. The standard definition is due to Freeman (1984) who states that:

> A stakeholder in an organisation is any group or individual who can affect or is affected by the achievement of the organisation's objectives.
>
> (p. 46)

For Donaldson and Preston (1995), stakeholder theory has descriptive, instrumental and normative aspects. The normative element is the bedrock in terms of recognition of interests and/or rights of stakeholders, that is, a recognition that stakeholders exist and that their interests are of intrinsic value.

Freeman supports this view. The corporation, or GSO in our case, is defined as a '...constellation of cooperative and competitive interests possessing intrinsic value...' (p. 66) and '...it establishes a framework for examining the connections, if any, between the practice of stakeholder management and the achievement of various corporate performance goals' (Donaldson and Preston, 1995, pp. 66–7). For Rowley this moves it beyond 'dyadic ties' but '...accommodates multiple, interdependent stakeholder demands' (1997, p. 887). Normative 'stakeholders are persons or groups with legitimate interests in procedural and/or substantive aspects of corporate activity' and 'the interests of all stakeholders are of intrinsic value' (p. 67).

While relevant to our concerns with the (formal) objectives of the GSOs, a broadening of Freeman's term is appropriate and consistent with Donaldson and Preston. Stakeholders are those affected by any actions of the organisation, including its actions not in pursuit of its objectives. This is similar to our arguments concerning managerial control. Furthermore Freeman's definition only considers those within the organisation. In the case of the GSO significant stakeholders, most notably the individual athlete, can be outside the organisation. At this point it is worth remembering that the principal–agent relationship excludes the possibility of the athletes being the GSO's principals. The potential for sport to be considered a stakeholder also has to be considered, although being neither a group nor individual, this poses difficulties.

However they are defined, the interests of the stakeholders are not the same as those of the members of the GSOs or their representatives in the General Assemblies. Critical among such stakeholders are those media entities holding contracts with the GSO who need not have any consideration for the GSO's success or failure. In this context, the problem of internal as opposed to external stakeholders may, by implication, define boundaries for the GSO that differ from those the organisation defines for itself. This is related to the organisational structures discussed in Chapter 6. Fans, for example, are stakeholders in a sport and hence the GSO, but they are definitely not internal to the GSO. Neither are the athletes although they are represented through the hierarchy of clubs, national associations and GSO relationships. In the case of FIFA, for example, soccer players are not members but FIFA rulings affect them directly through its interventions in the transfer market. Again this varies between team and solo sports being more direct in solo sports. Certainly it would appear strange to omit the athletes as stakeholders in the actions of a GSO.

In standard corporate governance theory there is a separation of interest from ownership. As we have already seen, the lack of direct ownership of the GSOs creates an accountability problem. However, this does not imply that some sectional stakeholders are not powerful, especially the media. This raises the question of stakeholder legitimacy and how their interests are to be both recognised and protected as legitimate. The absence of athlete's direct representation in the vast majority of GSO structures was shown in Chapter 6. This absence is of enormous importance given both the legitimacy and the directness of their stakeholdership in the GSOs. With some justification, however, the GSOs can point to how difficult this would be to achieve, but neither their actions nor their opacity indicate any willingness to solve it. Notwithstanding this problem, societies increasingly recognise that the interests of others must be taken into account in decision-making, and in some areas this is specifically mandated. Somehow the GSOs as members of global civil society appear to have exempted themselves from this concern.

A major challenge for the GSOs is that stakeholders are recognised as having legitimate and even legal rights with respect to an organisation. Increasingly stakeholders in a GSO and its sport are so entangled in economic and legal and other ways that the relationship is one of interdependency. Those with whom the GSO has long-term relationships are required to have specialised assets that open them to ex post exploitation. One way to get around this is to allow these stakeholders a more active role in the corporate governance of the company. This involves what Schmidt (1997) calls constitutional contracts. This, Schmidt states, '...would differ clearly from what is advocated by proponents of a "stakeholder approach", as it would limit the rights of other constituencies to those which would have been agreed upon in a constitutional contract...' (1997, Abstract). Thus rather than representation there is contractualisation and this seems to be the relationship between the GSOs and the athletes. In the case of the GSOs this contractualisation may not even be direct but indirect via contracts between the GSO and a hierarchy of organisations. The longer such chains of contracts the greater the potential for conflict between them. This has led to situations where the GSO has contracted exclusive sponsorship for one of its hallmark events to a company and the athlete and a national team may be contracted exclusively to other companies. This has proven a perennial problem in Soccer and RWCs and the Olympics. In these cases, the Schmidt argument is that some of these contracts would have to both establish precedence and rule out a role in governance.

Given the difficulty of interpreting GSOs in terms of the principal–agent relationship there is a need for some other form of analysis. This is especially the case in terms of the athletes who are excluded by any principal–agent interpretation. They are, however, embraced within almost any characterisation of stakeholdership. Nevertheless stakeholder analysis has its own problems. Mitchell *et al.* (1997) describe that it is an 'heuristic' that '...has not attained fully theoretical status' (p. 853). The major problem that stakeholder analysis faces in the GSOs is nevertheless one that is also faced by principal–agent analysis. This is the question of how sport is treated in the analysis? Our attitude is that it should be treated as a stakeholder, albeit an unusual one. Although not without critics, among them Phillips and Reichart (2000), this approach is not without precedent in that non-human elements, particularly the natural environment, have been regarded as stakeholders (Starik, 1995). What strengthens this possibility in the GSO case is that they have raised sport to a central level in their constitutions. What the GSOs have created is a substitute major stakeholder, which they claim is a proxy for all of the other stakeholders, but which is also voiceless. By suggesting that they work to the good of this abstract entity they can ignore other stakeholders as partial, thereby also rendering them impotent.

The ability of an organisation's members to express concerns about the direction it is taking is important. But for the GSOs – designed to allow national federations representation in the global governance of their sport or event – it is a key issue. Representation within organisations has been described and analysed as 'voice' and 'exit' as responses to decline by Hirschman (1970) in a now classic text, *Exit, Voice and Loyalty: Responses to Decline in Firms, Organizations and States*. Its potential application to INGOs (including the GSOs) has been overlooked.

This model was described in Chapter 6. Hirschman describes the only alternative to expressing voice as exit from the organisation. However exit is virtually impossible for the members of GSOs. This is because for a national sport federation to exit its GSO means that it puts itself outside international competition in the sport. This means that loyalty, the least developed of Hirschman's trio of factors, is not a consideration. Members of the GSOs, usually national federations (individuals in the case of the IOC and some solo sports) are largely powerless against the executive board or president of the GSO. For major GSOs this lack of members' voice is due to the size of the membership, the number of nations in the world is an approximate upper limit. This can mean between one hundred and two hundred members. Almost invariably the member federations have equal voting rights, enormously diluting the power of each member especially the larger federations. This is akin to the dispersed ownership of American corporations noted by Berle and Means (1932) where dispersion of shareholders was argued to put control in the hands of the managers rather than the shareholders. Not surprisingly, GSO presidents and boards have never moved to enhance the voice of the member federations despite their claims to being democratic. This both preserves the power of the GSOs with respect to the national federations and preserves the power of the individuals at the apex of the GSO.

We again have to remember that although the solo sports organisations are rather different and may be more commercially oriented organisations (PGA, ATP etc.), this does not mean that they are free from difficulties. Certainly the experience of chess and men's tennis indicates that there is a tendency for these organisations to splinter even though the athletes may be more directly represented.

Full circle: individuals and internal processes

In many ways this section brings us to the start of the previous chapter. There we began with personal politics but emphasised structures in order to redress an imbalance in the way that the GSOs have been examined up until now. We can now return to the individual, suggesting a variety of explanations of the behaviour of individuals within the GSOs. We argue that the structures, the non-profit status of the GSOs and their opacity will lead to predictable behaviour on the part of human beings. This is exacerbated by the huge revenues that are generated by some GSOs and an apparent lack of financial accountability to the outside world. These individuals are in practice largely unaccountable because of the degree to which they control the information provided by the GSOs.

Even when the members of a GSO are federations rather than individuals, it is individuals that are their representatives in the GSO. And it is most certainly individuals that are the GSO office holders. This discussion takes on a significance and focus it might not have had but for the corrupt behaviour of some individuals within GSOs. IOC members have been especially high profile in this area over recent years. While not all of the behaviour of such individual officers and representatives is corrupt, accusations have affected the elections and post-election staffing changes in GSOs such as FIFA. In cricket, the question of corrupt behaviour has dogged the ICC from individual player behaviour in national teams to some of the highest office holders in member federations. Unfortunately, any analysis in this area is extraordinarily difficult due to the lack of empirical information.

Here we have to distinguish between corruption and malpractice on the sporting field as opposed to that within the organisations themselves. With the possible exception of drugs, part of a much wider societal problem, the GSOs have dealt with corruption and misbehaviour on the playing field according to current societal tolerances. Concentrating on the governance of sports and sporting events, they have not provided much in the way of reasonable self-governance. Corruption and malpractice need not be important within the GSOs but where it has appeared the GSOs have seemed ill prepared to deal with it. Senior GSO officials have control over substantial funds, yet there seems to be little in the structures and processes of the GSOs that are designed for the governance of this aspect of their duties. There are several elements that lead to this. One is the structure designed to govern other elements rather then self-governance. Second are the very small bureaucracies that these organisations employ, which disallow the anonymity and impersonality of large organisations that let whistle-blowers operate. In addition, the GSOs are embedded into a Swiss legal system that gives them enormous protection against internal and external examination; witness the treatment of Jennings who was given a jail sentence. Also related to the Swiss system is the secrecy provided by a banking system that sees many millions of sport and other dollars flow through. A good many of these organisations exist as parts of the same networks and in the same locality. (Appendix lists the GSOs mentioned in this text including the location of their head quarters.)

Perhaps the most important factor of all is the non-profit status of these organisations. They have enormous sums of money in terms of revenue without shareholders. This means that there are few stakeholders directly related to money, as opposed to shareholders. The money is easily conveyed to friends, self or family under the cover of a variety of contracts for services. This has been alluded to in the cases in Chapter 5. Development funds going to nations where the sport is in a fledgling state or where the needs are greatest provide a less overt avenue for corruption. Essentially, the use of funds in this way can be used to ensure votes not only to support specific agenda but also to ensure re-election of officers (most notably Presidents) who are not appointees of the incumbent. It is reasonable to suggest that cash-poor Third World federations and their officers are especially vulnerable and open to exploitation in this way.

This happens in the absence of any real oversight that would be expected in any democratic assembly. There are few sports journalists that regularly cover the GSOs in the way that Jennings examined (in a very personal way) the IOC. Internal oversight is very difficult, in that the representatives of the member federations are normally located in other countries and not able to question immediately what happens inside the GSOs. In the absence of ownership of profits, except by the organisations itself, and with no formal mechanism for distributing surpluses, these become the prizes sought by a variety of individuals and federations. With little accountability and little information, it is not surprising that examples of problematic and unexplained use of funds abound.

One area that we touched upon in Chapter 6 was the role of structures and presidential power. What is much more difficult to examine is the degree to which lobbying occurs within the GSOs. Casual observation would suggest this is an enormous part of GSO internal activity, but if this is the case, we need to question how effective it is, and if it in anyway weakens or impinges upon executive powers. One possibility is that lobbying serves to strengthen presidential power by creating a body of supplicants whose own power bases, either inside the GSO or among the federations, tend to nullify each other.

In this context, how often the General Assemblies meet is important. Most meet annually or at even greater intervals. As we have seen, they can influence decision-making through their political deliberations. Having federation representatives meet only once a year is an enormous impediment to their ability to influence executives. Solo athletes are represented in very different ways and here the organisation tends much more to be based upon a CEO model rather than a presidential one. There is certainly a far greater tendency to bring someone in from outside based upon their commercial experience and success. In this sense, we note that F1, discussed in Chapter 5, is essentially a GSO of solo athletes, the athletes in this case being the team principals. This raises the question of how individuals make their careers in these organisations. Importantly, we need to ask how this affects the organisations. Given that internal bureaucracies are generally small, any 'career path' is through the political side and less to the administrative sides of the

GSOs. Only the very largest GSOs have bureaucracies and none approach the size of the IOC.

In the case of the IOC the path to the top is through the commission hierarchy. This career path applies not only to the Presidents but to those who reach rather less exalted positions, still with enormous influence. Within the IOC, the paths of the three contenders for the Presidency all followed such paths. The Commission path is where fiefdoms can be created and favours taken, earned and re-payed. Certainly the ability to offer and take patronage on a systematic basis is available. Patronage in this sense is a fact of life in many organisations and not necessarily any impediment to the efficiency of the organisation.

Given their significance, the opacity and apparent lack of accountability of the GSOs has a double impact. First, opacity and accountability are substantive issues in their own right providing a rationale for analysis. Second, they impose severe methodological constraints given that much information is missing and unobtainable. The consequence is that methods of what can best be described as organisational forensics and inference have to be used. In turn, this means that conclusions are to be cautiously drawn. Certainly, there is a need for the GSOs to become more open, especially in the light of the scandals and maladministration that have occurred. As a survival strategy, given the increasing ability of purely commercial organisations as well as rival GSOs to enter their realms, they will need to change their structures. This is especially true of their internal governance and the cultures this opacity creates. In terms of our analysis, this suggests that the member federations have to be prepared to use their voice for the benefit of their sport rather than narrow national advantage.

Conclusions

There is no single theoretical structure that is presently capable of providing even an adequate interpretation of the GSOs and their internal driving forces. Here we have only very briefly examined some of those theoretical analyses that may have a contribution to make to the understanding of the internal political economy of the GSOs. Welding them into some coherent single structure is, of course, unlikely to be achieved, given the mutually antithetical nature of some of their core ideas. However, we outlined some areas where there is an especial need for explanation to be strived for. One of these is the way, if any, their self-prescribed role in global society is either catered for or otherwise affects the internal workings of these organisations. Or, is it, as we venture to suggest little more than persiflage that obscures their real contribution to global culture in the form of sport. If so this makes the argument that ends and means of the GSOs have become inverted all the more important. Sport is no longer their objective but a means to other more economically oriented organisational ends. Certainly this makes their opacity all the more understandable.

8 Getting on with the neighbours
The external relationships of GSOs

Osvaldo Croci

Introduction

Sport serves both as an agent of socialisation and an instrument of diversion. Because it can promote national identity as well as confer prestige on those identified with it, sport can create 'politically useable resources' (Allison, 1986, p. 12). For these reasons governments, and not only authoritarian ones (Arnaud and Riordan, 1998), become involved with sport, trying to harness it to their objectives. Even if governments do not get involved, however, sport governance and control is political since it has its own power struggles. Thus, in an early treatment of sport and politics, Taylor (1986) distinguished between two standard definitions of politics: anything involving governments or public authorities or any activity involving power, influence and control over people's behaviour. No matter which definition is chosen sport is a political issue. This chapter pursues the external political relationships of GSOs under both these definitions.

Sports, especially those that are in any way commercialised, are regulated and controlled by a hierarchy of local, national, regional and global organisations. In doing so these organisations cooperate and compete among themselves. Equally importantly they do so with other types of organisations such as players' associations, some with their own claims to being GSOs, as well as with governments. Sport organisations compete among themselves to attract a following and media attention and, hence, revenues. Competition between organisations can occur within the same sport. Many of these elements are apparent in the cases of the DanceSport and soccer GSOs that are analysed here. It can take place at the same level as when a sport has competing sources of authority. This seems to be especially so at the GSO level, perhaps because of the greater rewards involved, both immanent and financial. It can also appear at different levels of a sport's organisational hierarchy.

A place in society (1): GSOs as INGOs

Within these contexts treating GSOs as INGOs is especially useful in analysing and understanding the external relationships of GSOs. This is because, unlike the MNCs and despite their commerce related functions, their external relationships are not always immediately or solely about commerce. INGOs are distinguished from International Governmental Organisations (IGOs) because they are set up and controlled by individuals and/or groups drawn from the population of at least two states and not by national governments. Introductions to the study of international politics recognise the increasing importance of INGOs but usually devote little attention to them, and none at all to the GSOs. Among the few exceptions is Papp (2002, p. 120) who mentions the IOC and IRB because of their involvement in politics between states. These texts alert the reader to the dramatic increase in the number of INGOs during this century, and particularly since the end of the Second World War.

Whereas it appears that fewer than 100 INGOs existed at the beginning of the twentieth century, their number had increased to some 19,000 by its end. There are also another estimated 40,000 INGOs who ostensibly limit their activities to their home country although at times with significant international repercussions (Union of International Associations, www.uia.org/uia/). Such an increase is usually explained in functional terms: an increase in the degree of international interdependence has required organisations that facilitate and coordinate trans-national interactions. At the same time, increased efficiency and decreased costs in communication have facilitated their activities and growth. Classifications of INGOs are usually framed in terms of their geographical scope (global or regional), size (big or small), purpose (multipurpose or functional e.g. human rights, environmental), and type of activity (operational or advocatory). Another classification is that used by the United Nations Economic and Social Council (ECOSOC): (1) General Status: global organisations with large membership and working on many different issues; (2) Special Status: regional organisations having one or few fields of activity but enjoying a high reputation in them; (3) Roster: small or highly specialised organisations usually working with UN agencies.

Many INGOs – especially the larger and more influential ones – are managed by permanent and hierarchically structured bureaucracies. In the case of the GSOs, however, the permanent bureaucracies that they employ are relatively small (see Yearbook of International organisations). The control exercised upon them by general assemblies is certainly not superior to that which corporate shareholders are able to exercise on executives. INGOs are usually formed in order to promote shared ideas and interests in specific functional issue-areas, rather than for profit. They regard their activities as political since their primary objective is to influence the policies of both national governments and IGOs. Thus, human rights INGOs for instance, monitor, investigate, and publicise the behaviour of states, lobby national governments and other IGOs, mobilise other interest groups, educate the public, and represent clients in their dealing with national officials or before courts and international organs.

Much like MNCs, GSOs manage and organise a specific (leisure, recreational) area of human activity within the commercial and economic spheres, as pointed out here and elsewhere in this text, and which they tend to regard as being separate from the political and hence beyond state regulation. Nevertheless, either because of, or in spite of the commodification and globalisation of sport and the consequent increased commercialisation of their activities, GSOs have increasingly encountered the political and have been obliged to deal and compromise with it. So while much like mainstream INGOs in being non-profit organisations, their ability to raise revenues has become extremely significant and increasingly follows the commercial lines used by MNCs.

The democratic family: representativeness of GSOs

The fact that INGOs might be unrepresentative does not deter their supporters from arguing that they should participate in international decision-making. Krut (1997) deploys a typical justification:

> While it may be fair to criticise some CSOs [Civil Society Organisations] as 'unrepresentative', as with national governments, this complaint may not be an appropriate basis for deciding on their right of access to global governance or to the UN. It would certainly be unreasonable to require that CSOs demonstrate greater representativeness than governments.
>
> (p. 24)

The argument basically is: if the UN does not mind the fact that some nation states are non-representative why should one mind if some INGOs are non-representative?

INGOs can be regarded in a very favourable light, as the cornerstone of a vibrant civil society and hence of a healthy democracy. This view of INGOs is rooted in the reflections of Alexis de Tocqueville. In his examination of American democracy in the early nineteenth century, he noted the high level of civic associations in the USA and linked them to the existence of a healthy democracy. An active civil society came thus be seen as a crucial prerequisite and contributor to democracy. Citizens' activism and participation came to be seen as necessary to prevent the potential abuse of state power and to guarantee the political accountability of the state. The only exception to this view was the 1975 report of the Trilateral Commission which maintained that democracy could be threatened by demand overload (i.e. too much civic engagement). Such roots have been more recently expanded by a new generation of Neo-Tocquevillian scholars (Putnam, 1993, 1995) who have developed and refined the link between civic associations and democratic governance.

From this perspective, INGOs are seen as the organised expression of a developing 'global civil society', which will eventually give birth to a 'global political society'. Always from this perspective, the development of a 'global civil society' is regarded as a necessary counterweight to the process of economic globalisation. Given that globalisation is seen as making democracy, or at least 'national democracies', increasingly impotent, the crucial role for a global civil society is to counter the anti-democratic tendencies of globalisation in general (and of global capital in particular), and work for democracy at the global level. The locus of democracy has traditionally been the nation state but today the fate of democracy is increasingly perceived to depend on a vibrant global civil society, organising itself and acting through its INGOs.

Putting aside for a moment the question of whether the existence and activities of INGOs does indeed promote global democracy, it is certainly ironic to realise that most INGOs hardly exhibit internal democratic procedures. That is to say, they are not representative bodies whose executive officers are clearly responsible and accountable to a democratic policy-making assembly. In some cases such as Oxfam and Greenpeace they are at best responsible to the public, rather than to a membership. Most human rights INGOs, for instance, consist of a small group of policy-makers and administrators without a broad membership. Some are effectively one-person organisations and have fallen prey to a kind of cult of personality. Few INGOs, despite the democratic aspirations of the work they perform, are run in a democratic manner. Even if formal democratic structures and procedures exist, moreover, the executive is almost always in a position to influence decisively the work of the assembly. This is something that is seen in Chapter 6. It is at least plausible to suggest that this has flowed into their organisational behaviour.

The IOC remains a self-recruiting body. Pierre de Coubertin, its founder and Second President (1896–1925), ran it as a personal property (and he did finance much of its early days) and invited his friends to join. He granted an independent team to whomever he pleased while ignoring existing sports federations. He chose his own successor, Henri de Baillet, on the basis that he had been impressed by his performance as organiser of the 1920 Antwerp games (Boulogne, 1994). It is also interesting to note that observers of GSOs usually explain changes in policy at the individual level of analysis; that is, focusing on the personal characteristics of individual executives, rather than on GSOs' responses and adaptation to their external environment. Thus, the IOC's abandonment of the idea of being an apolitical body and its recognition that it too was an actor in a political world is usually regarded as the result of the IOC presidency of Juan Antonio Samaranch beginning in 1980. On this subject he had different ideas to his predecessors (Morse, 1987, p. 3).

Distant cousins: GSO relations with sports organisations

Much like other INGOs there are often tensions in the relationship between the GSOs and their national constituents. The advent of commodification has been a major source of tension. In tennis, for example, the authority of the International Lawn Tennis Federation (ILTF) with its staunch amateur ethos was challenged first by the World Championship Tennis (WCT), the

Women's International Tennis Federation (WITF) and the formation of players' unions such as the ATP and WTA. Reconciliation took place through the formation of the MIPTC (Men's International Professional Tennis Council), a professional governing body representing all sectors of international tennis (Brasher, 1986). Not too much later, the ATP rebelled and the MIPTC lost its functions.

A persistent theme is what national member associations consider paternalism and excessive direction from GSOs. In football for instance, national federations, regional federations, and FIFA, are all theoretically responsible for regulation the game. In practice, however, because regional federations and FIFA are responsible for the organisation of international competitions at both club and national team levels, the system is presently skewed in their favour. As FIFA President Sepp Blatter put it:

> We [FIFA] have said clearly that, within their own country, they [national federations] can play football and organise it however they like, with whatever rules they like and with whatever president they like, but they cannot expect to go OUTSIDE their country and play in OUR competitions.
>
> (Radnege, 2000, p. 32, emphasis in original)

Another example is provided by the Media Partners' attempt to set up a European football competition in 1998 rivalling that organised by UEFA. Media Partners is a private Italian business group linked to the Finivest conglomerate that owns Milan AC, and hence to Italian Prime Minister Silvio Berlusconi. It launched a proposal for a European Super League that would officially compete with – and potentially replace – the current European-wide competitions organised by UEFA. Media Partners tried to convince the most successful European clubs to join its Super League by promising higher financial rewards than those provided by UEFA. UEFA, supported by FIFA, countered Media Partners' initiative by threatening to ban the players of the clubs that would join the proposed Super League from all other competitions, including those reserved for national teams.

The clubs contacted by Media Partners used the Super League proposal to bring pressure on UEFA both to change the format of its European competitions and to secure themselves a higher share of the financial returns they generate. When UEFA agreed to meet most of the demands made by the clubs they abandoned the idea of joining the proposed Super League. Media Partners, for its part, reacted by filing a complaint with the European Commission in which it argued that UEFA infringes European competition law by abusing its dominant position and preventing new organisations (such as Media Partners) from organising and marketing football competition in Europe. The EC in July 2003 gave UEFA an exemption until July 2009 in its marketing of TV rights. This ruling effectively maintains UEFA's dominant position in European soccer.

Some GSOs control sports which, while rarely direct competitors, have different interests. Frequently they have good reasons for cooperation, but the power relationships are not equal. The focus here is on the International DanceSport Federation (IDSF) and the way in which relationships between professional and amateur performers, commercial organisations and a GSO and between GSOs themselves, all affect each other. The major component of the methodology in this example is to let the organisations and their principal officers speak for themselves as much as possible. This they do extensively through their websites. The use of websites has become the major means by which the GSOs try to reach the general public as well as their own members, often unintentionally revealing as much by the 'tone' of their voice as by the context and content of what they say. That aside the set of quotations employed here gives some feel for an overall picture of the interrelationships between a small group of GSOs that is missing from just examining one in isolation. What is apparent in almost all of the statements is the power of the economic forces in operation. These forces erode and strengthen the positions taken as well as provide the primary motivation behind many of them. The nature of dance as an athletic and aesthetic exercise receives little attention. Nonetheless personal ambitions and desires to maintain or increase control and power are at least as apparent, and cannot be discounted.

The specific background is that DanceSport evolved from the more restrictive ballroom dancing to which it still has very strong affinities. Although only formed in 1957 the IDSF has a long series of precursor organisations, including the International Amateur Dancers Federation formed in Prague in 1935, with a world championship held as long ago as 1909 in Paris. It remains heavily European centred (in Germany especially) and has about eighty member national federations. In 2003 the principal elected officers were Rudolf Baumann (President) and Harald Frahm (First Vice-President). Baumann and Frahm play prominent roles in this case. The IDSF headquarters were in Lausanne, Switzerland. The IDSF claims to represent the sport in general, while there is a separate professional dancers association, the World Dance and DanceSport Council (WDDSC). However, the IDSF deleted the word 'amateur' from its title in 2002. This name change led to concern within the WDDSC. This was because the IDSF and WDDSC had had an agreement since at least the early 1990s on what can be termed their respective spheres of interest and overlapping responsibilities. In many ways this follows the global structuring of other solo sports but without the commercial pull of the leaders, tennis and golf.

More immediately our interest is in the relationship between the IDSF and the IOC. One of the major aims of Baumann has been to make DanceSport a full Summer Olympic sport. The IDSF Media Kit makes clear in a condensed form the case for inclusion. While Samaranch was president of the IOC the IDSF, and Baumann in particular, seemed to believe that there was a likelihood of this happening. Indeed in 2000 DanceSport was given a place in the closing ceremony of the Sydney Games. Unfortunately for the IDSF and Baumann's aims, shortly after the Sydney Olympics the incoming president of the IOC, J. Rogge, made it abundantly clear that he believed that the Olympics was becoming too big (see Chapter 6). This was for a variety of reasons, including complexity, cost, the time available to cover all events and sports and the sheer lack of commerciality of some sports. Given these criteria it seems abundantly clear that DanceSport is unlikely to be accepted. Nevertheless they have long lobbied to be included. Shortly after the Sydney Olympics the IDSF still had high hopes of inclusion in the Summer Olympics. The very first of 'The Aims of the IDSF' was 'To promote and advance the character, status and interests of DanceSport internationally and to be a well-regarded member of the Olympics' (www.idsf.net, IDSF Media Kit). One aspect of this statement is that the purely abstract concept of DanceSport is put above that of its members, that is, the national federations, as well as the individual DanceSport athletes. This is consistent with our analysis of Chapters 6 and 7. But, even though the IDSF remains an Olympic recognised international sport federation, its bid to be included in the 2004 Olympics was rejected. The IDSF website reproduces part of a letter from the IOC, which reads, in part:

> The IOC Executive Board decided on 13 December 2000 that no new sports would be admitted to the programme of the Athens 2004 Olympic Games. As always, the IOC commits itself to the continual development of the Olympic programme, and therefore this decision does not relate to Olympic Games beyond 2004.
> (15 December 2000, Gilbert Felli, IOC Sports Director)

This decision was announced after the IDSF had made its presentation to be included in the Athens games to the IOC on 11 December 2000. The IDSF interpretation of this decision and its wording comes in a press release signed by the IDSF Presidium. This release states:

> Please tell everyone, from the IOC and the IDSF: DanceSport hasn't been rejected from the Olympics. Anyone who suggests otherwise is completely wrong. No sport was added is more like it. No sport was rejected at all.

The reason for this emphasis on not being 'added' rather than being 'rejected' is that this is in part a response by the IDSF Presidium to an article by Harald Frahm, President of DTV. This was in the magazine Tanzspiegel (Hopes for DanceSport – thumbs down, May 2001) that claimed that the IOC had given the 'thumbs down' to the IDSF's bid for a place in the Summer Olympics. In this context inclusion in the closing ceremony at Sydney seems a hollow victory for the IDSF. The relationship to commercial matters appears in the statements in the same press release, that:

> Mr Drossart, the senior IG man dealing with IDSF, was also present and was also very pleased from the television point of view.
>
> Perhaps Mr Frahm was not pleased. It is well-known that Mr Frahm is a prominent German television man with a significant interest in maintaining his dominance. He knows IMG is directly linked to IDSF's Olympic initiative, and sees both as a threat. If our Olympic bid failed, it would be a huge disappointment to DanceSport, but might save him from the world's most powerful sport media company...
>
> ...As a busy executive Mr Frahm has unfortunately been unable to find time to serve on any IDSF Commission. Not one...
>
> ...Mr Frahm is not a hard working IDSF insider, but as DTV President he is too well-informed to make the statements he circulates in his federation's otherwise admirable magazine. [DTV is the German DanceSport Federation, which regards the German Open Championship (GOC) as the most important DanceSport event in the world]...As consequence to this the DTV cancelled the participation of its top couples at the World Games which will take place just a week before GOC in Akita/Japan.
>
> (Braun, W. GOC Press Release 1/2001, dated 02.04.01, 15. German Open Championships at Mannheim Congress Centre Rosengarten from 28.08.2001 to 01.09.2001)

Rather surprisingly perhaps, Mr Frahm is now very much an IDSF 'insider' having become its First Vice-President. Clearly some sort of agreement of mutual objectives became possible between the IDSF and Frahm for him to be elected to this position at the IDSF AGM of August 2002 in Singapore. Interestingly it appears that Baumann believes that Rogge has indicated that DanceSport needs to increase media and TV interest before it is considered a candidate for inclusion in the Olympics (IDSF President Baumann's New year's Message, 8 December 2002, www.ctdsa.org.tw/ct19-8.htm, accessed 11/03/2003).

The first and main part of this message, however, was concerned with a different but related issue. This was the failure in late 2002 of the IDSF and the WDDSC to agree terms to form a unified DanceSport GSO. The WDDSC is head quartered in London and describes itself as 'the exclusive body governing world-wide professional affairs for DanceSport, Social Dance (competitions/events, dance schools, teachers, trainers, adjudicators, competitors and organisers and the representation of these)' (Joint Statement of Position and First Stage Towards a Unified DanceSport, 13 October 2002, World Dance and DanceSport Council). It was formed in

Edinburgh in 1950 as the International Council of Ballroom Dancing (ICBD) (www.wddsc.com/council/council.htm). The Council, as a body for professionals also notes that the IDSF deleted the word 'amateur' from its title on 18th March 2002, in the memorandum that proposed the formation of a joint World DanceSport Federation (WDSF). Yet towards the end of 2002, Baumann stated:

> A meeting held in London on October 13. 2002 with representatives of the WDDSC made it clear to me, that the current leadership is determined to stick to their old entrenched positions.
>
> They say that they are bound by the views of their members as expressed at the WDDSC AGM, but there is little doubt that the WDDSC AGM was whipped up into a frenzy of fear and suspicion.

Baumann goes on to argue that this does not represent the views of the dance professionals that have spoken with him. Baumann points out that the argument used, that the 'only concern' of the IDSF is admission to the Olympic Games is incorrect, and that 'In fact the question of our participation in the Olympic Program will be placed down the agenda for the time being' (IDSF President Baumann's New Year's Message, 8 December 2002, www.ctdsa.org.tw/ct19-8.htm).

The WDDSC has problems of its own in that it regrets that many professionals compete in events sanctioned by neither the WDDSC nor any one of its national federations (www.wwdsc.com/presidium//president-report/2hy2002.htm). It is clear in the same message that there is encroachment by IDSF national member federations, especially in France and Russia, into areas that the WDDSC considers its own. In these two nations it appears that the national federations have created professional sections. It is suggested that the 1992 agreement between the WDDSC and the IDSF needs to be kept in operation but updated. In the same message, the WDDSC President Karl Breuer, takes issue with many of the statements of his IDSF counterpart in his New Year Message.

The IDSF, as a GSO, 'enjoys' a complex set of relationships with two other GSOs, the IOC and the WDDSC. To one it is a supplicant and a member of its Olympic family, while it has an agreement with another GSO concerned with the same sport. Yet it is clear that there is antagonism between the two DanceSport GSOs concerning encroachment. This is also true with respect to the WDDSC's concerns about IDSF national federations' members, especially those of France and Russia, moving into what it regards as its sphere.

So at least three GSOs including the IOC, several national federations and commercial companies seem to have a variety of conflicts. Through their GSOs even sports as disparate as the pentathlon and DanceSport are in many ways pitted against each other in terms of relationships with other organisations such as the IOC. The quoted material also indicates that personal politics very much comes into play in the inter-GSO relationships, as much as in the intra-GSO relationships examined elsewhere. The clash of amateurs and professionals seems to be a principal point of contention, especially as this distinction is transformed in the open era.

A place in society (2): relations with states and governments

One aspect of the relationship between states and governments has been examined with respect to global sporting events. There the governments were seen as supplicants to the GSOs. However that situation is often reversed.

INGOs are usually considered to have less political significance than IGOs due to the lack of direct governmental involvement, and to the predominantly technical focus of most INGOs. INGOs, and GSOs in particular, often stress the importance of being detached from political life or claim to be apolitical or above politics. Thus Oxfam in the Second Gulf War announced that it was to refuse any funding from any of the warring nations to avoid indicating that it supports the war aims. At best, INGOs acknowledge that they participate in the political process in a very general sense: they operate as pressure groups by seeking to influence those holding political power to act in particular ways. Willets (2001) goes as far as to state that the term NGO itself is a diplomatic smokescreen. He writes:

> Because diplomats like to claim that they are pursuing 'the national interest' of a united society, they will not admit to relations with interest groups or pressure groups and they prefer the bland title, non-governmental organisations or simply NGOs.
>
> (p. 369)

This is true not only of INGOs operating in the field of human rights or the environment but also of those operating in the sport field, including of course GSOs. In 1980 for example, US President Jimmy Carter called upon the US as well as the Western nations to boycott the Moscow Olympic Games to protest the decision of the Soviet Union to intervene militarily in the Afghani Civil War in 1979. The US Olympic Committee agreed to support the President's initiative. In 1984, the Soviet Union and its satellites retaliated by boycotting the Los Angeles Olympic Games.

Tensions often exist between INGOs and sovereign states and their governments and supranational governmental or quasi-governmental organisations such as the UN, IMF and the EU. In recent years most humanitarian INGOs have begun to push forcefully the idea that the 'international community' (often understood and used as a synonym for the humanitarian INGOs themselves) has a right of intervention, at least in countries that violate the rights of minorities or engage in violent repression. This notion of rightful intervention contrasts with the principle of sovereignty, which has been a cornerstone of international relations since the Treaty of Westphalia in 1647. Confrontations brought on by INGOs such as Greenpeace,

Amnesty International and Medecins sans Frontieres have been well publicised (Duncan *et al.*, 2002). Confrontations of course also exist between GSOs and states. If sport as apolitical was a sustainable myth during a period in which a corresponding myth of amateur sport existed, the commodification of sport has led to social relations in sport being perceived as falling within the jurisdiction of public authority. There has been in other words a process of sport 'juridification' (Foster, 1986). GSOs have resisted such a process given that formalised sport has traditionally enjoyed a high degree of self-regulation. In what follows the initial focus is on instances of confrontation between GSOs and states as well as cooperation on 'governance'.

Certainly sport has been unwillingly dragged into disputes between states, notably those that involved: the IOC and the boycotts of the Moscow or Los Angeles Olympics; IOC and the two Germanys; the PRC, Taiwan and Canada; and Indonesia. In the German case: two separate German Olympic Committees but only one German team in 1956, 1960 and 1964 with a special flag and Beethoven's 'Ode to Joy' as national anthem; two teams but one flag and anthem in Mexico, and two separate teams afterwards. In the case of the PRC: in July 1976 Prime Minister Trudeau announced that Taiwan would not be admitted to the Montreal Olympics under a name containing China. In the Indonesian case: President Sukarno attempted to challenge the IOC through GANEFO (Games of New Emerging Forces) for having been expelled following his refusal to accept Israel and Taiwan to the 1962 Fourth Asian Games. Also well documented are the relations between various GSOs and South Africa, as well as Arab states and the status of Israel. Palestinians used terrorism at the Munich games in 1972 and Arab states have continuously attempted to expel Israel from the Mediterranean games.

Beyond the state but also often in relation to the nation state, INGOs play a key role in what has been termed 'global governance' or 'governance without [an international] government' (Rosenau and Czempiel, 1992). The Commission on Global Governance (1995, pp. 2–3) reflected this view when it stated:

> Governance is the sum of the many ways individuals and institutions, public and private, manage their common affairs. It is a continuing process through which conflicting or diverse interests may be accommodated and co-operative action may be taken. It includes formal institutions and regimes empowered to enforce compliance, as well as informal arrangements that people and institutions either have agreed to or perceive to be in their interest. ... At the global level, governance has been viewed primarily as intergovernmental relationships, but it must now be understood as also involving non-governmental organisations (NGOs), citizen's movements, multinational corporations, and the global capital market.

Governments involve NGOs and INGOs in policy development both formally and informally because of the considerable expertise that they have in their own field and because consultation allows governments to claim that they are sensitive to the views and interests of stakeholders. In their neutrality INGOs can often be buffer zones between antagonistic governments, as the Red Cross and to a much lesser extent GSOs have dome. Having been consulted by governments, moreover, INGOs are less likely to criticise the policies that they have contributed to develop. Cooperation between governments and INGOs, however, can be difficult as they have different priorities and often speak a different language.

Close relatives: the case of EC, FIFA, UEFA and the governance of (European) football

The world of football has traditionally been regulated in all its aspects by a set of largely autonomous, albeit intricately interrelated organisations. That autonomy has to at least some degree been eroded by FIFA. In general football clubs are associated in various national leagues (professional, semi-professional and amateur). Leagues, as well as national professional associations (e.g. players, coaches, referees) are represented in national football federations, which are the constituent members of six continental and sub-continental supra-national regional federations, as well as the GSO, FIFA. The supra-national regional bodies include the UEFA. As with the other supra-national bodies UEFA is not a GSO on two counts: one, it does not cover the globe and second it is not the supreme body in its sport or any specialised aspect of sport. Nevertheless, all these organisations are responsible in different ways and to different degrees, for the regulation of football. These have been autonomous activities with states and government agencies hardly playing any role. In line with this as has already seen the rules of FIFA explicitly warn against bringing disputes to ordinary courts. They are to be solved internally. The formation of the continental bodies is an example of this. They have come into existence to develop, enhance and protect regional interests, very frequently running interference against FIFA on behalf of their regional members. UEFA, given the strength of European soccer, has long been a thorn in FIFA's side.

This situation has changed in the last decade: political authorities, and the EC in particular, have entered the field of sport, and of football in particular. This involvement has been justified in terms of the 'rapid [economic] development of sport, especially professional sport, and the important place occupied by sport in society' (European Commission, 1998, p. 3). The EC has become involved in four sports issue areas: freedom of movement, competition policy, audiovisual policy and public health and vocational training. This case study focuses on EC involvement in the first two of these issue areas.

The European Court of Justice (ECJ) first became involved in sport in 1974 with the 'Walrave case' and then again in 1976 with the 'Donà case'.

Both cases revolved around the question of nationality and free movement. The first concerned two Dutch pacesetters on motorcycles in cycle races with so-called 'stayers', who cycle in the lee of the motorcycle. They felt damaged by an ICU regulation providing that as of 1973, in world championship races the pacesetters had to be of the same nationality as the 'stayers'. The second case concerned a contract between the chairman of an Italian football club and a talent scout. The latter incurred some expenses while looking for talent abroad. The chairman refused to reimburse them as the Italian Football Federation's rules restricted the employment of foreign nationals. The scout then brought the case to court claiming that the Italian Federation's restriction on the employment of foreign players violated different articles of the Rome Treaty. In both cases the ECJ ruled that the activities of sport organisations were subject to EC legislation in so far as sport represented an economic activity. It also suggested, however, that sport because of its nature (i.e. qua sport) could be entitled to certain exceptions. Both ECJ decisions are contained in Blanpain (1996, pp. 355–79).

Following the Donà ruling, the Commission signalled to FIFA and UEFA the necessity to abolish a rule that put a limit on the number of foreign players a club could hire, which at the time was fixed at two. This 'nationality restriction' was justified in terms of the need to avoid the richest club being able to recruit all the best European players, to maintain a minimum of national identity, and to give more playing opportunities to young players, especially in those countries with strong leagues, and thus enhance the competitiveness of national teams. In Italy, for instance, it is common to blame any poor performance by the azzurri on the number of foreign players in Serie A. The presence of foreign players, the argument goes, makes it more difficult for promising Italian players to play at a high level and hence acquire experience that would improve their performance on the national team.

The Italian Football Federation (FIGC) closed its national frontiers to foreign players both after the 1966 World Cup (following defeat of the national team to North Korea) and 2002 (following defeat to South Korea). In 2002, however, the frontiers could be closed only to non-EU players. UEFA eventually agreed to revise such a rule and, in 1991, at the end of long negotiations adopted the so-called '3 + 2 rule'. According to this rule, a European team could field three 'foreign' players in any given match plus two 'assimilated players' (i.e. foreign players who had played in the country of the relevant national football association for an uninterrupted period of at least five years). UEFA left national federations free to adopt, if they so wished, an even more liberal approach, which the FA (England) did.

In 1995, however, the so-called 'Bosman ruling' of the ECJ declared also the '3 + 2 rule' illegal, at least when the adjective 'foreign' referred to other EC nationals. The same ECJ ruling declared illegal also the traditional FIFA/UEFA 'transfer system' whereby football clubs had the right to demand and receive payment for players moving to other clubs regardless of whether the player who moved was still under contract or the contract had expired. The ECJ ruling declared the system illegal when the transfer involved two clubs belonging to two different national football federations within the EU. Such a system has long been justified in terms of the need to maintain a sort of financial and competitive balance between smaller, less financially powerful clubs, which were usually the sellers, and richer ones, which were usually the buyers. This decision was reached following a complaint brought by an until-then little known Belgian player.

In mid-1990, the Belgian football player Marc Bosman, at the end of a two-year contract with RFC Liège and not wishing to accept the terms of a new contract, accepted an offer to move to the French club Dunkerque on a one-year loan. Due to some misunderstandings, however, the transfer did not go through and Bosman was unemployed as a result. He brought RFC Liège and the Belgian football federation (URBSFA) to court for failure to execute his transfer contract to Dunkerque.

RFC Liège refused to give the green light to URBSFA to issue the necessary transfer authorisation, as it feared that Dunkerque might not be able to honour the payment. It thus requested from the Dunkerque bank a confirmation that payment could indeed be made once the transfer authorisation was released. Since the contract did not mention that Dunkerque provide RFC Liège with what was for all practical purposes a letter of credit, the bank refused to provide confirmation. As a result the transfer did not go through by the set deadline, and the transfer contract became null and void. For details see Blanpain (1996), which contains the legal documentation. The court ruled that RFC Liège could not demand any compensation from a club willing to employ Bosman, and that it should keep him on its payroll until he found new employment. The legal battle made Bosman a pariah in the world of European football. He was eventually offered a contract by the club Saint-Denis in the French island of Réunion. Encouraged by FIFPro, the International Federation of Football Players (Blanpain, 1996, pp. 5 and 141), Bosman also initiated action against UEFA claiming that its transfer rules and nationality clauses had damaged his career. UEFA tried to have the case thrown out by arguing that as a Swiss legal entity (UEFA has its headquarters in Berne) it was beyond the jurisdiction of a Belgian court. The court, however, ruled that Bosman's action was receivable and requested a preliminary ruling from the ECJ as to the compatibility of UEFA's transfer system and nationality restrictions with Articles 48, 85 and 86 of the Rome Treaty (dealing with free movement of labour, competition and abuse of dominant position, respectively).

In late 1995, the European Advocate General declared that UEFA's transfer system and nationality restrictions violated both Articles 48 and 85 of the Rome Treaty. In its sentence of 15 December 1995, the ECJ reaffirmed that UEFA rules violated Article 48. The ECJ also pointed out that the justifications for the transfer rule put forward by the football authorities (i.e. they served to maintain a financial and competitive balance between clubs, and to support the development of young players) were not convincing since such objectives could be achieved by other means that would not impede the free movement of workers. The ECJ chose not to pronounce itself on Articles 85 and 86, since the violation of Article 48 was sufficient to make UEFA rules invalid. The Commission, however, made it known that, in its opinion, the transfer system was in principle contrary to Article 85 of the Treaty not only when transfers occurred between clubs located within two different EC member states but also in the case of transfers within the same member state, or between a member state and a third country.

On 19 January 1996, the Commission formally notified FIFA and UEFA that their transfer system and nationality restrictions that the ECJ had already found in violation of Article 48 were also in violation of Article 85 of the EC Treaty as well as Article 53 of the Agreement on the European Economic Area (Van Miert, 1996). The Commission gave the two football authorities six weeks to inform it of the steps they intended to take to comply with the ECJ's judgment. FIFA and UEFA informed the Commission that fees no longer would apply to the transfer of players at the end of their contracts between clubs within two different member states of the European Economic Area (EEA) (the EC and the European Free Trade Area (EFTA)). Likewise, the nationality restriction was going to be revoked, at least for what concerned UEFA-organised competitions between clubs. The issue thus remained open for what concerned transfers between two clubs within the same member state or between a club in one member state and one in a country outside the EEA.

On 19 June 2000, the Commission informed FIFA and UEFA that they had to bring additional changes to their transfer system by the end of the year or action would be commenced to have the ECJ rule it illegal. In September, FIFA agreed to revise the transfer system lest the Commission act on its threat and 'throw the European game into chaos' (*Financial Times*, 1 September 2000). The problem for FIFA in this is that it has to take into account the soccer labour market around the world. This means that rulings in one jurisdiction impede its ability to create a coordinated labour market policy across all of the regions. This affects individual minor soccer nations such as Australia, which supplies its best players to Europe but also important soccer regions in their own right such as South America under the Confederacion Sudamericana de Futbol (CONMEBOL). After lengthy negotiations an agreement was reached with FIFA in March 2001 ('Principles for the amendment of FIFA rules regarding international transfers' http://www.fifa.com/). It is a vital point that a court case brought by one player was enough to bring massive changes to the way a sport labour market could be operated by its GSO, especially one as powerful as FIFA. It is interesting to speculate what might have occurred if the case had been brought to court outside the EC.

The 'Bosman ruling' received an amount of attention by the media, the public and political authorities, that was simply unparalleled by any other

ECJ ruling. This publicity, moreover, went far beyond Europe to practically everywhere in the world where football is played and European football followed. From a strictly legal point of view, the ruling only reaffirmed what the ECJ had already established in the Walrave and Donà cases; that football qua business activity could not claim a special status but had to abide by the rules of the EC. More generally it destroyed any myth that the GSOs operated outside national jurisdictions. The ruling recognised that football is a business, that players are salary-earning labourers and that clubs are firms. How it regarded or treated football federations, be they national or international or global is more open to debate.

The reactions to the Bosman ruling were in general very negative. Just as with other sport organisations, football organisations felt invested with the mission of the defence and promotion of an activity that is supposed to unite humankind. Because of the character of such a mission, moreover, they have traditionally also felt above the reach of nation states and their laws. Following the Heysel disaster, for instance, UEFA was condemned by a Belgian court to pay some of the money allotted to the families of the victims. UEFA refused claiming that, as an association comprised or more than forty national football federations it was above Belgian laws and national laws in general. Only a threat from the Belgian Interior Minister to bring the issue to the TREVI group (and hence make it European) convinced UEFA to comply with the court order (on this episode, see Dupont 1996, p. 66). FIFA argued that its status as a global body placed it above a mere regional body such as the EC.

> In Fifa's view, it is clear that a small group of countries cannot be granted an exemption from sport regulations which are effective in all parts of the world and which operate successfully and efficiently and for the benefit of football at all levels.
>
> (quoted in Sugden and Tomlinson, 1998, p. 50)

Member state politicians also reacted rather sceptically. Belgian Prime Minister Dehaene, for instance, argued that while one should not disregard the principles of free movement of workers, one should also be sensitive to the needs of sport. The challenge was to find a way to reconcile EC rules with the continuing viability of football. Many critics agreed that the 'Bosman ruling' would destroy football, as it had been known for over a century. In part this was because: it would devastate the finances of smaller clubs by depriving them of a major source of revenue and, at the same time, make it almost impossible for them to compete in the bidding for top players. It would also lead to a sizeable increase in salaries, at least for star players, since clubs could offer in salary what they no longer have to pay in transfer fees. Even now it is probably too early to evaluate the consequences of the 'Bosman ruling', yet it would appear that its consequences have been greatly exaggerated. They will also have been overshadowed by far more important events in the economics of sport. For some national politicians the greater impacts lay outside sport. They lamented the excesses of a Europe that gave too much power to jurists and at least one member of the European Parliament denounced the 'Bosman ruling' as the result of 'pro-European legal delirium'. ('Hearing on Bosman judgment confirms differing opinions' Reuter Textline, Agence Europe, 22 March 1996.)

Why has the European Commission decided to tread on such dangerous ground as that of football? One possibility is that the Commission decided to intervene in this field because it regards sport, and football in particular, as an effective tool to build a European identity, which is part of its efforts to increase its legitimacy and thus solve the problem of the so-called 'democratic deficit'. That football could help in the construction of a European identity has also been argued by some entrepreneurs who have tried to set up a permanent European football league and, following UEFA's attempt to thwart their efforts, have appealed to the Commission on the basis of Article 85. Another possibility is that the EC institutions, and the Commission in particular, are essentially neo-liberal agents ideologically committed to the neo-liberal dismantling of institutional rigidities limiting market discipline that has already taken place in other sectors of the economy. For this possibility, see Miller and Redhead (1994) and Wright (1999). The degree of liberalism prevailing in the EC, however, is a matter of debate and is likely to vary with the eyes of the beholder. In the EC, liberalism coexists with protectionism and there is frequent and ample recognition of the necessity for occasional exceptions to general rules.

A third possibility is that the Commission is simply engaged in the process of 'international governance'. The term 'governance' is used differently, and in different areas of inquiry (e.g. Rhodes, 1996; Ronit and Schneider, 1999; Pierre, 2000). At the most general level 'governance' can be defined as a sustained process of competition and coordination, conducted both through formal structures and informal practices, by various actors, private and public, economic and political, national and trans-national, in order to regulate a specific sphere of collective activity. In the case of football, the Commission as the 'Guardian of the Treaties' is committed to liberal principles, but promotes them while taking into considerations the values, interests and preferences of all actors involved in a specific sector. A reading of the EC involvement in football, which focuses on a longer period than the last five years, provides support for this. In this context the 'Walrave and Donà cases' established sport as a legitimate area of EC activity but left other important questions unanswered since the ECJ admitted the possibility of 'certain exceptions' from EC rules for sport. As later pointed out by Advocate General Lenz in the Bosman case, those rulings did not explain clearly either the 'principle' or the scope of these 'exceptions' (Blanpain, 1996, p. 265).

The Commission, moreover, might not have been entirely convinced that UEFA rules did not have some merits and justification. Sport authorities after all did a considerable amount of lobbying to this effect and some member states were sympathetic to their views (Demaret, 1996, pp. 12–13). France, for instance, began trying to convince other member states to insert a brief protocol in the EC Treaties recognising sport as a sector with special needs and hence deserving exemptions. The Commission was thus more than likely to meet resistance and hence was very cautious in the way it proceeded. As explained by the then Competition Commissioner Karel Van Miert, the Commission wished to perform its duty as authority responsible for competition policy in the Community but preferred to leave the task of safeguarding the rights of individuals and firms to national jurisdictions. It limited itself to signal to football authorities that they needed to move in this field (Van Miert, 1996, pp. 6–7).

Another important reason why the Commission did not need to take a bold, legal approach to make sure that football authorities replace rules that violated Community law was that it could rely on some football actors to take, or threaten to take, legal initiatives and thus pressure football authorities to act. Following the 'Bosman ruling' in fact both players and clubs that would stand to benefit from the application of the 'Bosman ruling' to areas which the ruling itself had not directly addressed (e.g. transfers of players hailing from EFTA countries or other countries with which the EC had an association agreement covering the treatment of labour, transfers between clubs in the EC and clubs in EFTA or associated countries, etc.) could be expected to take initiatives (legal or otherwise) to have the 'Bosman ruling', and all the legal consequences that ensued from it, respected and applied. And indeed very soon the Commission began to receive complaints by EU clubs against UEFA/FIFA and national federations based on Articles 85 and 86 (Crespo Pérez, 1998). The cases that received most public attention concerned the transfer of Romanian Georghe Hagi from Barcelona to Galatasary of Turkey, the transfer of Croat Goran Vlaovic from Padova to Valencia, and the transfer of Ronaldo from Barcelona to Internazionale of Milan. In the end, none of these clubs went as far as seizing the ECJ against UEFA/FIFA and all cases were settled by means of a compromise that had little basis in law. The cases that UEFA/FIFA could expect to continue to be brought to the attention of the Commission (and possibly also to the ECJ) put pressure on them to establish new rules that would be acceptable to the Commission. Thus, UEFA first announced that the nationality clause would be suspended for what concerned UEFA-organised club competitions and then set up a working group that included representatives from national federations and leagues as well as FIFPro to find a suitable alternative to the existing transfer system. The setting up of the working group did not prevent the development of a rift between FIFA and UEFA (as well as thirteen European Leagues), which accused FIFA of giving up too easily to the Commission's pressures.

The interests and hence the views of all these football actors were rather diverse and thus negotiations were long-drawn and heated. Member states politicians, including Tony Blair and Gerhard Schroeder, also entered the field and expressed the desire that some kind of transfer fee system be retained. The governments of some member states tend to regard football as being more akin to a cultural industry than to business. Since national governments are concerned about the impact that the current evolution might have on the future of national teams, they are more inclined to treat football as a national industry deserving special treatment and exemptions. The view of member states carries weight and thus both the Feira (19–20 June 2000) and Nice (7–9 December) EU Councils recommended the Commission to consider giving the sport a special status on the basis of its social significance. The Commission's guidelines for Community action in sport explicitly recognise that any action should be concerned 'to respect the independence of cooperative effort in general and in sport in particular' (The European Community and Sport, SEC (91) 1438 of 31 July 1991). The Commission has also set up the European Sport Forum, which provides a permanent arena for discussion between the Commission, people involved in sport from national ministries and NGOs, as well as representatives of European and national sport federations. The Commission thus partially accepted the view that the rules for the organisation of sporting competitions are very different how those for competition between industrial firms, that sport represents not only an economic activity but also a social one. The Commission had to tread the fine line of trying to put a stop to the restrictive practices of sport organisations, which have a significant economic impact while, at the same time recognising that some of these practices might be necessary for a viable organisation of the sport (Pons, 1999, p. 6).

Member states governments can be said to have engaged in the same type of mediating activity at the national level. According to an Italian sociologist the dynamics of the Italian government intervention in the domain of sports can be explained as follows: the increase in earnings generated by TV has led some football super clubs to claim for themselves and football in general a bigger share of the pie. Such 'aggressively profit-oriented philosophy', however, 'has difficulty in coexisting with the principle of public support of the sporting movement'. Or, put in simpler words, in Italy by means of legal betting football provides 'public' financial support to many other sports. If football claims more for itself inevitably other sports will receive less. Hence, the intervention of the state aims primarily at curbing the 'strong powers', that is 'checking the separatist tendencies of spectator football in relation to the wider system of performance sport'. The state, in other words, is called upon 'to execute a complex role of both management and mediation'. Sport, and football in particular, constitute 'a political arena' in which very concrete interests are at stake and the management of which 'demands powers of arbitration'. The state can legitimise its 'regulatory' intervention through 'the very scope and the social dimension of the football phenomenon' (Porro, 1997, pp. 191–2). For a review of state intervention in English football, see Michie (2000). Indeed, Competition Commissioner Mario Monti, has referred to his role in these negotiations as that of a 'referee' explaining 'the ground rules and how they are applied'. He has also pointed out that the way to avoid old conflicts between the Commission and sport authorities is to adopt 'modern rules of governance' (Speech/01/84, 26 February 2001). FIFA President Joseph Blatter, on the other hand, in thanking Commissioner Monti gave the impression that he considered the Commission to have simply acted as a consultant to FIFA to improve its rules (Letter of Blatter to Monti, 5 March 2001 http://www.fifa.com/). A national judge or another national political authority would not have been capable of taking on FIFA or UEFA given the means of reprisal available to the latter (Demaret, 1996, p. 15). Demaret called this rescue 'récupération par l'ordre juridique communautaire de l'espace de liberté que les ordres juridiques nationaux étatiques avaient laissé au bénéfice des réglementations sportives privées'. As the Commission's paper on sport and competition of 24 February 1999 makes clear, Community sport policy is not yet sufficiently developed to answer all the issues that remain on the agenda. The governance process through which changes will be wrought is likely to remain the same; namely it will begin with actions by some of the football actors themselves.

Conclusions

The examples used demonstrate that the GSOs do not inhabit a calm world. In their relationships with each other there is a distinct impression of a form of inter-GSO diplomacy, not surprisingly allied to the use of power. This can be treated almost as if it was taking place in a world of super powers where a handful of the GSOs have hegemonic positions. The most notable of course is the IOC and its client GSOs, some of them more powerful than others. This could be seen in the DanceSport case. The fruits of this diplomacy are to be measured in the flourishing of a GSO and the survival of its oligarchy. For the sport the rewards are presentation in the global events and to become a commercial success where athletes can earn a living.

When it comes to their relationship to modern states and supra-national power such as the EC, whatever the GSOs may wish to believe, the treatment of them as quasi-states fail. Governments and states treat them with deference when the global events are on offer but it becomes clear that the GSOs have relatively little power except at those points in time when they are to award an event to some location. They can negotiate and bargain but as with other INGOs they do so with the decisive disadvantages of not controlling any real juridical or other powers. Where some other INGOs such as the Red Cross and Oxfam can sometimes claim a moral authority and a legitimacy derived from that authority, this is much more difficult for the GSOs. However, this has not prevented them from attempting to do so. In their dealings with states it appears that the nation state and its governments will increasingly treat the GSOs as MNCs rather than as INGOs, with more attention paid to the sport as a cultural entity than to the GSO as its guardian.

9 Yielding place to the new

Time future in time present and past

So far we have examined the GSOs with their existence, if not their status, taken as given. In this chapter we argue that their continued existence cannot be taken for granted, either singly or as a group. While we do not pretend to fully assess the future of sport, it will become clear that the GSOs face a set of challenges and potential threats to their existence. We arrive at this conclusion by examining trends in sport, making particular example of a set of five sports, at least one of which appears to be in terminal decline. Nevertheless, the primary focus is on new sports and sport activities. These are continually being created and developed, often under conditions that challenge the existence of GSOs. They also have the potential for establishing new GSOs.

The current global sport economy is such as to preclude the establishment of genuinely independent GSOs. New sports and sport activities are frequently invented and designed under private ownership, with specific economic objectives. Not surprisingly, owners attempt to retain both ownership and control of these sports. One means by which this is achieved is to ensure that the sport is difficult to play without the infrastructure that only considerable capital can provide. The electronic media, especially TV, are adept at this. *Gladiators*, of the 1980s, is one such invented-for-TV sport that involved genuine competition. It also, before its demise, demanded considerable athleticism from competitors. Originating in the USA, it was especially popular in the UK (www.lwt.co.uk, www.gladiatorszone.co.uk). Under license, it was seen around the world in various national guises. Cashmore argues that *Gladiators* is one of many activities that: '. . . owe far more to show-business than they do to traditional sports, but the suspicion grows that this type of activity is leading rather than following sports' (1996, p. 259). There is much to agree with in Cashmore's statement but the forces motivating and affecting new sports are much greater and varied than this, which is why the impacts on current GSOs can be so varied.

It will become clear that we regard the future as determining the fate of GSOs rather than the other way round. Nevertheless there are infinite strategies that GSOs can be expected to follow with respect to these trends. At the other end of the spectrum, rather than being consciously invented or designed, sport activities are being formed spontaneously. Often this occurs under near anarchic conditions. Initially at least, no one owns them. One of the most striking examples of this lies in extreme sports, many components of which began as street activities. These have now given rise to highly organised and tightly controlled world events. This leads to the inevitable questions of not only what defines a sport, but what is the contemporary viewpoint and how is that likely to change? In this context it is clear that much of what follows is necessarily suggestive and impressionistic.

What is a sport?

In contemporary society the impact of new sports can be accelerated and intensified because sports and sport events can so rapidly become global. This is often a matter of conscious strategy on the part of their progenitors, be they the grass roots competitors and organisers or global media interests that control them. Significantly, many of these new activities increasingly blur the edges of what is considered sport. TNN, for example, described its TV series Robot Wars as follows:

> *Robot Wars: Extreme Warriors* is a revolutionary sport in which teams design and build radio-controlled fighting machines to battle it out to see whose robot is supreme.
>
> (www.tnnonline.com/tnn/program/robot-wars/
> program-robot-wars. html, accessed 15/08/01)

Even allowing for the hyperbole of the network it is interesting that destructive machine vs machine contests – albeit radio-controlled by humans – are described as sport.

It is informative to compare *Robot Wars* with *Gladiators*. There are enormous similarities between their formats. Each was adopted from North America into Europe. Their competition is between contestants from the outside the network, who compete their robots against each other, as well as against the TNN network's robots. In common with individual *Gladiators*, the network's robots have different skills and are given aggressive names.

Because the boundaries of sport are incapable of precise categorisation, especially in the eyes of potential customers and practitioners – any blurring renders the domain of the GSOs less secure. This lack of precision in defining sport is intrinsic and is not new. For example, the psychologist Rosch (1973) asked over a hundred American students to rate six examples as to how well they fitted within a set of eight categories (Bird, Crime, Disease, Fruit, Science, Sport, Vegetable and Vehicle). They had already been placed in these categories and subjects were required to merely rate their appropriateness. In the ratings, a score of 1 would indicate a perfect example of the category, while a score of 7 would have indicated not at all an example. Within the sport category the six example sports were rated as:

Football (US)	1.2
Hockey (Ice)	1.8
Gymnastics	2.6
Wrestling	3.0
Archery	3.9
Weightlifting	4.7

Source: Rosch (1973).

While Rosch's concern was not with sport but categorisation processes, her results are striking. Clearly what constitutes sport is flexible. If a European audience had been asked the same questions using the same sports, the results may well have been different. In particular we would expect that US football would rate far lower. Not surprisingly, Wittgenstein (1953) also found problems in understanding what was meant by the related term, 'games'. So we feel safe in asserting that what constitutes sport is culturally determined and flexible. This flexibility is not just inter-cultural and inter-societal at a single point in time but also extends across time.

We have argued throughout that the political economy of contemporary sports cannot be understood without the GSOs. We, nonetheless, also argue that the social and economic conditions that gave birth to the original GSOs have long since disappeared. The intensely commercial framework of sport in the twenty-first-century world is unlike that of the nineteenth and early twentieth centuries. And it is a world that the GSOs themselves have helped create. With those originating conditions gone the legitimacy of GSOs, both individually and as a group, is more readily called into question.

As we have shown, questions of legitimacy of the GSOs relate to creation of surpluses, problems attendant upon distributing those surpluses, patronage, lack of accountability and secrecy. It is under these new conditions that infant sports have begun to appear. Paradoxically, this suggests an important reason for the continuing presence of GSOs: despite their own increasing problems of legitimacy they continue to help legitimise and protect their own sports.

A critical change in the modern sport economy is that the generation of new sports has become a matter of conscious design. This is often for specific economic purposes by media or other groups. In addition, this invention and design is increasingly subject to laws of intellectual property. At the same time, the GSOs have ossified their own sports in response to commercial demands and constituencies within their own polities. As a consequence, sport as a whole is being changed by the arrival of new sports and sport-like activities. This provides a massive challenge to the GSOs. They have redefined the purpose and economic nature of the sports that they govern, but remain wedded to sport's traditional forms. In the case of the IAAF, for example, many individual athletics events such as the discus have clear roots in antiquity, little prospect of change and have little following. So the GSOs are increasingly forced into the onerous task of defending the traditional against the new.

In order to reach some understanding of what is happening to sport – and later to make conjectures – we present five particular cases: (a) *cockfighting* (suffering decline and the absence of a GSO); (b) *boxing* (possible decline and its disputed control by several GSOs); (c) *computer games* (creation and growth of new sports and the absence of a GSO); (d) *robosoccer* (currently a primitive form of soccer between primitive autonomous robots, under the auspices of its own 'GSO', Le Federation International de Robot-Soccer Association (FIRA)) and (e) extreme sports (creation and growth of a 'family' of sports). Each of these activities has been strongly contested as belonging to the category of sport.

Cockfighting's treatment as sport or non-sport varies across cultures and time. Although found across the world it has no GSO, but there are associated national and sub-national organisations. In many places it is not just struggling with lack of recognition as a sport, but also with illegality. For *boxing*, unlike cockfighting, there is no shortage of GSOs. Several organisations simultaneously claim to be awarding, determining or recognising professional world titles. These competing claims raise questions about the external legitimacy of any and all of the claimants to the controlling body. This, of course, is in addition to those criticisms specifically directed at the activities of its controllers and promoters.

Computer games constitute a set of very different activities to cockfighting and boxing, with little or no recognition that they constitute a sporting activity, and certainly there is no GSO. However, a professional video game players association now exists (King, 2002). From the discussion in Chapter 3 we can expect this to emerge as a de facto GSO unless other associations emerge to challenge it. Computer games are activities that involve both intellectual and physical skills, and a contest (albeit between human and machine). Whatever the status, given rapidly increasing popularity at the global level, computer gaming's challenge to conventional sport for spectator and participant time and dollars is enormous.

The definition of sport is stretched by those sports that do not involve humans in the contest. In these activities it is normally animals (animal vs animal), as in cockfighting, that are the participants. Increasingly, however, as in chess tournaments restricted to computer programs, it is machines that are the contestants. Human involvement lies elsewhere, but specifically in the ownership, organisational, governance and spectatorship domains of such activities. A potentially important example is *robot soccer*, an adaptation of human soccer played by teams of autonomous robots.

Our interest in extreme sports, and *skateboarding* in particular, is in the way in which a group of sporting activities either created from scratch or as modifications of existing sports have gradually come together. It is regarded as a genuine grass roots movement in some quarters, and as a cynical and pre-meditated commercial enterprise in others.

The future past: cockfighting and boxing

Many sporting activities, especially those featuring animals as protagonists, are under moral question as 'blood sports'. Cockfighting is one such contested terrain. While it still exists, with its own sets of organisations in strongholds such as the Philippines, it has diminished enormously over the last one and a half centuries. In England it was first banned in the seventeenth century under Oliver Cromwell, but received royal favour under Charles II. It remained extraordinarily popular in England during the eighteenth century and, as with horse racing and many other sports, it was in eighteenth-century England that its formalisation began. The 1771 edition of Encyclopaedia Britannica refers to the 'Cock-pit', although cockfighting receives no other mention. Given that some other sports do rate mentions in some detail this may be read as indicating that the Scottish enlightenment saw little virtue in the practice. According to Porter (2000):

> ...the Enlightenment rethought the status of animals and man's relation to them...Urban society...manifested new sensibilities. Along with children, slaves, noble savages, orphans, the blind, the deaf and dumb and fallen women, animals became objects of sympathy...and cruel sports like bear-baiting, and cockfighting came under attack.
>
> (pp. 348–9)

Brailsford points to its association with horseracing, stating that the '*Rules for Matching and Fighting of Cocks* appeared regularly in the *Racing Calendar*' (1988, p. xi). As cockfighting began this process of formalisation – at about the same time as soccer, cricket and boxing – so moral sensibilities once again changed at what was a critical juncture. Massachusetts was the first state in the USA to declare cockfighting illegal under anti-cruelty laws passed in 1836, while it was finally banned in the UK in 1849. Given the central roles of Britain and the USA in the development of modern sports these were decisive blows to cockfighting's potential for global development. These state interventions prevented the conditions arising from which a GSO could be effectively created and legitimised. Nevertheless cockfighting is accepted in many nations such as the Philippines and Mexico and remains legal in three states in the USA. It is popularly televised in several nations and certainly operates in those nations where it is illegal (Simbeck, 2000).

The current fragmented organisation of cockfighting in the USA is a far cry from having a GSO. There is no central organisation in any formal sense, although there are organisations of breeders of game birds of the type used in cockfighting. None of these bodies makes any claims to be associated with the activity. They do, however, have a central body, The United States Gamebird Breeders' Association (USGBA), with affiliated state organisations. Over the past few years the USGBA and others have been lobbying to prevent the passage of federal bill S.345 which would ban the US Postal Service from the transportation of live game birds into the three states where cockfighting is still legal. In at least one of these three states, Oklahoma, there is a real possibility that the activity will be made illegal.

The governance of this 'sport' is necessarily localised. Nevertheless, the same rules of fighting and cock-pit governance appear to be generally understood throughout the USA, regardless of the legality or locale of its operation. Associated organisations have become lobby groups to defend what territory is left, mainly within the three states. There has also been a recent attempt to allow the fighting species of fowl to be continued to be transported interstate by the US Postal Service. Magazines such as *Grit and Steel* exist to cater for this audience. In the absence of any umbrella organisation the Internet plays a considerable role, not only for commercial sites catering to the 'cockers' but also as the basis of a network form of organisation. Conversely commercial gain has seen the breeders form organisations. In their websites, their PR and other information, they are careful to play down any link to cockfighting. Instead their mission statements emphasise their role in supporting breeding programs and scientific research, including vaguely specified links to universities.

Owing to the lack of a legitimising GSO, no international representation can be brought to bear upon legislators. Consequently no global resources or funding can be brought to bear within the USA in the interests of the sport as a whole. With only a small, barely legitimised body (the USGBA) the sport's protagonists have had to use the Internet to contact supporters. Another action was to create a mail campaign to legislators, threatening action at the ballot box. Supporters were urged to take these actions at their own expense. This was only weakly orchestrated but otherwise unsupported by organisations. A GSO or even some nationally recognised body seen by politicians as authoritative could more directly exert its power on politicians. The international dimensions of any decision could be emphasised by that organisation, since it is clear that politicians do have to negotiate with GSOs.

The implications of this example are that it provides a counterbalance to the majority of sports that come under the aegis of a GSO. One argument we have put forward is that a commercially successful sport helps legitimise the associated GSO, even while placing added pressures upon it. In turn the GSO helps legitimise the sport, especially if the GSO can claim membership of a fraternity of like bodies. This in part helps explain the co-location of so many GSOs in Switzerland. Observing the opposite in cockfighting reinforces the argument. The lack of legitimacy and commercial viability of the sport in many nations makes the creation of a GSO problematic. In turn, the lack of a GSO reduces further the chance of cockfighting regaining its legitimacy as a sport. The global fragmentation of cockfighting is simultaneously the result and the cause of the absence of a GSO. Most important, however, is the way in which it illustrates the moral element in the nature of sports. This argument applies to other animal based sports and to others that may in the future appear repugnant for reasons not yet considered. The GSOs have a vested interest in acting in this field. In this context we now turn to boxing.

Regarded by significant sections of the population as barbaric and a throwback to the past, boxing has many of the moral problems associated with cockfighting. But in other ways it is in a very different situation. It suffers not from an absence of GSOs but from a superfluity of them. It remains well supported, has influential allies and is commercially important. This section constitutes a brief analysis of boxing in terms of the fragmentation of its organisation. The emphasis is upon the reasons for the multiplicity of GSOs, the political economy of the impacts of this multiplicity, and an analysis of the forces that maintain this multiplicity.

The first element to note is that the multiplicity of GSOs does not extend to the amateur ranks. Here we see an example of the virtual college of GSOs, expressed most visibly in their Swiss co-location. The hegemony of the IOC is reflected in the need for national amateur boxing associations to belong to the sole global amateur boxing authority recognised by the IOC, the International Amateur Boxing Association (AIBA). The highest international boxing award available to an amateur boxer is Olympic selection.

A non-exhaustive list of current professional boxing GSOs includes the WBA; WBO; WBF; IBF; WBC; International Boxing Union (IBU) and the IBO. The criterion for inclusion is that they all lay claim to the right to sanction world titles and championship fights. One estimate is that: '...at least 15-world governing bodies...parade around their own set of world champions...' (ref. *Boxing Central* at wysiwyg://rbottom.zoffsitebottom.40/htt....boxing-central.com, accessed 16/10/01). In the majority of cases these are profit-making organisations and are, therefore, somewhat different to most GSOs. In addition they are virtually all USA based. Most importantly the vast majority have very close links with promoters, often appearing to operate at their behest. That there are numerous boxing GSO claimants means that they are individually weak in relation to the major promoters. Their profits are made by the fees they charge for sanctioning fights which then allow fighters to claim world titles. It is important to understand that many of these GSOs do very little, acting as self-appointed sanctioning mechanisms for meaningless world title fights. They have no control over the sport itself. This fragmentation is partly historical, related to the North America vs rest of the Globe split in the sports world. It is also both effect and cause of the economics of corruption in this sport, given the exploitable backgrounds of most boxers. The parallel of 'fixing' titles and fixing fights is irresistible.

The dynamics of the multiplicity of GSOs are such that once the monopoly of a group is broken there is a tendency to decay into multiple governing bodies. The reasons this has occurred in boxing include the following:

1   Professionals have always dominated the sport.
2   Consequently, there is a lack of disinterested parties to operate as administrators.
3   The college of GSOs did not initially operate in professional sports, so professional boxing was ignored.
4   The growth of for profit organisation led to a massive lack of accountability to the sport. (Note that this argument about lack of accountability is different from but consistent with comments about lack of GSO accountability.)
5   Professional boxers have little or no social status and are highly exploitable. This stems from problems of race and personal economic conditions.

Once the combination of legitimacy and monopoly enjoyed by a GSO breaks down it appears difficult to re-establish. Boxing can only survive as a major sport if there is some attempt to regulate it. This can be more readily done because of medical conditions. It also requires global rather than a North American approach. In the case of boxing the amateur – professional organisational divide may be crucial to its survival. It would appear extraordinarily difficult to conceive of a genuinely amateur world champion being able to defend his title on any fiscally sound basis. This is the same for many individual sports, implying a necessary split between competitions organised for amateurs and for professionals. As a result of this organisational fracturing is more likely.

The future present: computers, Xtreme games and robots

Ironically, even the seemingly innocuous electronic sports games, such as those based upon existing sports such as soccer, baseball and American football, pose their own moral dilemmas, at least for their designers. In attempting to make these sport games more realistic, given that they are based upon real sports, one of the most vexing questions in making them more realistic is whether or not to include foul play? The striking answer given by Adams, a virtual sports game designer, is that it is absolutely necessary to make such inclusions (Adams, 1999). In other words virtual sports games played in real time lose realism if there are not stoppages for infringements that have to be randomly assigned within parameters that give them realism. They are made to occur as defenders tackle opposition forwards who have the ball, or as forwards approach the goalkeeper. This then allows integral parts of the game such as free kicks, allowing banana kicks around walls of defenders, and penalties to occur that would not otherwise happen within the virtual game. And the potential for these infringements must be assigned not only to the computer's virtual team's players but to the human game-player's virtual team as well. This leads to a refereeing role for the computer, the potential dismissal of players from the field with impacts on game outcomes, and the ability of the human player to override such decisions. Even in the computer the philosophical and moral dilemmas of sport exist. As we shall see later these dilemmas re-appear in Robosoccer although this does not seem to have yet been noticed.

Computer games have no central organisation or equivalent of a GSO. This anarchic or chaotic element makes it impossible for other GSOs to negotiate with what may be one of their greatest opportunities (FIFA has computer soccer games that it puts its name to) and/or threats (as an alternative opportunity for participation/viewing).

Bryce and Rutter (2001) conducted a study of computer game participants, using questionnaires administered to top gamers at a tournament. They compared their psychological responses with those of top athletes at a physical meet. The questionnaire was designed to measure the pleasure that they get from play: what is termed the 'flow experience'. Very little measured difference existed between the two groups according to the responses. It was found that the gamers spent more time with friends than games, and only slightly less time in physical sports.

So on what grounds could computer soccer games be denied the status of being a sport? Perhaps because they are played on a machine, as opposed to use of a machine (such as an archer's bow or an F1 or Indy car). It may be because they are derivative of a real sport, soccer (as are Rugby forms, including American Football) or, because they involve relatively little physical exertion (like chess). Perhaps it is because the games and the opponents are virtual, and the human reactions are mere responses to coloured pixels. None of these seems completely adequate in philosophical terms and might provoke a derisory response from those who play the games at high levels of skill. As we have seen, the psychological and physiological reactions involved are remarkably similar to those of elite athletes. There are many activities (not regarded as sport) that involve competition between human beings via a technological medium such as a video game, a computer or hand held game. For many, the competition is against a technological arte-fact – Kasparov against *Deep Blue* at chess or against the more mundane artificial intelligence of a virtual opponent in a computer game such as FIFA2000 or F1-2001.

Does chess, classified as a sport in Russia and elsewhere, change its nature if it is human against machine? This argument is not inconsequential, given that 60 per cent of all Americans (USA) play video or computer games, while in 1998, 1999 and again in 2000, 35 per cent of all Americans (USA) rated the playing of computer and video games as 'the most fun entertainment activity' (http://www.IDSA.com/ffbox3.html). Of these games 15 per cent were classified as sports games, and 10 per cent as racing (http://www.IDSA.com/ffbox5.html). Reports from other nations suggest similar trends.

Nevertheless, there are practical problems with computer games as sport. A major one is the wide variety of game types and scenarios. This makes standardised competition extraordinarily difficult, especially over the long period as new games continue to be created. Closely related to this, and where games can differ from sports is that they often have a very strong narrative quality as in the exploits of Lara Croft. It is this that makes most game developers compare them to movies rather than sport. Sports competition styles of games that operate within a given and tight set of rules, such as soccer, are not especially highly considered.

Governance has the additional problem of development being in the hands of entrepreneurs. As we have already indicated, this is almost certain to change as professional players formally band together to become a GSO. The closeness of the spectators and the players in this area makes this even more likely.

While TV may invent sports the real changes to sport in the last half century have come from the preoccupations of youth, allowing many to legitimately say that they were there at the birth of a sport. In some cases these have moved to formalisation and organisational stages with rapidity. Some practitioners have already been acknowledged as having a status akin to world champions. Local organisations have arisen that will become a new generation of GSOs.

Skateboarding is unusual in being an intrinsically urban sport. It is a sport that illustrates invention, via technical innovations at the grass roots level (simply attaching a slab of wood to skates) and internal development and cultural shifts. It also links with commercialisation of sport both in its early relationship to roller-skating and to a lesser degree to surfing. It is an anarchically organised sport. While not having a GSO, it is still very different from the operation of cockfighting in its current success. Global in scope, it is organised via entrepreneurs and events for individuals. The major body is:

> The National Skateboard Association, headed by Frank Hawk, [which] held numerous contests across North America and eventually throughout the world.
>
> (Brooke, 2001)

This was set up with help from the Boy Scouts of America (Humphreys, 1996). There is also the United Skateboarding Association (http://unitedskate.com/mission.html) and the Northern California Downhill Skateboarding Association. The nature of this counter culture sport also makes a league structure antithetical to its culture. The idea of a skateboarding culture is one that occurs frequently in its literature. Its magazines are named accordingly. '*Rolling Stone's*, Trip Gabriel accurately described it as "...an anti-authoritarian sport virtually by definition; kids do it because they are told not to. In whatever town it becomes popular the local burghers ban it"' (www.wsu.edu:8001/vcwsu/commons/).

As with cockfighting and the computer game industry, it has had its ups and downs. However, it continues to grow and is now established with commercial sponsorship as a key ingredient of the Xtreme games. In skill terms it is linked to surfing, roller-skating, in-line skating, snow boarding and a variety of sub-variants such as downhill skateboarding. Its role as a marketing avenue into youth culture is crucial to its success and something of a contradiction of its image.

The symbiotic relationship between skateboarding, the extreme sport movement and the Xtreme games is clear. Skateboarding provided the extreme sports with a recognised set of organisations and governing bodies. This meant it had a set of journals and a customer base through which it could grow. Skateboarding had a posture of being anti-establishment. It had nearly achieved maturity as a sport, but one with attitude that went well with the extreme sports message. In its turn the Xtreme games promoters provided skateboarding, a sport that has gone through almost as many cycles of boom and slump as yoyos, with a new vehicle for its own promotion. It cemented its role as part of an urban youth sport movement. In turn the Olympics have had to adapt. The Winter Olympics have found this a lot easier than the Summer Olympics whose heyday may already have passed. The fact that extreme sports involve lots of risks, both for competition (spills are easy) and real physical danger adds a lustre to skateboarding which now has its own sub-species (luge). One major element in the economy of these sports is the rapidly escalating cost of insurance so that one of the main features of any GSO that emerges is going to be the control of dangerous activity, and the outlawing of some practices to increase the mainstream appeal. But, most of all, it will be necessary to reduce the insurance premiums and the lawsuits that they inevitably generate.

The definition of sport is further stretched by those sports that do not involve humans in the competition itself. In these non-human sports, animals (as in cockfighting) or machines (as in computer chess) compete for victory. Humans act as organisers, governors and spectators – not as participants. A primary example of this is the RoboCup series. Essentially it is a form of world soccer championship, played by increasingly autonomous robots. The first RoboCup championships, in 1997, were held in Nagoya, Japan, with the annual competition also held in Paris, Stockholm, Melbourne, and in Seattle in 2001 (www.cs.cmu.edu/~robocup2001/media/releases.html). The purpose is non-sport: to promote research in artificial intelligence and robotics, but the specific goal, according to the 'Robocup official site' is 'By the year 2050, develop a team of fully autonomous humanoid robots that can win against the human world soccer champions' (www.robocup.org).

To this end the RoboCup Federation is a non-profit body, based in Switzerland. The governing body is the (FIRA) (www.fira.net) based in South Korea. FIRA is essentially a new form of GSO. FIRA is modelled on the standard form of GSOs, being non-profit, having a constitution, by-laws, game rules, an assembly and an executive, yet its purposes are stated in purely scientific terms (www.fira.net/f2001/docs/overview/index.html). It is hosted by an academic institution. The Robot World Cup International Organising Committee is established within FIRA with its own constitution. The By-laws of FIRA state the following:

Local Chapters and Regional Associations
Local Chapters of FIRA shall be formed with the consent of the executive committee at the head quarters...
The local chapters/regional associations shall submit an Annual report on membership, meetings and activities to the Executive committee at the headquarters of FIRA, for their kind information (www.fira.net/ f2001/docs/overview/index.html).

This governance form gives power to the executive over the assembly and it also makes it clear that it is FIRA that gives legitimacy to its members and not the reverse. Similarly, being the first in the field has enabled FIRA to set the game rules that constrains the robots and their characteristics. A major element in the human vs robot sports that this organisation proposes, is that robots may need to be programmed not to cheat against their human opponents, or to take actions that might harm them. But, as with virtual games – if the robots do not infringe the rules, will a normal game be possible?

The computer game industry has not yet had any discernible impact on sports. However, it is suggested that the figures for growth indicate that not only is it already a mass phenomenon, but one that is growing. The time given over to games will affect support for sport in terms of (a) lack of spectators at either the screen or at stadia and (b) loss of advertising revenues as attention goes elsewhere and (c) lack of participants. Ultimately the implications of attention going elsewhere and the result of the lack of skills at sports and lack of participation will lead to declines in quality of players at the professional levels. The middle class may still watch sport but the players will be increasingly drawn from the Third World. Some sports, such as ice hockey may be especially affected as their player base is very much First World. If these games have no connection with sport other than the market, they still represent an enormous market lost to sport as a commodity. In both 2000 and 1999 there were over US$6 bn in software sales alone in the computer games industry, ignoring console sales, rental sales and other ancillaries (http://www.IDSA.com/ffbox7.html). This figure rose to $7.4 bn by 2001 (Marriott, 2001). By then, Microsoft was preparing to spend over US$500 mn in marketing alone for its new entry into the so-called 'Game Wars'.

Clearly not all of these revenues would have flowed to sport, but what is more important is that they represent the potential for a revolution in recreational activities. Being electronic these are intrinsically global activities that, regardless of their definition, are so close to being sports as to be a potential substitute activity. Sony Play Station 2 alone has sold nearly 10 mn units (Marriott, 2001). Electronic games compete with sports by claiming time and money and training the young for a very different kind of activity. Governance issues regularly occur and governance bodies, both global and local are arising spontaneously to cope with these issues. These organisations, allied with the financial power of the game manufacturers and their parent companies are a strange new phenomenon in the sports world.

Back to the future

The blurring of sport is taking on new dimensions, technological as well as moral. The act of participation and the meanings of spectatorship are being transformed as interactive technologies can potentially allow a viewer, remote from the action, to take part in decisions that determine outcomes. Interactive TV, invented and designed for TV sports, now in their earliest and crudest evolutionary forms are beginning to take on this aspect. The governance of such sports is extraordinarily problematic in ethical terms, and ultimately in legal terms when injuries or monetary loss can occur as a result. One question is whether any of these sports can be established or do they remain one or two network and one or two ratings season phenomena. If this seems unlikely then the example of the World Wrestling Federation (definitely not a GSO despite its title) has only to be brought forward, with its strong organisational base and its move into extreme football.

Increasingly, both directly and indirectly, technology is achieving a potentially commanding role in sport. To run a 10,000 m race, even allowing for high-tech shoes and incredibly energy returning track surfaces, is an extension of an entirely human activity. Horse racing combines human with animal but the propulsive force is the animal, and the horse's name, rather than that of the jockey describes the winner. At the same time it is recognised that many jockeys are superb athletes, quite apart from their affinity with the horse. In F1, the emphasis is much more ambiguous. Is it on driver, machine or team – 'Haakinen wins', 'McLaren wins' or the 'McLaren team wins'? All are used with some frequency. In some cases, such as cockfighting, greyhound racing and races, the competition is entirely between animals. Pigeon racing is still regarded as a sport by many, and has its own set of organisations although weak at the international and global levels.

One thing is striking in this discussion. The emergence of new GSOs is similar to the emergence of their forebears at the turn of the twentieth century. The evolutionary argument holds for extreme sports, computer games and robot games just as it did for athletics, motor sport and soccer. The dangers facing these sports are the same as those facing boxing and cockfighting. Failure to form a GSO will result in early demise, as with cockfighting. Forming a multiplicity of governing bodies will cause fragmentation and lend itself to corruption, as with boxing. With this in mind, in the next chapter we draw our final comments on the GSOs.

10 Postscript

The evolution of formalised sport, both amateur and commercial, lasted approximately from the initial development in the eighteenth century to the end of the nineteenth century. This took place before the GSOs arrived on the scene, but thereafter they played the dominant role in the international standardisation of sport. They both encouraged and facilitated sport's global expansion on a systematic basis and away from the random bilateral international competitions that had occurred up to that point. In turn this fed directly into increasing their own legitimacy and their role as legitimising forces. Since then they have played more indirect roles in increased globalisation of commercial sport while also adding to a global civil society – although almost certainly not to the extent that they claim. Unlike the IOC from Courbetin to Samaranch, FIFA under Blatter and other GSOs, we should not inflate the role that they have played. When sport is used as a global weapon (as through Olympic boycott and the boycott of apartheid South Africa) this is not so much an example of sport's importance, but of its convenience as a weapon and its ease of sacrifice.

The GSOs have expanded in numbers and influence and some in size right up to the present. They are more powerful now than they have ever been but in terms of the development of sport they were perhaps most influential in their early period – when they most resembled European gentlemen's clubs. This early Euro-centrism not only helped create biases in sport but in the development of the GSOs themselves. And although the relationship was symbiotic they were exploitable especially by the early electronic media. Conversely they managed to maintain their existence during the inevitable hibernations of international sport during the First and Second World Wars, increasing their importance and prestige as mass sport provided cheap mass entertainment in both post-war periods. In the early days of TV they had sufficient organisational capabilities to give them negotiating strengths, especially given seemingly unquestioned perceptions of their legitimacy. Until the 1980s, however, it appears they did not have commensurate marketing and financial skills and sold their 'product' for much less than it was worth to the media. The GSOs were created and staffed by amateurs and even now a business background is not the norm among the leaders of most GSOs. Eventually they were able to grasp what turned out to be a double-edged sword of enormous media revenues. These revenues created massive internal problems given that the governance structures of the GSOs were not designed for them. Even now they do not appear to have overcome these problems.

If the future of sport is uncertain then that of the GSOs is doubly so. In the second and third quarters of the twentieth century both amateur and professional sport were expanding and globalising. Alongside other elements such as the cinema, sport became one of the most important mass cultural activities around the world. The economic opportunities and threats this created are now at the core of the GSOs. They are either seeking to preserve and exploit their peak position or are trying to create that position for themselves. Sport in many ways has become the means to these ends rather than the end itself.

A major contradiction of the GSOs is that they are non-profit organisations, cultural and social objective INGOs, but which claim to control a major sphere of human economic activity. We have seen that that control is less than complete but these can be powerful organisations in their sports. Nevertheless, the GSOs have been instrumental in some of the most dramatic changes in sport. These include sport's commercialisation at the global level. The GSOs are the direct outcomes of the internationalisation of sport. Equally their existence is predicated upon the formalisation of sport, only able to appear after that process was largely completed. That formalisation was the achievement of national sports associations, and it was these associations that created the GSOs. So unlike most commentators we do not claim that the GSOs are self-appointed regulators of sport (with the notable exception of the IOC); they were created for that role by national bodies that knowingly gave up much of their own autonomy in so doing. Those national associations have now become the servants of their creation. This history has meant that most of the GSOs were on the scene before the universal commercialisation of elite sport. In athletics and tennis, for example, the amateur reigned supreme, and this amateur ethos has imbued virtually all of the GSOs for most of their existence. The contradictions this has created for the GSOs and for sport as a whole can be argued to lie at the heart of this book.

From these arguments we suggest what we believe is an important possibility – many of the changes that the GSOs have fostered and even helped create may yet hasten their demise as effective forces in sport. However we do not regard this as certain. The GSOs have extraordinary room for manoeuvre, even if some close. At their present stage in their history we have a view that they may already be past the peak of their influence, which came in the middle and late twentieth century. Some of the reasons for this can be characterised as part of historical forces over which the GSOs have little or no control. Globalisation and the continued increase in the commercialisation of sport undoubtedly rank as two of the most important. The GSOs have added to these factors a mixture of hubris, corruption and an inability to effectively strategise their longer term futures either individually or as a group.

It is not necessarily those GSOs that are the smallest and least commercially powerful that are the most vulnerable. In the small GSOs their very lack of attention in the mass media, the lack of superstars, and even the lack of a professional bureaucracy implies that costs are small and major revenues unnecessary for survival. This also places the GSOs and the national associations much more on a par in terms of their relationship. As a consequence in these sports gifts of time and effort from individuals are proportionately and potentially much stronger than in the larger GSOs. The most powerful GSOs, in commercial terms measured by both revenues and audience, seem to us to be vulnerable to a variety of internal and external forces. We do not mean that the sports or the global events for which they claim to be the controlling bodies will necessarily disappear – it is unlikely that the Professional Cyberathletes League and the Xtreme games will replace soccer and the Olympics. Rather the legitimacy, autonomy and privileges that the GSOs have enjoyed for around a century are under question. This is happening within the sports themselves, and within broader society and governments. In addition many of those that are largest may be vulnerable to both long- and short-term changes to their revenues.

One example of such a vulnerability flows from the analysis of events in Chapter 5. Although the ability to create such revenues must be counted as a strength, it is an ability that can deteriorate very rapidly. This is the ability to 'auction' the events they own to the highest bidder. In many cases we have seen this result in the host nation's taxpayers bearing the direct costs of the event while the GSO gains the mass of direct revenues from media rights to the event. In the past this has been accomplished by suggesting that governments will enjoy prestige and the uncertain and indirect revenues of increased tourism and business activity. Conversely we have seen that in other areas governments and states have the ability to make the GSOs bend to their wishes. If governments become more willing to use their greater powers or prove unwilling to underwrite the global events that are the major source of revenue to the GSOs, then these organisations are in a great deal of trouble. They have great incomes but these are potentially precarious, and even more so when one factors in elements such as terrorism.

The world's nation states increasingly take view that they should have some say in sport and its governance at least within their own borders. The increasing number of governments that have ministers of sport provides evidence for this. Of course, this does not represent either an underlying policy directed against the GSOs or a concerted move on the part of government. Rather it stems from their recognition of sport as a global cultural and economic force. The GSOs will rarely have the power to cope with nation states. Consequently the clashes will come indirectly in a variety of forms. For example, players and officials are now much more likely to ignore their GSOs and national sports bodies and go straight to law courts for redress of grievances. This may occur before using the sport channels provided for appeals and grievance or it may come after they have been exhausted. The CAS may find it increasingly difficult to play any role at all, even with governments' support if athletes seek redress in other courts. Certainly those subject to penalties can refuse to accept them and go to law which must be national or supra-national as in the case of the EU. In either case the status of the GSO is much reduced by being open to this form of indirect attrition of its authority. One of the most important factors in this will have impacts that will be felt beyond national boundaries. This is because those constrained in their livelihoods by the institutional framework of a sport, be they clubs, leagues or individuals, can go to the law in their own jurisdictions to have those rules voided. The GSOs may not only lose a case in a single jurisdiction but also find themselves forced to change their global rules because of actions in one state.

The existence of the EC makes this situation more difficult for the GSOs. Just as the individual GSOs are in many ways cartels of national associations, so the EC is a countervailing cartel of nations. Moreover, this is a massive group of sport consumers with enormous power and authority. The EC gains more importance at the global level because much of North American commercial sport lies outside the world's main team sports. The importance of the EC is further increased by the location of many of the GSOs in either the EC area or in neighbouring Switzerland. The EC appears to be evolving a specific sports policy that takes into account sport's cultural and social as well as economic nature. However, this does not necessarily favour the GSOs; much will be required of sports organisations in return. While this may exempt them from aspects of EC competition law many of the GSOs may be forced into actions that conform to EC regulations rather than to the desires of their member associations. In addition being headquartered in Switzerland will not be the protection that the GSOs may suppose. Rather it will mean that the EC will be determined to ensure that this cannot be used as a form of escape. In tackling the GSOs, this location means that the EC will come up against fewer vested national interests from within the EC. Almost certainly the GSOs will find themselves forced into greater and greater financial disclosure in order to operate in the EC.

This problem is exacerbated by numerous examples of cheating and deceptive behaviour in sport, both by athletes and the organisations. This is intensified by the GSOs' failing to stamp out their own internal problems, with some conspicuous cases of conflicts of interest and favouring of friends and close associates in the letting of contracts. The GSOs for a long period either turned a blind eye towards or were unable to prevent systematic cheating in the Olympics and other events. They allowed cheating to flourish in swimming, weight lifting, cycling and other sports where performance-enhancing drugs became widespread. It was only when the public outcry was large enough that the relevant GSOs took action: sometimes only after judicial or police bodies forced the issue. While WADA now seems determined to take firm action, this past record makes it difficult for governments to trust the other GSOs and national associations to self-regulate and police themselves.

Allied to this is their lack of frankness and openness. That they largely still do not publish accounts indicates that they are really not beholden to any group such as shareholders. However there are indications that this is about to change, the most important signal being that flowing from FIFA which now publishes audited accounts to international standards. This, of course, provides no absolute guarantees (as the collapse of Enron demonstrates). Nevertheless this is a step in the right direction and FIFA deserves credit for it. In the case of FIFA as a non-profit INGO there is the question of to whom the report is to be addressed. Quite reasonably FIFA makes this the presidents of those national associations that are its members. It is to be hoped this creates a new sense of critical stakeholdership on the part of these organisations. Even more it is to be hoped that other GSOs rapidly follow suit and in the current climate we believe this is likely – there is too much pressure for them to do otherwise. This does not immediately solve the problem that occurs for the major GSOs that the development funds can be used as a political tool within the membership of the GSO to create captive votes in presidential elections and other votes on crucial issues in general assemblies.

The GSOs will not be passive in the face of these threats to both themselves and support for their sports. It is apparent that the GSOs do not exist in isolation from each other. They are both competitors with respect to each other and are also cooperative. They have interests in common. Individually the GSOs operate as networks of national associations, while for solo sports it is the individual players and tournaments that provide the network's elements. As such the GSOs create and constitute a cartel of national associations within their own sport. They protect each other from market entry. Most jurisdictions treat the monopoly that this creates with increasing scepticism, although they also treat it with some benignity. This is because it is recognised that the GSOs genuinely perform other functions and that this powerful cartelisation is incidental to their original raisons d'être. Yet despite their mutual interests and commonalities the GSOs as a group are much less effective as a network than the national associations bound together in their GSO. This may be because they do not possess the cartel function as a group. Operating as a coherent network would re-create them as an enormously powerful lobby group. We examine some of the reasons why this is unlikely. This provides insight into the directions they are likely to take in protecting both their individual and collective futures.

The GSOs are a network only in some areas. In the case of the Olympic movement for summer and winter sports this is explicit and formalised and plays a part in the operation of the Olympic family. Their mutual interests are sufficient to overcome the indirect competition that they create for each other. These networks operate to the benefit of the IOC in the sense that it can be at the summit of a hierarchy of the sports organisations represented. The decision-making capabilities within the Olympic family remain well outside these networks. There are varieties of other links among the GSOs. Again the IOC is important in several of these. As far as the GSOs in their entirety are concerned, there are far too many to create anything other than a relatively informal umbrella organisation. The IOC has in many ways taken this task on and in doing so has helped preserve its importance beyond the Games themselves. Thus, much of the importance of the technical GSOs, most notably CAS and WADA, flows initially at least from the IOC. These technical GSOs are crucial for it is far more likely that, if independent and supported by government as they increasingly are, they will maintain a balance against the win-at-all costs attitude of many of the athletes and national associations. These technical GSOs must be strengthened and universalised and made independent of individual GSOs. At the moment they are too dependent upon the IOC in particular.

An example is Dick Pound who is the head of WADA but who is also a long-term member of the IOC. Arguably at least, this creates a conflict of interest. Given that we believe there are 200–300 organisations that would qualify as GSOs, all of varying shapes, sizes and formality and history, it seems unlikely that an umbrella organisation covering all GSOs will appear. At the same time this is made more complex as more and more sports are created, such as skateboarding, freestyle snowboarding, triathlons and computer gaming, they veer away from the more traditional forms of sport.

The consequence is that an umbrella organisation not only becomes less likely but also less meaningful. This means there may be key GSOs upon which most of the others depend for some form of leadership. Specifically there are very few that have the ability to successfully contact governments at the highest levels. These key GSOs have transcended the others either because of the universality of the sport or their ability to make it universal, with the Olympics as a special event case. FIFA, the IOC, IAAF and FIA may be among these. In addition there is a case to be made that the hegemony of the IOC, while serving the IOC's own purposes is vital to the other GSOs. The IOC is as much a global sports network administrator as an athletics event organiser. Nonetheless, it seems unlikely that the IOC can perform all of the leading tasks it has allotted to itself without reforming itself more than it has to date. Just as there are organisations such as WADA and the ICC corruption watchdog there should be a universal anti-corruption and ethics watchdog organisation for the GSOs. With WADA the IOC bans non-joining GSOs and their sports from becoming members of the 'Olympic Family' and hence for the Olympic Games. For some that are far removed from Olympic Games representation this may be little threat. This indicates a potential for making the network of GSOs tighter than at present.

A problem for the GSOs is the increasing wealth and income of individual elements of the sport scene. Some team clubs and even some individual athletes have the ability to challenge the power, authority and ultimately the legitimacy of the GSOs. An example of what is occurring is the formation of the G-14 group of the (currently eighteen) leading European soccer clubs. Individually they have little voice against FIFA and its control of international football but as a group they may be able to demand that FIFA recompense them for the free use of their players during the World Cup and other international appearance. In being European it also drives a wedge into FIFA that concerns the South American clubs, the other powerhouse of world soccer. Individually these clubs, be they European or South American, have little power to achieve this. Not surprisingly FIFA has supported national associations when they have called up players for international appearances and the clubs have resisted. In the past there has been little incentive for players to resist international calls, but now the rewards of club play are so much greater and the prestige of playing for Manchester United or Real Madrid is at least as great as playing for many nations. After all, the Manchester United and Madrid reserve benches are almost entirely composed of international representative players from around the globe. In such circumstance it is likely that the commercial interests will win out against the social and cultural proponents of a sport. In these circumstances the GSOs will perhaps have to give ground and the professional leagues will, either formally or informally, split from their GSOs. In this sense the North American style of sport governance is likely to gain ground.

At the other end of the commercial spectrum some GSOs will continue in existence but return to more informal organisations, as some already are, as their sport diminishes in importance. Given this diminution there will be little interest by the media and the sport will suffer financial loss at both the centre and the periphery. The GSO will become a part-time occupation of volunteers again and the athletes will be amateurs.

In both of the failure possibilities discussed earlier, the amateur–professional split reduces the GSO to being the 'rump' amateur arm. Much more likely and positive is the rise of two vehicles of amateur sport. The first of these relates to the 'open' nature of sport. In principal at least the amateur can compete in the same competition as the professionals and little distinction is made between the two. In some sports this is true but in terms of the operation of leagues, tournaments, events and the GSOs themselves there are distinct barriers placed in front of the amateur. They may need a tour card or the cost itself is just too prohibitive to be competitive in many sports. Previously it could be argued that the barriers were placed in front of the professional, as was the case in tennis and the Olympics and other athletics events. Now some GSOs, especially the solo sports, are specifically designed to promote the professional, as this is where sponsorship and other revenues lie. Where this occurs the development of a GSO dedicated to the amateur form of the sport or to the sport overall has occurred. This splitting can take an enormous variety of forms. This represents very much what has happened to the GSOs over time and it will almost certainly continue.

Rather more novel is the second form of amateur sport that we raised in terms of global events. These events flow from a different wellspring than the original amateurs who were interested in a sport for its own sake. The interest is now much more oriented towards using sport within some other community of interest that has a global sense. Such global community oriented events are the Gay Games, Police and Fire-fighter Games and transplant games. The very nature of these games indicates that they are not likely to be an avenue to elite professional sport for even the very best participants. While often based on the format of the traditional athletics meet they vary from these in ways that are significant to the community in question. Very often the sports are ones that are special to that community. While amateurs had events that ran in parallel for the same sport, now there is a professional equivalent.

What has been outlined as the possibilities are not so much looking into the future but outlining some of the forces that are presently at work. This has been the purpose of this text, examining for the first time this atypical, neglected but extraordinarily important set of organisations.

Appendix

Details of Global Sports Organisations in Text (Acronym: Full Title, Function/Sport, HQ, Date of Formation, web site address)

ASOIF: Association of Summer Olympics International Federations, forum of international federations, Lausanne, Switzerland, 1983, www.asoif.com

ATP: Association of Tennis Professionals, men's world tennis circuit and players, Ponte Vedra beach, FL, USA, 1972, www.atptennis.com

CART: Championship Auto Racing Teams, auto racing, Troy, Michigan, USA, 1978, www.cart.com

CAS: Court of Arbitration for Sport, sports arbitration and dispute settlement, Lausanne, Switzerland, 1984, www.tas-cas.org

CPL: Cyberathletes Professional League (Note: CPL is a for-profit company), professional computer gaming competition, Vancouver, Canada, 1997, www.cyberathlete.com

FGG: Federation of Gay Games, to hold quadrennial Gay Games, 1982, www.gaygames.com

FIA: International Automobile Federation, motor sports, Geneva, Switzerland, 1904, www.fia.com

FIBA: International Basketball Federation, basketball, Munich, Germany, 1932, www.fiba.com

FIDE: World Chess Federation, chess, Lucerne, Switzerland, 1924, www.fide.com

FIFA: International Federation for Association Football, Soccer-Association Football, Zurich, Switzerland, 1904, www.fifa.com

FIG: International Gymnastics Federation, gymnastics, Moutier, Switzerland, 1881, www.fig-gymnastics.com

FIIC: Federation Internationale d'Intercrosse, intercrosse, Montreal, Canada, 1985, www.intercrosse.tk

FIMS: International Federation for Sports Medicine, sport medicine (developed from AIMS: Association Medico-Sportive, 1920, St Moritz, Switzerland), www.fims.org

FINA: International Swimming Federation, swimming and diving, Lausanne, Switzerland, 1908, www.fina.org

FIRA: International Federation for Robot-Soccer, Robot-Soccer, Daejon, Korea, 1996, www.fira.net

GAISF: General Association of International Sports Federations, A Forum for international sports federations, Monaco City, Monaco, 1967, www.agfisonline.com

IAAF: International Association of Athletics Federations (formerly International Amateur Athletics Federation), track and field athletics, Monaco City, Monaco, 1912, www.iaaf.org

IBSA: International Blind Sports federation, sport for the blind and visually impaired, Madrid, Spain, 1981, www.ibsa.es

ICAS: International Council for the Arbitration of Sport, Took over governance of CAS from IOC in 1994, www.tas-cas.org (see above for CAS).

ICC: International Cricket Council, cricket, London, United Kingdom, 1909, www.cricket.org

IDSF: International DanceSport Federation, dance and dance as sport (amateur), Switzerland, originally FIDA founded in 1935, disbanded; eventually became ICAD and re-named in 1990 to IDSF in 1990, www.idsf.net

IFSA: International Federation of Sports Acrobatics, Acrobatics, Sofia, Bulgaria, 1973, www.fig-gymnastics.com (Note: no longer has a separate identity being incorporated into IFG in 1999. There is an IFSA currently operating as The International Federation of Strength Athletes but this GSO does not appear in the main text).

IFWHA: International Federation of Women's Hockey Associations, founded 1927 – no longer operates after amalgamating with IHF in 1982.

IFWLA: International Federation of Women's Lacrosse Associations, women's lacrosse, no apparent fixed location HQ, 1972, www.womenslacrosse.org

IGF: International Golf Federation, Amateur Golf and amateur golf events, Far Hills, NJ, USA, 1958 (founded as the World Amateur Golf Council (WAGC) – renamed as IGF in 2003), www.internationalgolffederation.org

IHF: International hockey federation, hockey, Brussels, Belgium, 1924, www.fihockey.org

IIHF: International Ice Hockey Federation, Ice hockey and in-line hockey, Zurich, Switzerland, 1908, www.iihf.com

IJF: International Judo Federation, Judo, Seoul, 1951, www.ijf.org

ILF: International Lacrosse Federation, men's lacrosse (small membership but includes the Iroquois Nation as a national federation full member – apparently no fixed HQ location), www.intlaxfed.org

IMTA: International Men's Tennis Association, Male professional tennis players (contesting at least on of the ATP's roles), 2003, no website found.

IOC: International Olympic Committee, Olympic Games, Lausanne, Switzerland, 1894, www.olympic.org

IRB: International Rugby Board, rugby union, Dublin Ireland, 1886, www.irb.com

ITF: International Tennis Federation, promotes tennis, Roehampton, England, 1913 (founded as International Lawn Tennis Federation, changing title in 1977), www.itftennis.com

ITU: International Triathlon Union, triathlon, Vancouver, Canada, 1989, www.triathlon.org

MIPTC: Men's International Professional Tennis Council – supplanted by the ATP (see above).

WADA: World Anti-Doping Agency, Anti-doping and testing for banned drug use, Montreal Canada, 1999, www.wada-ama.org

WAF: World Armsport Federation, Arm-wrestling, Calcutta, India, 1967, www.armsport.com

WAGC (see IGF above).

WDDSC: World Dance and DanceSport Council, dance and dance as sport (professional), originally founded in 1950, London, England, www.wddsc.com

WDSF: World DanceSport Federation (proposal only for almagamating WDDSC and IDSF).

WTA: Women's Tennis Association, women's professional tennis and tour, 1970, St Petersburg, Florida, www.wtatour.com

WTGF: World Transplant Games Federation, organises international sport events for organ donors and recipients, Winchester, England, 1978, www.wtgf.org

Sports organisations with some GSO functions and/or features

NBA: National Basketball Association, premier North American professional basketball league with global organisation and market presence.

St Andrews: St Andrews, golf, rules of golf world-wide in conjunction with USGA, Scotland, 1754, www.randa.org

USGA: United States Golf Association, golf, rules of golf world-wide in conjunction with St Andrews, www.usga.org

Wimbledon

WCT

Sources: (1) Union of International Associations Yearbook of International Organisations, K.G. Saur, Munich (2) List compiled in part by Osvaldo Croci (private communication) (3) GSO web sites.

Notes

1 Titles change with some frequency. For example in 2002/3 the IAAF changed its name and the WAGC became the IGF. Amalgamations also occur, notably as men's and women's a federations combine.

2 Full titles are usually given in English but acronym may relate to French form of the full GSO title.

Bibliography

Adams, E. (1999) Designing and Developing Sports Games, *Gamasutra*, 3: 38 (www.gamasutra.com).

Adler, M. (1985) Stardom and Talent, *American Economic Review*, 208–12.

Adonnino Committee (1985) A People's Europe, *Bulletin of the European Communities*, Supplement 7.

Akerlof, G. (1970) The Market for 'Lemons': Quality Uncertainty and the Market Mechanism, *Quarterly Journal of Economics*, August, 488–500.

Aldred, C. (1996) Court Tackles Referee, Opens Liability Question: Sport Associations Examine Coverage After Rugby Ruling, *Business Insurance*, 30(19): 63–4.

Allison, L. (1986) Sport and Politics in L. Allison (ed.) *The Politics of Sport*, Manchester: Manchester University Press, pp. 1–26.

Allison, L. (ed.) (1986) *The Politics of Sport*, Manchester: Manchester University Press.

Ananova (2003) British Squash Open is Saved, www.ananova.com/sport/story/, 6 February 2002.

Andrews, J. (1998) Survey: The World of Sport: The Paymasters, *The Economist*, 347, 8071, S14–S19.

Anheier, H., Glasius, M. and Kaldor, M. (eds) (2001) *Global Civil Society 2001*, Oxford: Oxford University Press.

Anonymous (1999) Growth in Youth Sports Participation, *Journal of Physical Education, Recreation and Dance*, 70(9): 6.

Anonymous (2000) Moreover: Why There is No Soccer in America, *The Economist*, 355, 8173, 84–5.

Anonymous (2001) The Joy of Lara, *The New Scientist*, No. 2301, 28 July, 10.

Arnaud, P. and Riordan, J. (eds) (1998) Sport and International Politics: The Impact of Fascism and Communism on Sport, London: E & FN SPON.

Arthur, W. (1989) Competing Technologies, Increasing Returns, and Lock-in by Historical Events, *Economic Journal*, 99(1): 116–31.

Arthur, W. (1996) Increasing Returns and the New World of Business, *Harvard Business Review*, 74(4): 100–9.

Ashworth, G. and Goodall, B. (1988) Tourist Images: Marketing Considerations, in B. Goodall and G. Ashworth (eds) *Marketing in the Tourism Industry: The Promotion of Destination Regions*, London: Belhaven, pp. 213–38.

Atkinson, S., Stanley, L. and Tschirart, J. (1988) Revenue Sharing as an Incentive in an Agency Problem: An Example for the National Football League, *Rand Journal of Economics*, 19: 27–43.

Australian Olympic Foundation (2001) *Annual Report 2000*, Sydney: Australian Olympic Committee Incorporated.

Baade, R. (1996) What Explains the Stadium Construction Boom, *Real Estate Issues*, December, 5–11.

Baade, R. and Sanderson, A. (1997) The Employment Effects of Teams and Sports Facilities, in R. Noll and A. Zimbalist (eds) *Sports, Jobs and Taxes*, Washington: Brookings Institution, pp. 92–118.

Babin, H. Jr (1996) Sports Franchises – The Real Key to the City, *Real Estate Issues*, December, v.

Baltake, J. (2002) 'Z-Boys' Captures skateboarding's Gritty Roots (Review of the film *Dogtown and Z-Boys*), www.movieclub.com, accessed 29 July 2002.

BBC Sport (2002) Zen-Ruffinen to Leave FIFA, 31 May 2002, http://news.bbc. sport.co.uk

Beal, B. (1995) Disqualifying the Official: An Exploration of Social Resistance through the Subculture of Skateboarding, *Sociology of Sport Journal*, 12: 252–67.

Beaver, D. (2000) USOC – Bowing to Pressure or Honoring Amateur Sports Act, *Palaestra*, 16(2): 4–5.

Bell, D. (2003) *Encyclopaedia of International Games*, Jefferson, NC, McFarland.

Berle, A. and Means, G. (1932) *The Modern Corporation and Private Property*, New York: Macmillan.

Bernath, C. (2002) Outside the Ropes (www.secondsout.com/uk/column_5651.asp) (accessed 2 December 2002).

Bess, P. (1996) Urban Ballparks and the Future of Cities, *Real Estate Issues*, December, 27–30.

Bird, P. (1982) The Demand for League Football, *Applied Economics*, 14: 637–49.

Blanpain, R. (1996) *L'affaire Bosman: la fin de l'ère des transferts?* Leuven: Peeters.

Boli, J. and Thomas, G. (eds) (1999) *Constructing World Culture: International Nongovernmental Organizations since 1875*, Stanford: Stanford University Press.

Boulogne, Y.-P. (1994) The Presidencies of Demetrius Vikelas and Pierre de Coubertin in The International Olympic Committee – One Hundred Years, vol. 1, Lausanne: IOC, pp. 13–207.

Bowers, B. (2000) Extreme Risks, *Best's Reviews*, 100(11): 28–34.

Bowles, P. and White, G. (1994) Central Bank Independence: A Political Economy Approach, *The Journal Of Development Studies*, 31(2): 235–64.

Boyle, M. (1997) Civic Boosterism in the Politics of Local Economic Development – 'Institutional Positions' and 'Strategic Orientations' in the Consumption of Hallmark Events, *Environment and Planning A*, 29: 1975–97.

Brailsford, D. (1988) *Bareknuckles: A Social History of Prize Fighting*, Cambridge: Butterworth Press.

Brasher, K. (1986) Traditional versus Commercial Values in Sport: the Case of Tennis in L. Allison (ed.) *The Politics of Sport*, Manchester: Manchester University Press, pp. 198–215.

Brewer, J. (2001) This Sporting Life, *Corporate Governance International*, 4(3): 2–3.

British Sports Council (1995) British Sports Council Report, London: Independent Television News, 19 May 1996.

Brower, J. (1976) Professional Sports Team Ownership, *Journal of Sport Sociology*, 1(1): 15–51.

Brooke, M. (1999) *The Concrete Wave: The History of Skateboarding*, Warwick Publishing.

Brooke, M. (2001) *The History of Skateboarding in Less than 1700 words*, www.interlog.com/%7Embrooke/history.htm, accessed 2 September 2001.

Bryce, J. and Rutter, J. (2001) In the Game – In the Flow: Presence in Public Computer Gaming, Computer Games and Digital Textualities Conference, IT University of Copenhagen, www.digiplay.org.uk

Buchanan, J. and Tullock, G. (1962) *The Calculus of Consent*, Ann Arbor: University of Michigan Press.

Carlos, A. and Nicholas, S. (1993) Managing the Manager: An Application of the Principal–Agent model to the Hudson's Bay Company, *Oxford Economic Papers*, 45(2): 243–57.

Carmichael, F. and Thomas, D. (1995) Production and Efficency in Team Sports: An Investigation of Rugby League Football, *Applied Economics*, 27: 859–69.

Carmichael, F., Thomas, D. and Ward, R. (1999) Team Performance: The Case of English Premiership Football, *Aberystwyth Economics Research Papers*, 99–10.

Carraro, F. (2002) Review of the Olympic Programme and the Recommendations on the programme of the Games of the XXIX Olympiad, Beijing 2008, Report by the Chairman, Franco Carraro, IOC Executive board, August 2002, Olympic Programme Commission.

Cashmore, E. (1996) *Making Sense of Sports*, 2nd edn, London: Routledge.

Cave, M. and Crandall, R. (2001) Sports Rights and the Broadcast Industry, *The Economic Journal*, Special Issue – The Economics of Sport, February, 111, 469, F4–F26.

Chain Store Age (1997) NIKE Marries Brand and Retail, *Chain Store Age*, March, 90–2.

Chaudhary, V. (2001) World Cup at Risk as Insurer Backs Out, *Guardian Online*, 13 October 2001, http://www.guardian.co.uk/Archive/Article/0,4273,4276479,00. html, accessed 14 October 2002.

Coakley, J. (1978) *Sport in Society*, St Louis: Mosby.

Coates, D. and Humphreys, B. (1999) The Growth Effects of Sport Franchises, Stadia, and Arenas, *Journal of Policy Analysis and Management*, 18(4): 601–24.

Coates, D. and Humphreys, B. (2000) The Stadium Gambit and Local Economic Development, *Regulation*, 23(2): 15–20.

Commission on Global Governance (1995) *Our Global Neighbourhood: The Report of the Commission on Global Governance*, New York: Oxford University Press.

Cornwell, B. (1995) Sponsorship-Linked Marketing Development, *Sport Marketing Quarterly*, 4(4): 13–24.

Cornwell, B., Pruitt, S. and Van Ness, R. (2001) The Value of Winning in Motor Sports: Sponsorship-linked Marketing, *Journal of Advertising Research*, 41(1): 17–31.

Crawley, S. (1995) Murray Sacked as Murdoch Raises the Stakes to $300m, *The Australian*, 6 April, 22.

Crespo Pérez, J. (1998) Análisis de los últimos conflictos juridicos en la era post-Bosman del fútbol profesional, Revista General de Derecho, 642 (March), available on line at http://www.iusport.es/OPINION/crespo97.htm

Croci, O. (2001) Taking the Field: The EC and the Governance of European Football, ECSA-USA International Conference, Madison, Wisconsin, 31 May–2 June, 2001.

Crone, J. (1999) Toward a Theory of Sport, *Journal of Sport Behavior*, 22(3): 321–31.

Crompton, J. (1995) Economic Impact Analysis of Sports Facilities and Events: Eleven Sources of Misapplication, *Journal of Sport Management*, 9(1): 14–35.

Cyert, R. and March, J. (1963) *A Behavioral Theory of the Firm*, 2nd edn 1992, reprinted 1996, Cambridge, MA: Blackwell Publishers.

Daly, G. and Moore, W. (1981) Externalities, Property Rights, and the Allocation of Resources in Major League Baseball, *Economic Inquiry*, January, 77–95.

Davidson, J. (1985) Sport and Modern Technology: The Rise of Skateboarding, 1963–1978, *Journal of Popular Culture*, 18(4): 145–57.

Dawson, P., Dobson, S. and Gerrard, B. (2000) Estimating Coaching Efficiency in Professional Team Sports: Evidence from English Association Football, *The Scottish Journal of Political Economy*, Special Issue – The Economics of Sport, September, 47(4): 399–421.

Demaret, P. (1996) Quelques observations sur la signification de l'arrêt Bosman, *Revue du Marché Unique Européen* (1): 11–15.

Demmert, H.G. (1976) *The Economics of Professional Team Sports*, New York: Joint Council on Economics.

Dennett, D. (1995) *Darwin's Dangerous Idea*, New York: Simon and Schuster.

De Vany, A. (2004) Hollywoood Economics: How Extreme Uncertainty Shapes the Film Industry, Routledge, London.

De Vany, A. and Walls, W. (1997) The Market for Motion Pictures: Rank, Revenue and Survival, *Economic Inquiry*, XXXV: 783–97.

Department of Industry, Science and Resources (DISR) (2000) Latest Inbound Visitor Movements, *Impact*, October (2), http://www.isr.gov.au/sport_tourism/publications/impact/oct20002.pdf, accessed 19 January 2002.

Department of the Prime Minister and Cabinet (DPMC) (2001) The Australian Government and the Sydney 2000 Games, http://www.dpmc.gov.au/docs/display-contents1.cfm?&ID=125, accessed 17 February 2002.

Diehl, P. (ed.) (2001) *The Politics of Global Governance: International Organizations in an Interdependent World*, 2nd edn, London: Lynne Rienner Publishers.

Dietz-Uhler, B., Harrick, E., End, C. and Jaquemotte, L. (2000) Sex Differences in Sport Fan Behavior and Reasons for Being a Sport Fan, *Journal of Sport Behavior*, 23(3): 219–31.

Dixit, A. and Stiglitz, J. (1977) Monopolistic Competition and Optimum Product Diversity, *American Economic Review*, 67(2): 297–308.

Dobson, S. and Gerrard, B. (1999) The Determination of Player Transfer Fees in English Professional Soccer, *Journal of Sport Management*, 13(4): 259–79.

Donaldson, T. and Preston, L. (1995) The Stakeholder Theory of the Corporation: Concepts, Evidence and Implications, *Academy of Management Review*, 20(1): 65–92.

Doyle, D. (2000) The Sinews of Hapsburg Governance in the Sixteenth Century: Mary of Hungary and Political Patronage, *The Sixteenth Century Journal*, 31(2): 349–60.

Duncan, R., Jancar-Webster, B. and Switky, R. (2002) *World Politics in the 21st Century*, New York: Longman.

Dunning, E. and Sheard, K. (1979) *Barbarians, Gentlemen and Players*, Oxford: Martin Robertson.

Dupont, J.-L. (1996) Le droit communautaire et la situation du sportif profession-nel avant l'arrêt Bosman, *Revue du Marché Unique Européen* (1): 65–77.

Dwyer, L. (1996) A Framework for Assessing the Economic Significance of Cruise Tourism, in *Highlights of the 27th Annual TTRA Conference, Las Vegas*, Boise, Idaho, Travel and Tourism Research Association.

The Economist (1997) Mr Formula One, 15 March: 72.

The Economist (2000a) Formula One's Finances: Grand prix, grand prizes, 15 July, 97–100.

The Economist (2000b) The Secret Finances of Formula One, 15 July, 18–19.

The Economist Intelligence Unit (2000) Bernie Ecclestone and the Finances of Formula 1, *The Economist*, 15 July, 356, 8179, 67–70.

Edwards, H. (1973) *Sociology of Sport*, Homewood: Dorsey Press.

El Hodiri, M. and Quirk, J. (1971) An Economic Model of a Professional Sports League, *Journal of Political Economy*, November–December: 1302–19.

Etzioni, A. (1961) A Comparative Analysis of Complex Organisations: On Power, Involvement, and their Correlates, New York: The Free Press.

European Commission (1998) The Development and Prospects for Community Action in the Field of Sport, Commission Staff Working Paper, Directorate General X (29 September).

Fatsis, S. (2002) Fans of Olympic Pentathlon Fight to Save It, *Naples Daily News*, 27 November, www.naplesnews.com

Ferrari, G. (1990) *Il padrone del diavolo: storia di Silvio Berlusconi*, Milano: Camunia.

FIFA (2001) World Cup and Television, *Info Plus*, Zurich: FIFA.

Financial World (1997), 17 June, 47–9.

Fishbein, M. and Ajzen, I. (1975) *Belief, Attitude, Intention: An Introduction to Theory and Research*, Reading: Addison Wesley.

Fisher, J. and Price, L. (1992) An Investigation into the Context of Early Adoption Behavior, *Journal of Consumer Research*, 19: 477–86.

Fletcher, J. (1989) Input–Output Analysis and Tourism Impact Studies, *Annals of Tourism Research*, 16: 514–29.

Flynn, M. and Gilbert, R. (2001) The Analysis of Professional Sports Leagues, *The Economic Journal*, Special Issue – The Economics of Sport, February, 111, F27–F46.

Forster, J. and Pope, N. (2002) A Comparative Study of Market Entry Strategies in Sport Leagues: Two Australian Examples, *International Journal of Sports Marketing and Sponsorship*, 4(1): 403–19.

Fort, R. (1997) Direct Democracy and the Stadium Mess, in R. Noll and A. Zimbalist (eds) *Sports, Jobs and Taxes*, Washington: Brookings Institution, pp. 146–77.

Fort, R. (2000) European and American Sports Differences, *The Scottish Journal of Political Economy*, Special Issue – The Economics of Sport, September, 47(4): 431–55.

Foster, K. (1986) Sporting Autonomy and the Law in L. Allison (ed.) *The Politics of Sport*, Manchester: Manchester University Press, pp. 48–65.

Frank, R. (1998) Driving Ambition, *The Wall Street Journal* (Eastern edn), 3 December: A1.

Fredline, E. and Faulkner, B. (2000) Host Community Reactions: A Cluster Analysis, *Annals of Tourism Research*, 27(3): 763–84.

Freeman, R. (1984) *Strategic Management: A Stakeholder Approach*, Cambridge, MA: Ballinger.

Gamage, A. and Higgs B. (1997) Economics of Venue Selection for Special Sporting Events: With Special Reference to the 1996 Melbourne Grand Prix, *Asia Pacific Journal of Tourism Research*, 1(2): 15–25.

Gambetta, D. (1993) The Sicilian Mafia: The Business of Private Protection, Cambridge, MA: Harvard University Press.

Gauthier, P. and Haman, A. (1992) Amateur Sport in Canada, *Canadian Social Trends*, 25: 21–3.

Gilpin, R. (2001) *Global Political Economy: Understanding the International Economic Order*, Princeton, NJ: Princeton University Press.

Giulianotti, R. (1999) *Football: A Sociology of the Global Game*, Cambridge: Polity Press, pp. 86–107.

Goff, B., Shughart, W. and Tollison, R. (1989) Disqualification by Decree: Amateur Rules as Barriers to Entry, *Journal of Institutional and Theoretical Economics*, 144(3): 515–23.

Golden, M. (2000) Political Patronage, Bureaucracy and Corruption in Postwar Italy, Paper presented at the Annual Meeting of the American Political Science Association, 2000.

Goldlust, J. (1988) *Playing for Keeps*, Melbourne: Longman Cheshire.

Gorman, J. and Kirk, C. (1994) *The Name of the Game*, New York: John Wiley.

Greenspan, A. (1996) Remarks at the 80th Awards Dinner of the Conference Board, 16 October 1996, Federal Reserve Board Speech, www.bog.frb.fed.us/boarddocs/speeches/1996/19961016.html

Greppi, M. (2001) NBC Ads Promise Olympics with Attitude, *Electronic Media*, 20(43): 3.

Griffiths, J. (2003) Car-makers Nose Ahead, *Financial Times*, 5 March.

Gratton, C. and Dobson, N. (1999) The Economic Benefits of Hosting Major Sports Events, in *Tourism Intelligence Papers*, A-31, London: English Tourism Council.

Guha, R. (2002) *A Corner of a Foreign Field: The Indian History of a British Sport*, London: Picador.

Hall, C. (1993) The Politics of Leisure: An Analysis of Spectacles and Mega-events, in A. Veal, P. Jonson and G. Cushman (eds) *Leisure and Tourism: Social and Environmental Changes*, Sydney: World Leisure and Recreation Association.

Hamburger, T. and Binkley, C. (2001) No Contest: Bid to Outlaw Betting on College Sports Faces Very Long Odds – Nevada Gambling Interests Lobby Hard to Keep a Cherished Exemption, *Wall Street Journal*, 3 April, A1.

Hamlen, W. Jr (1994) Variety and Superstardom in Popular Music, *Economic Inquiry*, XXXII: 395–406.

Hamzeh, A. (2001) Clientalism, Lebanon: Roots and Trends, *Middle Eastern Studies*, 37(3): 167–78.

Harris, K. (1988) What do we See When we Watch the Cricket? *Social Alternatives*, 7(3): 65–70.

Hart, R., Hutton, J. and Sharot, T. (1975) A Statisitical Analysis of Association Football Attendances, *Journal of the Royal Statisitical Society*, Series C, 24, 17–27.

Harverson, P. (1997) The Business of Sport, *Financial Times*, 33(253) 14 March, 14.

Hechter, M. (1987) Principles of Group Solidarity, Berkeley, CA: University of California Press.

Hinch, T. and Higham, J. (2001) Sport Tourism: A Framework for Research, *International Journal of Tourism Research*, 3: 45–58.

Higham, J. (1999) Commentary: Sport as an Avenue of Tourism Development: An Analysis of the Positive and Negative Impacts of Sport Tourism, *Current Issues in Tourism*, 2(1): 82–90.

Hiller, H. (1998) Assessing the Impact of Mega-events: A Linkage Model, *Current Issues in Tourism*, 1(1): 47–57.

Hinings, C., Thibault, L., Slack, T. and Kikulis, L. (1996) Values and Organisational Structure, *Human Relations*, 49(7): 85–99.

Hirschman, A. (1970) Exit, Voice and Loyalty: Responses to Decline in Firms, Organisations and States, Cambridge, MA: Harvard University Press.

Hobbes, T. (1651) The Leviathan; or, The Matter, Forme, and Power of a Commonwealth Ecclesiasticall and Civill, London.

Hultkrantz, L. (1998) Mega-event Displacement of Visitors: the World Championship in Athletics, Goteborg 1995, *Festival Management and Event Tourism*, 5: 1–8.

Humphreys, D. (1996) Skateboarding, in D. Levinson and K. Christensen (eds), *Encyclopaedia of World Sport: From Ancient Times to the Present*, ABC-CLIO, Oxford, pp. 350–51.

IAAF (1999) www.iaaf.org/InsideIAAF/History Inside IAAF – History: International Amateur Athletic Federation (IAAF).

Ingle, S. (2000) England: A Diary of a Failed World Cup Bid, *Guardian Online*, 6 July 2000, http://www.guardian.co.uk/Archive/Article/0,4273,4037672,00.html, accessed 14 October 2002.

International Rugby Board (IRB) (2001) 1999 World Cup Tournament Report: Rugby World Cup Limited, http://www.irfb.com/www.irfb.com/report.htm, accessed 7 January 2002.

IOC (2001) Olympic Marketing Revenue Distribution, http://www.olympic.org/ioc/e/facts/finance/fin_mark_intro_e.html, accessed 11 May 2001.

Jacobson, H. (1984) *Networks of Interdependence*, 2nd edn, New York: Alfred A. Knopf.

Janssens, P. and Kesenne, S. (1987) Belgian Soccer Attendances, *Tijdschrift voor Economie en Management*, XXXII, (3): 305–15.

Jennett, N. (1984) Attendances, Uncertainty of Outcome and Policy in the Scottish Football League, *Scottish Journal of Political Economy*, 32(2): 176–98.

Jennings, A. (1996) *The New Lords of the Rings*: *Olympic Corruption and How to Buy Gold Medals*, New York: Simon and Schuster.

Jensen, M. and Meckling, W. (1976) Theory of the Firm: Managerial Behavior, Agency Costs and Ownership Structure, *The Journal of Financial Economics*, 3, 305–60. Reproduced in abridged form in L. Putterman (ed.) (1986) *The Economic Nature of the Firm: A Reader*, Cambridge: Cambridge University Press, pp. 209–29.

Jog, V., Kotlyar, I. and Tate, D. (1993) Stakeholder Losses in Corporate Restructuring: Evidence from Four Cases in the North American Steel Industry, *Financial Management*, 22(3): 185–202.

Jones, C. (2001) Mega-events and Host-region Impacts: Determining the True Worth of the 1999 Rugby World Cup, *International Journal of Tourism Research*, 3: 241–51.

King, B. (2002) Video Game League on the Verge. *Wired News*, 8 August 2002 (www.wired.com).

Knowles, G., Sherony, K. and Haupert, M. (1992) The Demand for Major League Baseball: A Test of the Uncertainty of Outcome Hypothesis, *The American Economist*, 36(2): 72–89.

Krüger, A. (1999) The Unfinished Symphony: a History of the Olympic Games from Coubertin to Samaranch in J. Riordan and A. Krüger (eds) *The*

International Politics of Sport in the 20th Century, London: E & FN SPON, pp. 3–27.

Krut, R. (1997). Globalization and Civil Society. NGO Influence in International Decision-making, discussion paper no. 83, Geneva: United Nations, Research Institute for Social Development.

LaFeber, W. (2002) *Michael Jordan and the New Global Capitalism*, New York: W.W. Norton.

Leonard, W. (1997) Some Economic Considerations of Professional Team Sports, *Journal of Sport Behavior*, 20(3): 338–42.

Lever, J. and Wheeler, S. (1984) The Chicago Tribune Sports Page, 1900–1975, *Sociology of Sport Journal*, 1: 299–313.

Levinson, D. and Christensen, K. (eds) (1996) *Encyclopaedia of World Sport: From Ancient Times to the Present*, ABC-CLIO, Oxford.

Lewney R. and Barker, A. (2002) Preliminary Results from 3 Pilot Studies 10 October, *CambridgeEconometrics*, http://www.sportengland.org/whatwedo/research/strategic/summary_reports/Value-of-sports-in-economy-Final%20pilot.pdf accessed 6/5/03, London: Sport England.

Li, B. and Walder, A. (2001) Career Advancement as Party Patronage: Sponsored Mobility into the China's Administrative Elite, 1949–1996, *The American Journal of Sociology*, 106(5): 1371–408.

Loomis, J. (2001) Lessening the Risks at High-Risk Venues, *Rough Notes*, 144(7): 56–8.

Lucifora, C. and Simmons, R. (2001) *Superstar Effects in Italian Football: An Empirical Analysis?*, www.unicatt.it/economiaimpresalavora/quaderni/Quad29-2001.pdf

McAllister, M. (1998) College Bowl Sponsorship and the Increased Commercialization of Amateur Sports, *Critical Studies in Mass Communication*, 15: 357–81.

McCarville, R. and Copeland, R. (1994) Understanding Sport Sponsorship Through Exchange Theory, *Journal of Sport Management*, 8: 102–14.

MacDonald, G. (1988) The Economics of Rising Stars, *American Economic Review*, March, 155–66.

McElroy, M. and Cartwright, K. (1986) Public Fencing Contests on the Elizabethan Stage, *Journal of Sport History*, 13(3): 193–211.

McNeill, D. and Freiberger, P. (1993) *Fuzzy Logic*, New York: Touchstone Books, Simon and Schuster, pp. 85–6.

McPherson, B. (1975) Sport Consumption and the Economics of Consumerism, in D. Ball and J. Loy (eds) *Sport and Social Order: Contributions to the Sociology of Sport*, Reading: Addison-Wesley.

Maguire, J. (1999) *Global Sport: Identities, Societies, Civilizations*, Cambridge: Polity Press.

Marriott, M. (2001) Let the Game Wars Begin, *New York Times*, 26 April.

Marglin, S. (1974) What do Bosses Do? The Origins and Functions of Hierarchy in Capitalist Production, *The Review of Radical Political Economy*, 6: 33–60.

Marshall, D. and Cook, G. (1992) The Corporate (Sports) Sponsor, *International Journal of Advertising*, 11: 307–24.

Meenaghan, T. (1991) The Role of Sponsorship in the Marketing Mix, *International Journal of Advertising*, 10(1): 35–47.

Melaniphy, J. (1996) The Impact of Stadiums and Arenas, *Real Estate Issues*, December, 36–9.

Michie, J. (2000) The Governance and Regulation of Professional Football, *The Political Quarterly,* 71(2): 184–91.

Miller, F. and Redhead, S. (1994) Do Markets Make Footballers Free?, in J. Bale and J. Maguire (eds) *The Global Sports Arena: Athletic Talent Migration in an Interdependent World*, London: Frank Cass, pp. 141–52.

Mitchell, R., Agle, B. and Wood, D. (1997) Toward a Theory of Stakeholder Identification and Salience: Defining the Principle of Who and What really Counts, *The Academy of Management Review*, 22(4): 853–86.

Miyazaki, A. and Morgan, A. (2001) Assessing Market Value of Event Sponsoring: Corporate Olympic Sponsorships, *Journal of Advertising Research*, 41, January–February, 9–15.

Moorehead, C. (1998) *Dunant's Dream: War, Switzerland and the History of the Red Cross*, New York: Carroll and Graf.

Morse, E. (1987) Sport and Canadian Foreign Policy, Behind the Headlines Series, 45(2), Toronto: CIIA.

Moxey, N. (2002) Moxey Unhappy at Transfer Window, www.soccernet.com/england/news/2002/0721/wolverhampton_20020721_moxeyunhappyattransfer window.html

Nachmias, D. (1991) Israel's Bureaucratic Elite: Social Structure and Patronage, *Public Administration Review*, 51(5): 413–21.

Neale, W. (1964) The Peculiar Economics of Professional Sports, *Quarterly Journal of Economics*, 78: 1–14.

Neirotti, L., Bosetti, H. and Teed, K. (2001) Motivation to Attend the 1996 Summer Olympic Games, *Journal of Travel Research*, 39, February, 327–31.

Nelson, R. (1977) Firm and Industry Response to Changed Market Conditions: An Evolutionary Approach, *Economic Inquiry*, XV, 179–202.

Nelson, R. and Winter, S. (1982) *An Evolutionary Theory of Economic Change*, Cambridge, MA: Harvard University Press.

New South Wales Treasury (2000) *Budget Summary,* http://www.treasury.nsw.gov.au/bp00-01/other/budsum.htm#14Anchor, accessed 19 January 2002.

Nogawa, H., Yamaguchi, Y. and Hagi, Y. (1996) An Empirical Research Study on Japanese Sport Tourism in Sport-for-All Events: Case Studies of a Single-Night Event and a Multiple-Night Event, *Journal of Travel Research*, 34(Fall): 46–53.

Noll, R. (1974) Attendance and Price Setting in R. Noll (ed.) *Government and the Sports Business*, Washington, DC: Brookings Institution.

Noll, R. and Zimbalist, A. (1997a) Build the Stadium – Create the Jobs!, in R. Noll and A. Zimbalist (eds) *Sports, Jobs and Taxes*, Washington, DC: Brookings Institution, pp. 1–54.

Noll, R. and Zimbalist, A. (1997b) The Economic Impact of Sports Teams and Facilities, in R. Noll and A. Zimbalist (eds) *Sports, Jobs and Taxes*, Washington, DC: Brookings Institution, pp. 55–91.

Noll, R. and Zimbalist, A. (1997c) Sports, Jobs and Taxes: The Real Connection, in R. Noll and A. Zimbalist (eds) *Sports, Jobs and Taxes*, Washington, DC: Brookings Institution, pp. 494–508.

Nossal, K. (1998) *The Patterns of World Politics*, Scarborough: Prentice Hall.

O'Brien, T. (2002) $25 Million Wave House opens Doors in South Africa: First of Several Planned, *Amusement Business*, 114(2): 7.

Ogrodnik, L. (1997) Towards Comprehensive Sport Statistics, *Quarterly Bulletin from the Culture Statistics Program*, 9(4): 4–6.

Olds, K. (1998) Urban Mega-events, Evictions and Housing Rights: The Canadian Case, *Current Issues in Tourism*, 1(1): 2–46.

Ouillon, C. (1999) Analysis of the Impacts of Mega-events and Stadia on Tourism Destinations – Case Study of the Rugby World Cup in Cardiff, unpublished MSc thesis, Bournemouth University.

Ozanian, M. (1995) Suite Deals, *Financial World*, 9 May: 42–3, 46–8, 50, 52, 54, 56.

Papp, D. (2002) *Contemporary International Relations: Frameworks for Understanding*, 6th edn, New York: Longman.

Persson, C. (2002) The Olympic Games Site Decision, *Tourism Management*, 23: 27–36.

PGA (2000) Chronolgy of Events, 1980–1989, http://www.pga.com/FAQ/History/chronolgy_8.html, accessed 19 January 2002.

Phillips, R. and Reichart, J. (2000) The Environment as Stakeholder? A Fairness Approach, *Journal of Business Ethics*, 23(2): 185–98.

Pierre, J. (ed.) (2000) *Debating Governance: Authority, Steering, and Democracy*, Oxford: Oxford University Press.

Pitts, B. and Stotlar, D. (1996) *Fundamentals of Sport Marketing*, Morgantown: Fitness Information Technology.

Polston, P. (1997) Sport Dollar Impact on the Economy, Indiana DNR news release, 24 November, www.great-lake.net

Pons, J.-F. (1999) Sport and European Competition Policy, paper presented at the 26th Annual Conference on 'International Antitrust Law and Policy', New York: Fordham Corporate Law Institute, 14–15 October, http://europa.eu.int/comm/competition/speeches/text/sp1999_019_en.pdf

Pope, N. and Ransley, J. (1995) Government as Entrepreneur: A Case Study of the Surfers Paradise IndyCar Grand Prix 1990–1994, *Accountability and Performance*, 1(1): 57–72.

Porro, N. (1997) Politics and Consumption: The Four Revolutions of Spectator Football, in R. D'Alimonte and D. Nelken (eds) *Italian Politics: The Center-Left in Power*, Boulder, CO: Westview Press, pp. 183–97.

Porter, R. (2000) *Enlightenment: Britain and the Creation of the Modern World*, London: Penguin.

Prichard, G. (1995a) ARL Fires in $21m Reply, *The Australian*, 5 April, 22.

Prichard, G. (1995b) Pressure Mounts to Seek Deal Over Split, *The Weekend Australian*, 8 April, 38, 41.

Putnam, R. (1993) *Making Democracy Work: Civic Traditions in Modern Italy*, Princeton: Princeton University Press.

Putnam, R. (1995) Bowling Alone: America's Declining Social Capital, *Journal of Democracy*, 6(1): 65–78.

Quah, D. (1996) The Invisible Hand and the Weightless Economy, Centre for Economic Performance, Occasional paper no. 12, May 1996, London School of Economics.

Quercateni, R. (1964) *A World History of Track and Field Athletics, 1864–1964*, London: Oxford University Press.

Quirk, J. and El Hodiri, M. (1974) The Economic Theory of a Professional Sports League, in R. Noll (ed.) *Government and the Sports Business*, Washington, DC: Brookings Institution.

Quirk, J. and Fort, R. (1992) *Pay Dirt: Business of Professional Team Sports*, Princeton: Princeton University Press.

Rader, B. (1984) *In Its Own Image*, New York: The Free Press.

Radnege, K. (2000) Blatter: the Millennium Interview, *World Soccer*, January, 32–3.

Rather, J. (1999) On Sunday, 'Let Us Pray' or 'Let Us Play', *The New York Times*, 4 April, 1.

Rhodes, R. (1996) The New Governance: Governing Without Government, *Political Studies*, XLIV(4): 652–67.

Riordan, J. and Krüger, A. (eds) (1999) *The International Politics of Sport in the 20th Century*, London: E & FN SPON.

Ritchie, J. and Smith, B. (1991) The Impact of a Mega-event on Host Region Awareness: A Longitudinal Study, *Journal of Travel Research*, 30 (Summer): 3–10.

Roche, M. (1992) Mega-events and Micro-modernisation: On the Sociology of the New Urban Tourism, *British Journal of Sociology*, 43: 563–600.

Ronit, K. and Schneider, V. (1999) Global Governance Through Private Organisations, *Governance: An International Journal of Policy and Administration*, 12(3): 243–66.

Rookwood, D. (2001) Silverstone Safe for Now, 14 December 2001, *Guardian Online*, http://www.guardian.co.uk/Archive/Article/0,4273,4320183,00.html, accessed 14 October 2002.

Rosa, J., Porac, J., Runser-Spanjol, J. and Saxon, M. (1999) Sociocognitive Dynamics in a Product Market, *Journal of Marketing*, 63: 64–77.

Rosch, E. (1973) On the Internal structure of Perceptual and Semantic Categories, in Moore, T. (ed.) *Cognitive Development and the Acquisition of Language*, New York: Academic Press, pp. 111–14.

Rosch, E. (1978) *Principles of Categorisation*, in E. Rosch and B. Lloyd (eds) *Cognition and Categorization*, Hillsdale NJ: Lawrence Erlbaum, pp. 27–48.

Rosen, S. (1981) The Economics of Superstars, *American Economic Review*, 71(4): 845–98.

Rosen, S. (1983) The Economics of Superstars, *American Scholar*, 52(4): 449–59.

Rosen, S. and Sanderson, A. (2001) *Labour Markets in Professional Sports*, The *Economic Journal*, Special Issue – The Economics of Sport, February, 111, F47–F68.

Rosenau, J. and Czempiel, E.-O. (eds) (1992) *Governance without Government: Order and Change in World Politics*, New York: Cambridge University Press.

Ross, J. (2000) *The Pyramid*, www.zfeweb.com.uk, last updated: 20 April.

Rottenberg, S. (1956) The Baseball Player's Labour Market, *Journal of Political Economy*, June, 242–58.

Rowley, T. (1997) Moving Beyond Dyadic Ties: A Network Theory of Stakeholder Influences, *The Academy of Management Review*, 22(4): 887–910.

Rozin, S. (2000) The Amateurs Who Saved Indianapolis, *Business Week*, 2676: 126–30.

Ruggiero, J., Hadley, L. and Gustafson, E. (1996) *Technical Efficiency in Major League Baseball*, in J. Fizel, E. Gustafson and L. Hadley (eds) *Baseball Economics: Current Research*, Praeger, Westport.

de Ruyter, K. and Wetzels M. (2000) With a Little Help From my Fans – Extending Models of Pro-social Behaviour to Explain Supporters' Intentions to Buy Soccer Club Shares, *Journal of Economic Psychology*, 21: 387–409.

Sammons, J. (1988) *Beyond the Ring*, Camden: University of Illinois.

Sandler, D. and Shani, D. (1993) Sponsorship and the Olympic Games: the Consumer Perspective, *Sport Marketing Quarterly*, 2(3): 38–43.

Sandler, T. (1992) *Collective Action: Theory and Applications*, Hemel Hempstead: Harvester Wheatsheaf.

Sbragia, A. (2000) The European Union as coxswain: governance by steering, in J. Pierre (ed.), *Debating Governance: Authority, Steering, and Democracy*, Oxford: Oxford University Press, pp. 219–40.

Schmidt, R. (1997) Corporate Governance: The Role of Other Constituencies, J.W. Goethe-Universitat, Frankfuet am Main, Working Paper Series, Finance and Accounting, No. 3, to be published in A. Pezard, and J.-M. Thiveaud (eds) *Workable Corporate Governance: Cross Border Prespectives*, Paris: Montchrestien.

Schofield, J. (1983) The Demand for Cricket: The Case of the John Player League, *Applied Economics*, 15: 282–96.

Schofield, J. (1988) Production Functions in the Sports Industry: An Empirical Analysis of Professional Cricket, *Applied Economics*, 20: 177–93.

Scully, G. (1974) Pay and Performance in Major League Baseball, *American Economic Review*, December, 915–30.

Scully, G. (1994) Managerial Efficiency and Survivability in Professional Team Sports, *Managerial and Decision Economics*, 15: 403–11.

Scully, G. (1995) *The Market Structure of Sports*, Chicago: University of Chicago Press.

Seeley, A. (1996) Skating, Roller, in D. Levinson, and K. Christensen (eds) *Encyclopaedia of World Sport: From Ancient Times to the Present*, ABC-CLIO, Oxford, pp. 356–7.

Shank, M. and Beasley, F. (1998) Fan or Fanatic: Refining a Measure of Sports Involvement, *Journal of Sport Behavior*, 21(4): 435–40.

Short, N. (1989) *Nigel Short's Chess Skills*, London: Hamlyn.

Simbeck, R. (2000) Feathers and Blood: The Shadowy Allure and Complicated Politics of Cockfighting, *Nashville Scene*, 12 June (http://www.weeklywire.com), accessed April 2001.

Singer, P. (1975) *Animal Liberation*, 2nd edn 1990, New York: New York Review Books.

Sleight, S. (1989) *Sponsorship*, McGraw Hill: Maidenhead.

Smith, A. (1776) An Inquiry into the Nature and Causes of the Wealth of Nations, in A. Cannan (ed.) New York: Modern Library, 1937.

Smith, C. (1992) *Voices of the Game*, New York: Fireside Books.

Snyder, E. and Spreitzer, E. (1983) *Social Aspects of Sport*, Englewood Cliffs: Prentice Hall.

Spence, M. (1976) Product Selection, Fixed Costs and Monopolistic Competition, *Review of Economics and Statistics*, 217–36.

Spilling O. (1998) Beyond Intermezzo? On the Long-term Industrial Impacts of Mega-events: The Case of Lillehammer 1994, *Festival Management and Event Tourism*, 5: 101–22.

Starik, M. (1995) Should Trees have Managerial Standing? Towards Stakeholder Status for Non-Human Nature, *Journal of Business Ethics*, 14(2): 207–17.

Strange, S. (1996) The Retreat of the State: The Diffusion of Power in the World Economy, Cambridge Studies in International relations, Cambridge: Cambridge University Press.

Stotlar, D. (1993) Sponsorship and the Olympic Winter Games, *Sport Marketing Quarterly*, 2(1): 35–43.

Sugar, B. (1978) *Hit the Sign and Win a Free Suit of Clothes from Harry Finklestein*, Chicago: Contemporary Books.

Sugden, J. and Tomlinson, A. (1998) FIFA and the Contest for World Football: Who Rules the Peoples' Game? Cambridge: Polity Press.

Sydney Olympic Park Authority (2001) *About Us,* http://www.sydneyolympicpark.nsw.gov.au/sop/html/aboutus.cfm#Mission, accessed 19 January 2002.

Szymanski, S. (2001a) *Economics of Sport: Introduction, The Economic Journal,* Special Issue – The Economics of Sport, February, 111, F1–F3.

Szymanski, S. (2001b) *Income Inequality, Competitive Balance and the Attractiveness of Team Sports: Some Evidence and a Natural Experiment from English Soccer, The Economic Journal,* Special Issue – The Economics of Sport, February, 111, F69–F84.

Szymanski, S. and Smith, R. (1997) The English Football Industry: Profit, Performance and Industrial Structure, *International Review of Applied Economics,* 11(1): 135–53.

Szymanski, S. and Kuypers, T. (1999) *Winners and Losers: The Business Strategy of Football,* London: Viking.

Taylor, T. (1986) Sport and International Relations: a Case of Mutual Neglect, in L. Allison (ed.) *The Politics of Sport,* Manchester: Manchester University Press, pp. 27–48.

Tourism Forecasting Council (2001) Forecast: the 13th Release of the Tourism Forecasting Council, Sydney, Tourism Forecasting Council.

Trevithick, A. (1996) Takraw, in D. Levinson and K. Christenesen (eds) *Encyclopedia of World Sport,* Oxford: ABC-CLIO, pp. 389–91.

Union of International Associations (1993/1994) Yearbook of International Organisations, Munich K.G. Saur.

Viner, P. (2003) Chess, *The Weekend Australian,* 22–23 February: 55.

Van Miert, K. (1996) 'L'arrêt "Bosman": la suppression des frontières sportives dans le Marché unique européen', *Revue du Marché Unique Européen* (1): 5–9.

Varney, W. (1999) Howzat! Cricket from Empire to Globalization, *Peace Review,* 11(4): 557–63.

Vrooman, J. (1995) A General Theory of Professional Sports Leagues, *Southern Economic Journal,* April, 971–90.

Vrooman, J. (1997a) A Unified Theory of Capital and Labor Markets in Major League Baseball, *Southern Economic Journal,* 63(1): 594–619.

Vrooman, J. (1997b) Franchise Free Agency in professional Sports Leagues, *Southern Economic Journal,* 64(1): 191–219.

Vrooman, J. (2000) The Economics of American Sports Leagues, *The Scottish Journal of Political Economy,* Special Issue – The Economics of Sport, September, 47(4): 364–98.

Wales Tourist Board (2000) Annual Report, *1999–2000,* Cardiff: Wales Tourist Board.

Wales Tourist Board (2001) Visitor Statistics 1999, URL: http://www.wales-tourist-board.gov.uk/entries/en/8/26/30, accessed 19 January 2002.

Ward, A. and Waller, A. (eds) (1907–1921) *The Cambridge History of English and American Literature: An Encyclopedia in Eighteen Volumes,* Volume XIV: section on The Literature of Pugilism and Hunting, Cambridge: Cambridge University Press.

White, G. (1996) Creating the National Pastime: Baseball Transforms Itself, 1903–1953, Princeton, NJ: Princeton University Press.

Wittgenstein, L. (1953) *Philosophical Investigations,* Oxford: Basil Blackwell.

World Travel and Tourism Council (2001) Year 2001 TSA Research – Variance Report: World, London: World Travel and Tourism Council.

Whitson, D. and Macintosh, D. (1989) Rational Planning vs. Regional Interests: The Professionalisation of Canadian Sport, *Canadian Public Policy*, 15(4): 436–49.

Willetts, P. (2001) Transnational Actors and International Organisations in Global Politics, in J. Baylis and S. Smith (eds) 2nd edn, *The Globalizations of World Politics: An Introduction to International Relations*, Oxford: Oxford University Press, pp. 356–83.

Woodford, J., Baines, P. and Barn, S. (1998) Football Relationship Marketing: Can football market the 'sizzle'? in Proceedings of the 27th EMAC Conference, Stockholm: EMAC, pp. 57–76.

Worsnop, R. (1995) The Business of Sports, *CQ Researcher*, 10 February.

WTA Tour Inc. (2002) The 2003 WTA Tour Official Rulebook, www.wtatour.com

Wright, G. (1999) 'The Impact of Globalisation' in 'Debate: the New Political Economy of Sport', *New Political Economy*, 4(2): 268–73.

Zak, T., Huang, C. and Siegfried, J. (1979) Production Efficiency: The Case of Professional Basketball, *Journal of Business*, 52: 379–92.

Zech, C. (1981) An Empirical Estimation of a Prodcution Function: The Case of Major League Baseball, *American Economicst*, 25: 19–23.

Zimbalist, A. (1992) *Baseball and Billions*, New York: Basic Books.

Zimmerman, D. (1997) Subsidizing Stadiums: Who Benefits, Who Pays?, in R. Noll and A. Zimbalist (eds) *Sports, Jobs and Taxes*, Washington, DC: Brookings Institution, pp. 119–45.

Index

Date Due
